STUDIES IN WELSH HISTORY

43

EMLYN HOOSON AND THE WELSH
LIBERAL PARTY, 1962–1979

'General Election declaration, Welshpool' – Emlyn Hooson being congratulated on his re-election (Don Griffiths Collection, Photographer of Newtown, 1970). By permission of Llyfrgell Genedlaethol Cymru/The National Library of Wales

EMLYN HOOSON AND THE WELSH LIBERAL PARTY, 1962–1979

by

NICHOLAS K. ALDERTON

UNIVERSITY OF WALES PRESS
2025

© Nicholas K. Alderton, 2025

All rights reserved. No part of this book may be reproduced in any material form (including photocopying or storing it in any medium by electronic means and whether or not transiently or incidentally to some other use of this publication) without the written permission of the copyright owner. Applications for the copyright owner's written permission to reproduce any part of this publication should be addressed to the University of Wales Press, University Registry, King Edward VII Avenue, Cardiff CF10 3NS.

www.uwp.co.uk

British Library CIP Data
A catalogue record for this book is available from the British Library

ISBN   978-1-83772-297-6
e-ISBN   978-1-83772-298-3

The right of Nicholas K. Alderton to be identified as author of this work has been asserted in accordance with sections 77 and 79 of the Copyright, Designs and Patents Act 1988.

For GPSR enquiries please contact: Easy Access System Europe Oü, 16879218
Mustamäe tee 50, 10621, Tallinn, Estonia.
gpsr.requests@easproject.com

Typeset by Richard Huw Pritchard
Printed and bound by CPI Group (UK) Ltd, Croydon, CR0 4YY

SERIES EDITORS' FOREWORD

Since the foundation of the series in 1977, the study of Wales's history has attracted growing attention among historians internationally and continues to enjoy a vigorous popularity. Not only are approaches, both traditional and new, to the study of history in general being successfully applied in a Welsh context, but Wales's historical experience is increasingly appreciated by writers on British, European and world history. These advances have been especially marked in the university institutions in Wales itself.

In order to make more widely available the conclusions of original research, much of it of limited accessibility in postgraduate dissertations and theses, in 1977 the History and Law Committee of the Board of Celtic Studies inaugurated this series of monographs, *Studies in Welsh History*. It was anticipated that many of the volumes would originate in research conducted in the University of Wales or under the auspices of the Board of Celtic Studies, and so it proved. Although the Board of Celtic Studies no longer exists, the University of Wales Press continues to sponsor the series. It seeks to publish significant contributions made by researchers in Wales and elsewhere. Its primary aim is to serve historical scholarship and to encourage the study of Welsh history.

CONTENTS

SERIES EDITORS' FOREWORD	v
LIST OF TABLES	ix
LIST OF FIGURES	xi
NOTE ON PLACE NAMES AND INFLATION	xiii
ABBREVIATIONS	xv
ACKNOWLEDGEMENTS	xvii
INTRODUCTION	1
1 The fall and rise of the Welsh Liberals, 1918–1966	23
2 The organisation and finances of the Welsh Liberal Party, 1967–1979	89
3 Policymaking in the Welsh Liberal Party	135
4 The electoral legacy under Emlyn Hooson	203
CONCLUSION	247
BIBLIOGRAPHY	257
INDEX	267

LIST OF TABLES

Table 1: BLP – British general election results, 1945–59
Table 2: LPW – General election results in Wales, 1945–59
Table 3: Montgomery general election results, 1950–9
Table 4: Montgomery by-election result, 15 May 1962
Table 5: SLP, LPW and BLP elected MPs, 1955–64
Table 6: State of WLP constituencies
Table 7: Constituency questionnaire response
Table 8: Income and expenditure of the WLP, 1966–70
Table 9: Affiliation fees and subscriptions received by the WLP, 1971–3
Table 10: WLP income and expenditure, 1972–3
Table 11: Income and expenditure, 1975–9
Table 12: Bank balance, 1975–9
Table 13: Affiliation fees, 1976–9
Table 14: Financial cost of the organising secretary
Table 15: Population change (+/-)in mid-Wales, 1903–65
Table 16: Migratory changes to mid-Wales, 1951–61
Table 17: Total income and policy expenditure by the four main parties in Wales, 1970–6
Table 18: Total income and policy expenditure for the Federated Liberal Party, 1970–6
Table 19: Total unemployed in Wales, 1971–6

Table 20: Professions of 1970 general election candidates

Table 21: Results of identifiable Welsh-language candidates in direct competition with Plaid Cymru, 1970–9

Table 22: Weakness of WLP or PC in seats where either took first or second placing

Table 23: LPW and PC positions in every constituency with a candidate, 1966

Table 24: The relative strength of the WLP in nineteen direct contests with Plaid Cymru, 1970

Table 25: The relative strength of the WLP in thirty-one direct contests with Plaid Cymru, February 1974

Table 26: The relative strength of the WLP in thirty-six direct contests with Plaid Cymru, October 1974

Table 27: The relative strength of the WLP in twenty-eight direct contests with Plaid Cymru, 1979

Table 28: Montgomeryshire electoral expenses by party, October 1974

Table 29: Montgomeryshire general election results, 1945–59

Table 30: Montgomeryshire general election results, 1962–6

Table 31: Montgomeryshire general election results, 1970–9

Table 32: WLP and Plaid Cymru seats gained under FPTP, 1970–9 general elections

Table 33: WLP and Plaid Cymru seats allocated under the D'Hondt method, 1970–9 general elections

LIST OF FIGURES

Figure 1: The organisation of the Welsh Liberal Party
Figure 2: 1967–75 Policy-enacting process of the WLP
Figure 3: 1975–9 Policy-enacting process of the WLP

NOTE ON PLACE NAMES AND INFLATION

Throughout the book, I have kept the constituency names as they were during this period, meaning that several constituencies use the English title rather than the Welsh. Although my choice would have been to use the Welsh version, as Beti Jones did in her book *Etholiadau'r Ganrif/Welsh Elections 1885–1997*, it would not have been historically correct. Therefore, I have used 'Cardigan' instead of 'Ceredigion', and 'Merioneth' instead of 'Meirionnydd'. The book uses the Welsh spelling for Llanelli, as the English 'Llanelly' was changed prior to the 1970 general election.[1]

In terms of Emlyn Hooson's seat of Montgomeryshire, it is customary to refer to it as Montgomery. So, to avoid confusion, especially when the constituency became part of the county of Powys, rather than 'Montgomeryshire', I have referred to it simply as 'Montgomery' throughout the book. The only difference has been when using texts and quotes that refer to 'Montgomeryshire'.

High inflation was an issue throughout the 1970s, and for the reader of this book, I believe it is useful to see how much the amounts quoted are worth now. It allows the reader to have a better idea as to how much, or little, money the LPW and WLP had, especially when dealing with pre-decimalisation amounts. All converted amounts quoted in the footnotes come from the Bank of England's online inflation calculator and are adjusted for 2023. The annual inflation percentage rate is quoted next to the converted number in the endnotes. A note on the Bank of England's online inflation calculator website states:

---

1 *The London Gazette*, 'Llanelli Borough Council: Change of Name of Borough', 4 March 1966; available at: *https://www.thegazette.co.uk/London/issue/43915/page/2444* (accessed 1 August 2024).

The calculator uses Consumer Price Index (CPI) inflation data from the Office for National Statistics from 1988 onward. Monthly calculations of the current year are based on the latest CPI level, whereas previous years use their calendar year averages. CPI estimates before 1988 are modelled based on data collected for the Retail Price Index (RPI).

The calculator uses the Consumer Price Index (CPI) as this is the measure used by the Government to set the Bank of England's target for inflation. An alternative credible measure, which is the ONS' lead measure of inflation, is the Consumer Price Index including Owner Occupiers' Housing Costs (CPIH).

Please note: the estimates in the calculator from 1949 onwards have been updated with revised CPI estimates from the ONS published in May 2022.[2]

---

2 Bank of England inflation calculator; available at: *https://www.bankofengland.co.uk/monetary-policy/inflation/inflation-calculator* (accessed 1 August 2024).

ABBREVIATIONS

BLP	British Liberal Party
LPO	Liberal Party Organisation
LPW	Liberal Party of Wales
NLW	National Library of Wales
NLYL	National League of Young Liberals
Plaid	Plaid Cymru
PLP	Parliamentary Liberal Party
PPC	Prospective Parliamentary Candidate
SLP	Scottish Liberal Party
WLP	Welsh Liberal Party

ACKNOWLEDGEMENTS

No matter what anyone thinks, you are never the 'finished product'; this has been just as true in academia as it was in the dozen or so jobs that I have had or the father that I am. There is always something new to learn and another way of doing things. Also, no one accomplishes anything without the aid of others; I certainly haven't. This book is based on my PhD thesis. I started that journey in April 2012 and I am forever grateful for the help and support that I have received in those ten years.

My supervisors have been at the top of their field and I have been very lucky to have them as my mentors. Professor Peter Dorey has been there since day one and it has been a genuine pleasure to spend time in his company, talking about the thesis, history and politics in general – always a guiding hand and I look forward to many more chats. Professor Clare Griffiths has been supportive of me and invariably willing to put me on the right path. I have always enjoyed discussing the ideas for the thesis with her. It's been a long journey with many highs and lows but having two supervisors who are always willing you on and want to see you succeed has been a great experience. I could never have done this without you, so, thank you both. Likewise with my two previous supervisors, Professors Scott Newton and Chris Williams – we had a brief time working together, but made good memories. Sadly, we lost Chris in 2024. He was a formidable, passionate historian and a charming man, who is greatly missed.

I'd like to thank Professor Russell Deacon and Dr Johnathan Kirkup. Additionally, Dr Sam Blaxland deserves a special mention for allowing me to have sight of his thesis prior to publication. He embarked on a similar journey, in that we started our PhDs at the same time and chose two very overlooked political parties

– he chose the Welsh Tories. I have learnt a lot, so, thank you. My thanks, too, to Llyfrgell Genedlaethol Cymru/The National Library of Wales board and staff for their kind permission to use the archival material included in this book. It is a wonderful institution that needs to be protected. I would also like to thank the Welsh Liberal Democrats for their help and permission to use their archive material.

To my family, Tammy and Tomos, you two are just wonderful and beyond words. I love you both. To the rest of my family, Dad, Edwina, Kelly, Ray, Hana, Rowena and Stephen (not forgetting their spouses and children), thank you for the love and support as well. I look forward to a glass of wine with you all.

Inevitably, over the course of a decade, people leave us. My mother, Elizabeth, died in 2016 and this book is dedicated, with love, to her memory. We also lost my father-in-law, Trevor R. Turke, in 2020, such a sad loss. He was certainly a character. He loved Tomos and Tomos loved him. I am glad you both got to know him. You are both missed, as are other members of my family: Angela McIlroy, Robert McNeil, Gerald Alderton, Jim McNeil and Betty Moore.

There are too many people to thank and I apologise for any omissions. Likewise, any mistakes or omissions within this book are my own.

Diolch yn fawr. Cymru am byth!

Nicholas K. Alderton, Ponthenri, November 2024

INTRODUCTION

Historians have viewed the Welsh Liberal Party (WLP) and Emlyn Hooson's role within it as footnotes in Welsh history. Rarely is a reason given for ignoring the WLP and, like the Welsh Conservatives, they are conspicuous by their absence within the literature. Of the historians who have made the unconscious decision to omit the Liberals, many of them were writing during the period when the press treated the Liberals in Wales as bystanders to Plaid Cymru's rise.[1] It would not be controversial to point out that Welsh historians of the post-war period tended to write from a leftist perspective, but with a focus on Labour history rather than Liberal and, as such, began to consign the Liberal Party of Wales, (LPW, the former name for the WLP), to background noise. It is not hard to understand why this would be the case, as by the end of the 1950s, Labour's usurpation of the LPW's position as the leading radical party within Wales was complete. Secondly, the ascent of Plaid Cymru, which happened in conjunction with a rise in Welsh national consciousness during the 1960s and 1970s, was deemed to have finished off the Liberal Party's chances in its former heartlands.[2] Third, Plaid fought every seat in Wales throughout the 1970s, with the party taking Labour seats that had recently been Liberal. Fourth, to these historians, the WLP's fortunes were tied to those of the British Liberal Party (BLP).[3] So, writing off the WLP by ignoring it and focusing on the battle between Plaid and Labour seemed natural: the dominant party of Wales fending off the attack from the nationalists. The WLP, like the Conservatives, were thought irrelevant to Wales during this period, so it was an omission due to perceived irrelevance and not malice.

However, latter-day historians go further and have consciously decided to ignore the WLP, arguing that they were not a challenge to Plaid in north-west Wales or, by extension, in the rest of Wales.[4] Johnes argued that his focus on national identity meant that 'nationalists get more attention than their electoral fortunes maybe deserve and Liberals might feel short-changed'.[5] It is these attitudes and biases that this book seeks to address.

In recent years the Welsh Liberal historiography has experienced a slight increase, although none of the works has really challenged the assumptions of the period under review. Which is why Johnes's passing nod that the Liberals would feel 'short-changed' by his approach is welcome, because it is an acknowledgment that the WLP may have a story to tell. Additionally, and this is probably more important to the broader historical debate of the 1960s and 1970s, it has also had its nationalist credentials ignored. Hooson looked to reassert and emphasise these credentials, pointing to the WLP's sense of Welshness which, in turn, shaped the party's policy outlook. It became the WLP's raison d'être. Historians have minimised the contribution of the WLP, brushing aside the fact that from 1945 onwards (with the exception of the 1970 General Election), it was a much more popular party within Wales than Plaid. Coupled with the vagaries of the British electoral system, the party has been relegated to the position of an electoral 'also-ran'.

Apart from the obvious link to Welsh political history and the history of political parties and organisations, this book is also a work of British political history. The political history of Britain during the late nineteenth and early twentieth centuries was shaped by the Liberal Party and David Lloyd George. From 1923 until 2015, the Liberal Party and its successor, the Liberal Democrats, was the UK's third largest political party. The Liberal Democrats regained that position in 2024. No record of Britain during the pre-Second World War period can afford to leave out the Liberal Party in its assessment of the rise of

Labour or the welfare state. Also, it cannot be left out of any post-1960s examination of British politics. Likewise, due to the prominence of Lloyd George, British history is not complete without considering Wales and its impact on Liberalism in these isles. The abundance of books and articles on this period is a testament to the Liberal Party's position in pre- and post-First World War British politics. Historians such as Kenneth O. Morgan have highlighted the prominence of the Welsh influence on British Liberal policy. Even if they limit this to nonconformist policies, such as the disestablishment of the Church in Wales or Lloyd George's 1909 'People's Budget', the influence is there.

However, the Welsh influence is reduced or non-existent in the post-1945 historiography, though the British Liberal Party does feature at significant junctures. In very simplistic terms, the fate of the post-war British Liberal Party has had a direct bearing on people's lives and this can be shown by its role and influence on national politics. The revival that started in the late 1950s under Jo Grimond, which reversed the almost terminal decline of the party, would enable the success of the 1962 Orpington by-election. This by-election saw the Liberals overturn a sizeable Conservative majority to take the seat, which created shockwaves within the Tory Party. A further revival in 1974, under Jeremy Thorpe, would eventually lead to the Lib-Lab Pact, initially agreed to ease the passage of devolution legislation through Parliament. The failure of the 1979 devolution referendums, which was a key Labour policy, would be one of the factors in the fall of the Callaghan government. What followed was a Conservative landslide victory and, in 1981, a split within Labour that would lead to the founding of the Social Democratic Party (SDP). The SDP would form an electoral alliance with the Liberals, briefly challenge Labour's position within British politics, and lead to the eventual formation of the Liberal Democrats in 1988. The 2010 general election would see the Liberal Democrats form a coalition government with the Conservative Party before suffering a catastrophic general election defeat in 2015. These milestones can be traced back to the rehabilitation of the BLP under Jo Grimond.

The survival of the post-war BLP was crucial in enabling these events and it is no exaggeration to say that the LPW and the WLP were affected by them and played a part. The revival under Grimond can be seen to have been a factor in the retention of Montgomery as a Liberal seat during a by-election in 1962. Emlyn Hooson gained a more significant majority than the former Liberal leader, and previous holder of the seat, Clement Davies. As will be examined later in the book, Hooson and Geraint Howells were able to affect both the BLP's and the Labour government's policies on agriculture. Hooson's status as agricultural spokesperson for the BLP had a significant effect on policy, whilst the government's position was changed through Howells's insistence that the Farmers' Union of Wales be placed on the list of approved negotiators. When it comes to devolution and the EEC referendum debates, the WLP and Hooson should not be written out of the primary political events of the 1960s and 1970s. They remained an influential voice on Europe, devolution and Welsh nationalism beyond this period. Although subjected to an unfair portrayal in the 2018 TV miniseries *A Very English Scandal*, Hooson played a significant role in the Jeremy Thorpe scandal and stood for the leadership of the BLP twice. Most importantly, when the Liberals were on the verge of being overshadowed and wiped out in Wales, the reforms under Hooson ensured that the party survived and did not concede to Plaid. In this way, the book will also fit into the broader historiography of how a remarkable person could affect the direction of an organisation, political party and country.

The significant themes of the book will focus on the nationalistic nature of the WLP and its Welshness. These themes will fit into the historiographies of Welsh nationalism and nationalist parties within the UK. As a sense of place and nationhood is a political and personal construct, we should give a definition of 'Welshness' and what it means. A dictionary defines Welshness as 'the quality or state of being Welsh'.[6] However, this is vague and does not give us an idea of what 'being Welsh' means. To some, the ability to speak Cymraeg is a symbol of 'Welshness'. Yet, this leaves out a significant proportion of the Welsh population that does not speak the language. So, in this context, the WLP took the approach that speaking the language was desirable but was not the only indicator of Welshness, so an inclusive language policy was needed (see chapter three). A much better interpretation would be that there was a sense of nationhood or an understanding that Wales politically and culturally differed from its more dominant neighbour. Defining a nation also means showing that something sets the country apart, culturally, emotionally or through its growing institutions. Hooson, a fluent Welsh speaker himself, understood that the party had to appeal to an idea of Wales and its people. The WLP's concept of Welshness and nationalism was just as valid as those of Plaid and the Labour Party. These parties recognised that Wales was different from England, with Plaid wanting dominion status for Wales and Labour advocating devolutionary measures; Hooson's concept emphasised keeping Wales within the wider United Kingdom but under a parliamentary federalist structure. The WLP offered a significant degree of autonomy to Wales whilst retaining its historical ties to the United Kingdom.

This study of the Welsh Liberals under Emlyn Hooson is multifaceted. It will add to the historiography and our growing understanding of the place of the party in Welsh and British politics. On this note, although this book will fit into the broader knowledge of Liberalism within these isles, it is just as important to point out that Welsh democracy needs to have a rounder knowledge of its political past. The democratic changes currently occurring within Wales, with its own legislative Senedd/Parliament and First Minister, would not have taken place without people like Hooson taking the first steps. This book echoes Deacon's dedication at the start of his book and pays a debt of acknowledgement to the pioneers who kept the Liberal flame alive in Wales and never abandoned hope in what Wales could be.[7]

AIMS AND CHAPTERS

The aim of this book is to show that the formation of the WLP was needed for the Liberal tradition to survive in Wales. Additionally, the new organisation offered an alternative to the unionist and independence visions for Wales. As already explained, this is a work of British political history that will examine a particular section of the British Liberal Party, which became a state party in its own right, how it fared in Wales, and the decisions that were taken to ensure a Liberal presence remained in Wales.

This book will provide a more in-depth analysis of the WLP, focusing on the top-down reorganisation that was overseen by Emlyn Hooson. It challenges some of the orthodoxies of the Welsh political historiography of the late 1960s and 1970s, arguing that the WLP was just as crucial to the burgeoning Welsh consciousness as Plaid was. In some instances, for example, through the Lib-Lab Pact, the WLP could directly influence the direction of the devolution debate and Wales itself.

Offering a comprehensive analysis of the upper echelons of the WLP, it will detail the organisational and financial issues that bedevilled the party during this period. It also sheds new light on some lesser-known characters within the party, such as Winifred 'Freddie' Whitaker. It offers a re-evaluation of Emlyn Thomas's role in the financial issues the WLP experienced just prior to the 1970 general election. The policies and policymaking processes of the WLP will be examined, as well as the general election records of Hooson and the WLP. The book utilises little-used archival sources to produce a revisionist perspective of the WLP and Hooson. It will not be revisionist for the sake of it, but to show that the history of the WLP during this period has more to offer than has previously been thought.

Chapter one will set the book in its historical context. It will begin with an overview of the decline of the LPW and will refer to the BLP's own decline. It will argue that the LPW was in a grave state by the 1950s, with several causes: the first was the organisation itself. The Welsh party was separated into two federations under the nominal umbrella of the Liberal Party of Wales. Both federations were mutually suspicious of each other and there was no coordination on policies or elections. The chapter will also examine the rise of Emlyn Hooson, how he identified the problem and his plans for reform. Hooson's decision to reform the WLP, the type of reforms enacted, the new structure of the party and the reaction it garnered from the local associations will all be evaluated.

Chapter two will continue assessing the organisation but will show how the changes that took place worked in practice. It will review the roles of the General Secretaries and offer a revised understanding of their time in office. The chapter will also assess the role of the Cardiff headquarters in building the local associations and the influence the party had on candidate selection. In turn, it will highlight the little-known figure of Winifred 'Freddie' Whitaker and her efforts to build up the organisation. The role of the executive will be discussed and the financial issues the party faced will be examined. It will highlight the decisions that the Honorary Treasurer, Rhys Gerran Lloyd, took, and how his accounting hampered the WLP when he resigned from his post. These first two chapters situate the book within the historiographies of organisations and political parties.

Chapter three will spotlight the policy process of the WLP, highlighting the work of the policy directorate and allowing the WLP's focus on Welshness to come to the fore. The chapter will link back to the previous chapter, arguing that financial issues hampered policy formation after the 1970 general election. A discussion on the manifestos and policies formulated between 1967 and 1979 will follow, showing that the burst of energy before the 1970 general election sustained the party throughout this period. The chapter will argue that the WLP's policy programme was predicated on the premise that Wales would gain a legislative parliament/senedd in the not-too-distant future.

Finally, chapter four will assess the general election record under Hooson. It will offer a revisionist interpretation of the results and will not shy away from reaching some controversial conclusions. The results will be compared with those of Plaid and will argue the WLP was disadvantaged by the UK electoral system. As with the earlier chapters, an emphasis will be placed on redefining the WLP's position, and it will argue that the neglect of the WLP, within the historiography of Wales, is detrimental to gaining a proper understanding of Welsh politics in this period. This chapter will inform future historiographies that place a focus on elections.

The above themes will run through all four chapters. The WLP was a nationalist party focused on promoting the party's Welshness through its policies and organisational structure. Other themes include identifying how the WLP was marginalised and why this needs rectifying within the various historiographies. It also needs to be pointed out that the WLP's main rival was Plaid, which will be highlighted throughout the book. Very little attention is given to the Labour Party and the Conservatives, as neither posed a significant threat to the WLP. These two parties were well ahead of the WLP and Plaid, although both smaller parties posed a threat to the larger parties in certain areas. This book is concerned with the jostling for third place and what it shows about the actual popularity of political parties under the 'first past the post' system.

METHODOLOGY

When my PhD began in 2012, the intention was for the thesis to encompass the full history of the Welsh Liberal Party from its establishment in 1966, ending with the formation of the Welsh Liberal Democrats in 1988. It was to be a history of the party that would include analysis of the local constituencies, but would be a top-down examination of those twenty-two years. It would focus on the changes made within the party and how that affected the electoral fortunes of the WLP. However, it was soon realised that such a history could quickly lose focus, be too broad and would lack the necessary depth required of a doctoral thesis. Also, in 2014 Deacon's book *The Welsh Liberals* was published, examining the WLP via an overview of the main events and the issues the party faced. This was carried out, in the main, through interviews with the main actors and some archival work. In a conversation with Deacon, he advised me that the archive was incomplete due to much of the WLP material being stored in damp conditions before being passed to the NLW. This obviously necessitated a reliance on interviews, backed up with the incomplete archival material.

In 2011, I had already started the process of looking into who could be interviewed for the project. Contact was made with people who had been active within the WLP during the 1960s and 1970s, asking if they would be willing to be interviewed at some point. This met with a mixed reaction, with some stating that they would be willing to be interviewed, whilst some of the responses mentioned that Deacon had already interviewed them and his book was soon to be published. Around this time, a call was received from Helen Roberts, a friend of Hooson's and his secretary during the 1970s. She wanted to make contact to say that Hooson was suffering from Alzheimer's disease and would not be able to take part. This call was greatly appreciated and it gave some insight into Hooson as a person. As it was a personal call, the details are not being used here and, sadly, Hooson died soon afterwards. However, during the call, Ms Roberts informed me that a substantial amount of Hooson's archival material was now available at the National Library of Wales, without needing to gain his, or the family's, permission to view them.

However, when I started my own archival search, it became clear that the archive was more complete than previously realised. There were several different depositors, including Hooson, Merfyn Jones, the WLP and Lord Ogmore, all of whom had held a considerable amount of relevant material. A lot of the papers, particularly in the case of Hooson, had remained untouched and became available for viewing only after Deacon's book had been completed.[8] Whereas the historiography, up to this point, had relied upon interviews, the primary evidence within these archives, which included correspondence, constituency papers, minutes and election material, meant that the project could be based upon these findings. Coupled with other primary evidence, such as other Liberal archives, newspapers, government publications and Hansard, it meant a more in-depth study of the WLP could be produced.

Although he was referring to governmental policy research rather than that of an individual political party, we can modify Lowe's four main advantages of conducting archival research:

> First is that they contain the widest possible amount of information on which policy is based. Second, in the bulk of records created by the 'lower levels' of government we can trace policy implementation and therefore see how decisions taken by the 'core executive' are acknowledged, discussed and refined. Third, by sifting through departmental records it is possible to find clearly stated views of ministers and officials . . . Finally, the files allow researchers to identify an important variable in policymaking, 'a distinctive "departmental" view transcending individual ministers and officials'.[9]

Although he is specifying governmental research, the basic principles of Lowe's statement are just as true for other political research projects. In the context of this project, as the archives were organised in such a way that it was easy to find information on policy, elections and finances, the archives produced the widest amount of information on the various themes of the thesis. The 'lower levels' that Lowe references can also be found within the WLP, namely those who sat on the various committees, such as the policy committee, how they formed the policy, who was spoken to and the final documents that were produced. The private views, for example via letters, of those within the WLP were very candid and on a range of issues. From the formation of the WLP to policy and the party's financial situation, it is possible to garner not only the views expressed but also how they differed from the published remarks made to Deacon and others. Additionally, the archival search established how the members of the WLP defined themselves in relation to Plaid Cymru, Labour, the Conservatives and even the British Liberal Party. What emerged from the archives is an extensive view of how the WLP was run, how it was financed and its decisions on policymaking.

This book, as already established, is not based on interviews with any of the actors within the WLP. It became apparent early on that the top-down approach to the thesis meant having to understand the actions of the key players within the organisation and why they took the decisions they did. The fact is that the thesis was undertaken too late to interview people such as Hooson, Geraint Howells, Lord Ogmore and Lord Lloyd of Kilgerran (Rhys Gerran Lloyd). Hooson died in 2012, Howells in 2004, Lloyd in 1991 and Ogmore in 1976. These were the people at the top of the WLP, upon whose leadership decisions the thesis is partly based. The thesis had to use the archives to establish the motives and decisions made by each of them. Another factor was the age of the people involved. Although those still alive were still astute and mentally strong, many are now in their eighties and the fact that they had already spoken to Deacon meant that challenging their role within the organisation could have caused them unintended distress. One must also face the fact that they had built up their own myths of the events of almost sixty years ago. For example, Deacon interviewed Martin Thomas,[10] among others, who reinforced the popular opinion (within the WLP) that Emlyn Thomas had nearly bankrupted the WLP, prior to the 1970 general election.[11] Deacon established the 'facts', as far as his interviewees were concerned, and this was backed up with the limited amount of archival material available to him. However, there is a danger that the limited archival material then available would have just confirmed their opinions, rather than challenged them. This book, based on a larger amount of archival material than was previously available, looks to challenge those views and build upon the work of Deacon and J. Graham Jones.

This last point feeds into one of the many criticisms of oral history. As Hobsbawm pointed out, oral history is a 'remarkably slippery medium for preserving facts',[12] and this is a charge that has been levelled at oral historians since the 1950s. Peneff, for example, went further and argued that the oral historian had to identify the myths that people convey and try to find the authenticity within them.[13] Another way to look at this is that oral testimonies are essentially the individuals' take on their own life stories and can be coloured by how they want to be viewed. Also, oral histories, like documents in an archive, are not without their biases. Yet it can be difficult to verify the accuracy of someone's recollection decades after an event, especially if it is contradicted by the archival material.

However, it must be said that oral history can be a very valuable tool for historians and political researchers. Pierce points out that historians use interviews to confirm our understanding of the documentary material, clarify grey areas, understand their beliefs or mindset, and to find others to interview.[14] This is important, as it can help to clarify certain points, for example what the atmosphere at a certain meeting might have been like, or why something had been said. In this sense, it is right to reflect on the words of Louis Starr, the first president of the Oral History Association, when he stated that 'oral history is more than a tool and less than a discipline'.[15] This tool has its limitations; in the case of the thesis it was decided that the age of the living members, coupled with the death of the higher profile actors, presented challenges that could be better compensated for by paying due attention to those interviews conducted and published in the work of other historians, such as Deacon and Jones. A more complete history of the WLP can be produced only if all the historians' tools have been utilised. This book complements the work of those historians who came before and adds to their findings by increasing the use of the available sources.

SOURCES

As already noted, the book has extensively used the Hooson, Merfyn Jones, Lord Ogmore and WLP archives at the National Library of Wales in Aberystwyth. The problem with such a large number of personal papers is the repetition of documents, especially leaflets relating to the general elections. On the other hand, there is an issue with the scarcity of some records. For example, the minutes of the various committees are dotted around the archive and many are missing. It can be frustrating if one comes across an interesting piece of information only to find the follow-up information is in a different set of papers or missing entirely. One must also consider that the minutes have been written by someone who must keep them concise by including only what they believe to be relevant. Unfortunately, those compiling the minutes did not have one eye on posterity and probably had no interest in piquing the interest of a future historian. These were collected as a record for the committee and anything else was an afterthought.

Having pointed this out, what is in the archive has proven to be very useful and relevant to this study, whilst being a lot more complete than was initially believed. For example, the handwritten notes detailing which local associations had paid their affiliation fees could be cross-referenced to a list of association officers, providing a picture of the Liberals' strength in that area. The minutes of the executive and the sub-committees provided information about the activities the WLP were involved in. They showed that this was not an amateurish party but a professional, albeit financially stretched, organisation. For example, although not used in the book, the EEC referendum was meticulously documented, with 'link-men' being chosen to liaise between the constituencies and the Liberal European campaign headquarters, and detailing the potential dangers of working with other parties.[16] It was a lot of (expensive) work going through the archives, but the information that has survived does indicate that there were individual Welsh Liberals with their eye on posterity. The completion of this book was only possible because of what has survived, and it makes one wonder about the content of the information that was destroyed.

Newspapers are also valuable, not only for this book but for the historian in general. The online British Newspaper Archive has proven to be an excellent source, having digitised many local and national newspapers. The local newspapers from this period have provided details of meetings that Hooson and others attended. Details given include the speeches they made and how many people were there, which have gone unmentioned in the traditional archives. There is rarely any commentary in the local press, other than a simple report of what was said at a meeting. Yet, the historian must question what has been left out and be aware of the inherent bias in newspapers, in particular, those with broader circulation, such as the Conservative-leaning *Western Mail*. However, it is striking how much coverage the WLP received, and more so how many times Hooson appeared in the columns for his legal work. The local and national Welsh newspapers seemed more than happy to include reports of events within the WLP, although, in the case of the local press, it was because there was very little else going on. Yet, it is interesting to note that the party was not ignored. We see Hooson being reported upon in the national papers, and even writing the odd column for the *Daily Mirror*.[17]

The Hansard website is beneficial, providing details of Hooson's speeches in the House of Commons and links to government publications, such as Hooson's 1967 Government of Wales Bill. Another helpful online resource has been the *Internet Archive*, a non-profit depository of books and other publications, allowing items to be digitally 'borrowed' – a beneficial source if looking for an out-of-print book.

As mentioned throughout this introduction, secondary sources on the WLP are somewhat limited. The main influences on this book have been the works of Russell Deacon, John Graham Jones, David Roberts, K. O. Morgan, Andrew Edwards, Laura McAllister and Martin Johnes. Apart from the first three authors, the rest touch only briefly on the WLP, and their contribution to this book has been through other avenues and parties. If a person wanted to understand why the Welsh Liberals declined before 1950, they would find an abundance of literature on the subject, although, it must be said, most of the literature places the primary focus on England and the enigmatic figure of Lloyd George. However, before 2014, if that person wanted to understand why the Welsh Liberals endured, what policies they had and how the party later became a coalition partner in the Welsh government,[18] they would be disappointed by the lack of an established historiography.

Before 2014, the closest one had to a history of the post-1945 party was a chapter by David Roberts in *The National Question Again*, and J. Graham Jones's article 'The Liberal Party and Wales, 1945–79', published in the *Welsh History Review* in 1993. Of the two, Roberts's chapter has a deeper analysis of the period and was based on an interview with Hooson, a few newspaper articles and some secondary literature.[19] The strength and weakness of Roberts's chapter are that he was writing within six years of Hooson losing his seat. Although an interview with Hooson gives some context to what was happening in the party at the time, the lack of available archival material meant that it was difficult to counter Hooson's assertions. For example, Roberts argued that the 1966 reorganisation of the party, and subsequent events, were in response to Plaid Cymru, with Roberts stating that there were calls for the two parties to work closely together, but Hooson dismissed this.[20] Yet, as this book will argue later, Hooson was very open to working with Plaid Cymru. This highlights the limitations of historians trying to write a proper account within a few years of the described events by relying on just interviews, beneficial as they are. There is no doubt that the addition of archival sources can help to correct any inaccuracies.

As such, it was Jones's article that began to provide the detail that was missing in Roberts's account. The article is the first to give an in-depth understanding of the history of the LPW and WLP and it has been an invaluable resource to historians. It, along with Roberts's chapter, set the template for much of the research that followed, although, like Roberts, Jones does lean heavily on the argument that the WLP was formed in response to the threat posed by Plaid Cymru,[21] which this book argues was only one of the reasons. As the first chapter of this book makes clear, whilst acknowledging the undeniable threat posed by Plaid Cymru, the WLP was set up because the LPW required urgent organisational reform if the party and Liberalism were to survive in Wales. The more detailed nature of Jones's article is understandable, as it used material that had not been seen or used before, for which he gained Hooson's permission to consult his archive. Yet, the detail was at the expense of any in-depth analysis; there is a feeling it was more critical to get the material out there and tell the story. By having to tell the party's history in the confines of an article or, in Roberts's case, a chapter,[22] there is a limit as to how much of that history can be told.

Jones has been a prolific publisher of articles on the LPW, preferring to focus on the Lloyd George family and the 1950s Parliament for Wales campaign, although, in recent years, he has written several articles on Hooson's time as the party leader. The most relevant have been published in the *Journal of Liberal History*[23] and in other journals, such as the *Montgomeryshire Collections*.[24] These articles continued in the tradition of his earlier article in that they were heavily detailed and used material from the Lord Ogmore and Hooson archives held at the National Library of Wales. These articles have been a valuable resource, as they have provided details about many events and have been a good starting point for this book. However, it must be said that these are very much concerned with telling the story of events rather than providing a thorough interpretation of them.

In 'Montgomeryshire's Liberal Century',[25] K. O. Morgan produced one of the more interesting articles and analysed how Hooson lost his parliamentary seat. Although Morgan dedicates just three pages to Hooson's tenure in the seat, he argues that Hooson was ousted by a constituency that had become more anglicised since 1974. Hooson was removed for his support of the Lib-Lab Pact and devolution.[26] This analysis has proven influential, informing the works of Jones, in particular. However, Roberts had suggested this interpretation[27] before Morgan's article was written. Still, it was the latter who assessed the population statistics and was able to provide the evidence for this plausible thesis.

Before the publication of *The Welsh Liberals*, Deacon had authored a couple of articles, the first of which examined the party's history from 1906 and the general election.[28] At just four pages in length, 'The Steady Tapping Breaks the Rock' was a whistle-stop tour of the period and gave just one page to the 1962–79 period. However, this article reinforced the argument that Hooson's seat was lost due to his support for devolution and the Callaghan government.[29] Deacon's other paper, 'The Slow Death of Liberal Wales',[30] analysed why the Liberals declined in Wales between 1906 and 1979 and is the more influential. This article examines events such as the Liberal schisms, the 1922 general election, the rise of the Labour Party and the Liberals' inability to adjust to socialism and Plaid Cymru. The article explains why the party declined and argues that the Liberals were woefully unprepared to respond to each crisis.

Deacon's book, *The Welsh Liberals*, was published in 2014 and examined the Liberals in Wales from the nineteenth century up until 2011. This book was a sorely needed addition to the political historiography of Wales and proved why the party deserved its history to be written. It was a work that takes the reader through the various personalities and history of the LPW, the WLP, the Alliance, the Welsh Liberal Democrats and into the devolution years. Before this work's publication, the post-1959 historiography was patchy and, as we have seen, amounted to a handful of articles. What was missing was a bedrock on which the historiography could grow, which it could take issue with, agree with and use as a reference for further research. Deacon's work provides that foundation. As the first significant work to examine the history of the Liberals in Wales it can, nonetheless, rely on a well-established historiography for its first half. Still, the second half is where the new ground is broken and this is where the originality of the work is shown. The period that coincides with this book is quite detailed but does allow room for other historians to reinterpret the events and take issue with some of the oral history elements.

Outside of these works, other studies on the wider politics of Wales have been used for context. First is Alan Butt Philip's *The Welsh Question*,[31] which provides a detailed history of Welsh nationalism in general and of Plaid Cymru's rise in the 1960s and 1970s. This book should also be read in conjunction with Andrew Edwards's *Labour's Crisis*.[32] Edwards's work examines the Welsh Labour Party in north-west Wales during the 1960s and 1970s. Using the growing threat from Plaid Cymru and the Conservatives to show how both parties infiltrated areas associated with Labour and, before them, the LPW, it is one of the first works to correctly argue that the Conservatives had more of a Welsh following than has been previously acknowledged; however, it is the fear that Plaid Cymru provoked within Welsh Labour that stands out, describing Plaid's move away from the politics of the language and how it matured as a political party in the 1970s. The book is essential for any student interested in Welsh and national politics during this turbulent decade. Martin Johnes, in his *Wales Since 1939*,[33] like Edwards has sought to dispel some of the myths surrounding the nationalist history of Wales, particularly in his revision of the Tryweryn debate. As in much of his work, Johnes tackles the mythology built up around Plaid Cymru and Welsh nationalism in a bid to reclaim a narrative that has sometimes been reduced to an 'us and them' fight.

As can be seen, the historiography is limited, but the justification for further research is sound. It is the contention of this book that any future history of Wales, during this period, should include the WLP. This book places the WLP in its rightful place as the popular nationalist party of Wales during the post-war period, demonstrating that it was Plaid Cymru that was lagging behind the Welsh Liberals.

Notes

1 For example, Kenneth O. Morgan, *Rebirth of a Nation: Wales 1880–1980* (Oxford, 1990), pp. 307–411, and John Davies, *A History of Wales* (London, 1994), pp. 612–79.
2 Russell Deacon, *The Welsh Liberals: The History of the Liberal and Liberal Democratic Parties in Wales* (Cardiff, 2014), p. 187.
3 I have used BLP or the British Liberal Party to distinguish between the party that was the national federal party HQ for the UK and the Welsh Liberal Party or the Scottish Liberal Party (SLP). BLP has also been used to reference the British-wide party, which was in existence before the SLP, became the first

federal Liberal Party and nominally controlled the LPW, before it too became federated. I have kept the same term to avoid confusion and because there was not a separate English Liberal Party.
4   Andrew Edwards, *Labour's Crisis: Plaid Cymru, The Conservatives and the Decline of the Labour Party in North-West Wales, 1960–74* (Cardiff, 2011), p. 9.
5   Martin Johnes, *Wales Since 1939* (Manchester, 2012), p. 4.
6   Merriam-Webster dictionary, 'Welshness'. Available at: *https://www.merriam-webster.com/dictionary/Welshness* (accessed 1 August 2024).
7   Deacon, *The Welsh Liberals*, dedication, p. vi.
8   In fact, a large amount of his constituency correspondence is still not able to be viewed until 2030, due to the possible sensitive nature of the material.
9   Peter Burnham, Karin Gilland Lutz, Wyn Grant and Zig Layton-Henry (eds), *Research Methods in Politics* (Basingstoke, 2008), p. 201. Quoted from R. Lowe, 'Plumbing New Depths: Contemporary Historians and the Public Record Office', *Twentieth Century British History*, 8/2 (1997), 242.
10 Now Lord Thomas of Gresford.
11 Deacon, *The Welsh Liberals*, p. 177.
12 Quoted in Anna Green and Kathleen Troup, *The Houses of History* (Manchester, 2012), p. 230.
13 Green and Troup, *The Houses of History*, p. 235.
14 Roger Pierce, *Research Methods in Politics: A Practical Guide* (London, 2008), pp. 119–20.
15 Enid H. Douglas, 'Oral History and Public History', *The Oral History Review*, 8 (1980), 5.
16 NLW, Merfyn Jones Papers, File 35, Minutes of the WLP Executive, 22 February 1975.
17 *Daily Mirror*, 10 July 1962, 7, for example.
18 Following the 1999 Welsh Assembly election. The Welsh Liberal Democrats entered government in a coalition with the Labour Party.
19 David Roberts, 'The Strange Death of Liberal Wales', in John Osmond, *The National Question Again: Welsh Political Identity in the 1980s* (Llandysul, 1985), pp. 97–8.
20 Roberts, 'The Strange Death', p. 92.
21 J. Graham Jones, 'The Liberal Party and Wales, 1945–79', *Welsh History Review*, 16/3 (June 1993), 347.
22 Jones gave just shy of twelve pages in an article of thirty pages to Hooson's time, and Roberts provided eight out of a possible twenty-three pages.
23 J. Graham Jones, 'Emlyn Hooson (1925–2012)', *Journal of Liberal History*, 86 (Spring 2015), 30–7.
24 J. Graham Jones, 'Emlyn Hooson and Montgomeryshire Politics 1962–79', *The Montgomeryshire Collections*, 97 (2009), 165–204. Also, J. Graham Jones, 'Emlyn Hooson's Parliamentary Debut: The Montgomeryshire By-Election of 1962', *The Montgomeryshire Collections*, 81 (1993), 121–9, and J. Graham Jones, 'Emlyn Hooson, the Devolution Debate and the General Election of May 1979', *The Montgomeryshire Collections*, 106 (2018), 145–67.

25 Kenneth O. Morgan, 'Montgomeryshire's Liberal Century', *Welsh History Review*, 16/1 (June 1992), 93–109.
26 Morgan, 'Montgomeryshire's Liberal Century', 107–8.
27 Roberts, 'The Strange Death', pp. 94–5.
28 Russell Deacon, 'The Steady Tapping Breaks the Rock', *Journal of Liberal History*, 22 (Spring 1999), 14–17.
29 Deacon, 'The Steady Tapping', 15.
30 Russell Deacon, 'The Slow Death of Liberal Wales, 1906–1979', *Journal of Liberal History*, 49 (Winter 2005–6), 12–23.
31 Alan Butt Philip, *The Welsh Question: Nationalism in Welsh Politics 1945–1970* (Cardiff, 1975).
32 Edwards, *Labour's Crisis*.
33 Johnes, *Wales*.

1
THE FALL AND RISE OF THE WELSH LIBERALS, 1918–66

INTRODUCTION

'*To a marked degree, Liberalism and nationalism were fused, and in a real sense the Liberals were the party of Wales and the vehicle for its growing national consciousness*'[1]
(Kenneth O. Morgan, *Modern Wales*, 1973).

In just one sentence, K. O. Morgan deftly describes what Welsh Liberalism meant to the nascent Welsh sense of nationhood. This chapter will begin with a short introduction to how the Liberals were able to become the 'Party of Wales' in the late nineteenth century and why Wales and Liberalism were intertwined. This will then be followed by a brief discussion on the background to why Welsh Liberalism began to experience difficulties and how Labour overtook the Liberals in Wales. It will be argued that, despite the rise of Labour, Welsh Liberalism was able to maintain a sizeable following. The post-1945 decline saw the party reach its pre-Hooson nadir in 1959. This occurred two decades after the BLP suffered a similar fate. The chapter will argue that the reason for the longevity was due to the party's electoral base now being in the rural and less industrial areas of Wales. Voter support in these areas was large enough for the Liberals to keep its third-party status. Additionally, the lack of an organised political challenger to the position of the LPW in the post-1931 period gave the perverse impression that Liberalism in Wales was secure, and the Liberal leadership perceived this security as a strength.

During his leadership of Cymru Fydd (Young Wales), Lloyd George recognised that the LPW needed significant organisational reform. The main issue was that the two federations, the North Wales Liberal Federation (NWLF) and the South Wales Liberal Federation (SWLF), acted independently of one another. However, when he abandoned Cymru Fydd, Lloyd George's plan to seek Home Rule for Wales and enact the necessary reforms the LPW needed, in turn creating an independent organisation, were also jettisoned. Almost seventy years later, it would be Emlyn Hooson who would wield the axe to the LPW and enact a root-and-branch reorganisation making the party independent of the wider BLP. Hooson was only able to do this once he became leader of the LPW, and because he had the understanding and ambition to drive through the much-needed reforms. Additionally, the policy platform that accompanied the reforms placed an emphasis on rediscovering the party's Welshness. As such, a significant portion of the chapter will be given to the rise of Emlyn Hooson within the LPW and will argue that Hooson had shown the reforms that were needed long before he was able to enact them.

The chapter will show that the new WLP was formed at the point when the Liberals in Wales were facing several existential crises. The first threat came from Plaid Cymru, which had reorganised its own internal structure, was making inroads into Labour territory and was seeking to overtake the Liberals as the third party in Wales. The second, as Hooson perceived it, would come from Jo Grimond, the BLP leader, who sought a 'realignment of the Left' and was prepared to work with other parties to achieve that aim.

LIBERALISM IN WALES PRIOR TO 1918

The sudden decline experienced by the BLP, particularly in England, was not a universal experience and the decline in Wales was an extended and drawn-out affair. This is not to suggest that the events of the interwar period did not affect the Liberals in Wales, because they did, but the nature of the decline was different from that experienced in the rest of the UK. To understand why we need to know what the Liberal Party meant to a large proportion of Wales. As K. O. Morgan stated, Wales and Liberalism were intertwined for much of the late nineteenth and early twentieth centuries, to the extent that Liberalism 'permeated Welsh life at every point during this period. Every major transformation of Welsh life owed something to it.'[2] R. Merfyn Jones has argued that the Liberal Party was successful in Wales because it and, later the Labour Party, gave:

> Wales a sharply delineated political identity, but in both cases, this was not based on a sense of all the Welsh as a constituency. Rather was it a case of a large section of that constituency choosing to ally with particular worldviews that then . . . effectively [created] a Welshness in its own image.[3]

Although Jones does highlight the sectarian nature of the identities that both parties fostered,[4] the Liberals dominated Welsh politics in the latter half of the nineteenth and early twentieth centuries because they gave the fledgling nation a sense of its own identity. They carried this identity to Westminster, where the Welsh Liberal MPs were able to champion the issues that mattered to Wales and nonconformists in general.

The reason for this is that many of the Liberal leaders within Wales came from a nonconformist background, significantly influencing their politics, which were of a radical colour. Yet, non-conformity was not just a feature of the LPW but had become a crucial part of Welsh national identity. By the middle of the nineteenth century, Wales had sufficiently deviated from the established Anglican religion, embracing other Protestant-based religions, such as Methodism, Calvinism and Baptism. In the process, the country had become an openly nonconformist society in its religion and politics. Of course, not everyone in Wales was a nonconformist,[5] but the religious difference from England was integral to Welsh identity and to many Liberals.

Politically and culturally, the Liberals were viewed as the defenders of Wales and Welshness. They defended the Welsh language, campaigned for the disestablishment of the Church in Wales and promoted the nonconformist tradition (including pacifism and temperance). Additionally, they provided the infrastructure and ceremonies that would help define the fledgling nation, such as founding the National Library of Wales and the universities. Liberalism had a long tradition of adopting Welsh issues and fighting for a cause, and these causes were radical and Welsh in nature. As Deacon states, 'Campaigning on one issue or another was the *raison d'être* for Welsh Liberal radicals. To be a "radical" meant that you were wedded to a cause or causes that would be at the very soul of your political being.'[6]

Further, labour interests were intertwined with the Liberals. As Cyril Parry argues, the labour movement, as we would understand it today, appeared later in Wales than in the rest of Britain, and initially reflected a Welsh radical ideology rather than a socialist one.[7] This meant that the LPW was in a unique position and could ensure that incremental steps towards better conditions and pay were taken, rather than pressing for an immediate overhaul of society.

An example of a cause that epitomised the relationship between the Welsh Liberals and nonconformism was that of education. Education became a rallying point for the

Welsh Liberals and the nonconformists, taking up the cause following the 1847 publication of the three-volume 'Reports of the Commissioners of Enquiry into the State of Education in Wales'. The reports, with their blue covers, ignited a scandal commonly referred to as the 'Treason of the Blue Books' or 'Brad y Llyfrau Gleision'. Despite noting their native intelligence, the Commissioners considered that nonconformism and the Welsh language, in particular, kept the people in a state of ignorance.[8] Despite the uproar caused by the ignorance displayed within the reports, which was accompanied by some rather salacious newspaper coverage,[9] the bulk of the reports accurately and studiously evidenced the nature of the education system in Wales. However, for nonconformist Wales, the lasting effect of these reports was that the authors and, by extension, the British state were making no secret of their disdain for the Welsh, their language and the religious differences from England. Education became one of the Welsh Liberals' chief battle-cries, and the passage of the Education Acts of 1870[10] and 1902 engendered a considerable amount of hostility within Wales. The 1902 Act was particularly egregious as it gave financial benefits to Anglican schools that were denied to those in the nonconformist sector. The battle to stop the 1902 Act was a defining political moment for Lloyd George.[11]

This sense of identity was an important factor when we consider how long the Liberal Party was able to hold on in Wales compared with its decline in England. Much of this identity was embodied by the popularity of men such as Tom Ellis and David Lloyd George. Lloyd George was at the forefront of many of the campaigns that were linked to the Liberals in this period, including education, the fight against landlordism, Welsh-language rights and Cymru Fydd (Young Wales), which campaigned for a form of Welsh home rule. Additionally, he enjoyed his greatest success, in Wales and the UK, as the 'man who won the war', following the cessation of hostilities in 1918.

It is a testament to his popularity in Wales that, even after being ousted as prime minister by his coalition partners, any opposition to him was localised. Even the animosity caused by the 1918 'Coupon Election' had little bearing on his status.

The results of the 1906 general election allowed the Liberals to lay claim to being the 'Party of Wales', as all but one of the seats in Wales took the Liberal whip. Further afield, as well as in Wales, the informal electoral pact with Labour also meant that the Liberals were able to keep the younger party in check and incorporate aspects of socialism into the so-called 'New Liberalism'. However, by the end of the First World War and despite David Lloyd George's personal popularity within Wales, this status had changed. By the time of the 1931 general election, the LPW had slipped from being the largest political party in Wales to the third, behind Labour and the Conservatives.[12] The reason for the Welsh decline is linked with the UK-wide collapse of the Liberal Party, but it was a markedly different decline that took longer.

THE WELSH LIBERAL COLLAPSE
– THE HISTORIOGRAPHY

The decline of the Liberal Party in Britain following the First World War is one of the most researched and contentious areas of British political history. The bare 'facts' of the decline appear to be straightforward: the BLP, having won a landslide general election in 1906, entered the First World War with Asquith as prime minister and Lloyd George as chancellor. By the end of the conflict, the BLP had been in a coalition with the Conservatives since 1916, with Lloyd George becoming prime minister, following Asquith's resignation that year. Parliament had passed the illiberal Defence of the Realm Act in 1914 and the Military Service Act in 1916, the latter of which introduced conscription. Lloyd George would lead the coalition until 1922.

Due to the way that the handover of power occurred, Asquith believed that Lloyd George had usurped his position; the BLP fractured into two groups, one led by Asquith and the other by Lloyd George. Lloyd George's group remained loyal to the coalition and Asquith's grouping was on the sidelines, although they generally supported the war effort. The two Liberal groups were often hostile towards each other and the animosity between the leaders became increasingly bitter, particularly following the 1918 'Coupon Election'.[13] Lloyd George was eventually ousted by his coalition partners in 1922, with both Liberal factions separately contesting the general election that followed. However, in 1922, the Labour Party had overtaken the Liberals, becoming the official opposition to the Conservative government. The election results showed that the Liberals were better together than apart.

The decision to reunite the party in time for the 1923 general election was due, in part, to the Conservative government's plan to impose tariffs, thereby abandoning the principle of 'Free Trade', an issue that united both the Liberals and the Labour Party. Although the Liberals regained some lost ground, the Labour Party entered government, albeit for a short time, with Liberal backing. The general elections of 1924 and 1929 confirmed that the Liberals were no longer a government in waiting and had been usurped by Labour. The party was now entrenched as the third party in British politics. There was a further split in 1931, this time a three-way split, caused by the collapse of the second Labour government. Lloyd George's opposition to a general election, which he believed would only benefit the Conservatives, was precipitated by the resignation of the prime minister, Ramsay MacDonald. MacDonald's resignation was due to a worsening economic situation and high unemployment.[14]

From August 1931, MacDonald would lead a coalition known as the National government, with no fewer than three Liberal groupings contesting the subsequent general election.

Herbert Samuel led the bulk of the Liberal Party, often referred to as the 'Samuelites'. Sir John Simon led a group that had begun aligning themselves with the Conservatives and supported the National government. They were known collectively as the Liberal Nationals (sometimes known as the 'Simonites'), then from 1947 they became the National Liberals. The party would be entirely subsumed into the Conservative Party in 1968. Finally, David Lloyd George led the third grouping. This small group included his daughter, Megan, and son, Gwilym. Lloyd George retreated from front-line Liberal politics at this point. Lloyd George's grouping would reunite with Samuel's BLP in time for the 1935 general election. The BLP declined further over the course of the next twenty-five years and six general elections. The fifty-nine MPs elected in 1929 would be reduced to a rump of six in 1959.

As mentioned, these are the bare facts of the collapse of Liberalism within the UK. Yet, debate on the exact cause of the collapse has been ongoing since George Dangerfield released his classic, but derided, work, *The Strange Death of Liberal England* (1935).. It is not the intention of this current book to comment on the debate, as it will send us down a rabbit warren that is not needed to understand the Welsh Liberal experience. Suffice to say, from a Welsh perspective, the issue with the debate on the decline of the BLP is that many of the texts and arguments pay scant attention to the individual nations within the UK, preferring to focus on England. This is not unexpected as, by population size, most of the Liberal support was based in England. However, England was not as intertwined with the Liberal Party as Wales was.

Within Wales, the historiography for the LPW is concentrated chiefly on the period up until the Second World War. This is because Welsh historians have mainly focused on the post-1918 rise of the Labour Party. Historians have neglected the continued post-war history of the LPW, as it was seen as a minor political party, unable to challenge Labour. The only other political party that has received a notable level of academic research, comparable to the Labour Party, is Plaid Cymru, albeit most of it centred on the 1950 to 1980 period. In terms of its share of the vote, it must be reiterated that the LPW maintained its status as the third party in Welsh politics until the 2015 general election.[15] However, due to the inbuilt unfairness of the UK electoral system, the LPW and its successors never gained the parliamentary representation that reflected its support. Plaid, on a smaller share of the Welsh vote, had more MPs. This will be explored in the final chapter.

One of the main features of the historiography of Welsh Liberalism is that most of the studies focus on a particular aspect of the decline. For example, J. Graham Jones has written extensively on the Lloyd George policy documents of the 1920s and the effect they had on the 1929 general election, whilst others have regionalised their studies. Cyril Parry's influential micro study *The Radical Tradition in Welsh Politics* focused on the rise of Labour and the decline of the Liberals within Gwynedd. It argued that through most of the pre-1914 period, Labour and socialism found it challenging to gain a foothold because of the Liberals' dominance. He argues that most of the socialist ideas, particularly those emanating from the Fabian Society, were seen as 'English' and of little relevance to the isolationist tendencies of the Gwynedd workforce. One of Parry's main arguments was that the Liberals had adopted an understanding of labour politics and promoted the New Liberalism creed, thereby appeasing any potential trouble.[16] Even if Parry's work was regional, rather than Wales-wide, his argument goes some way towards refuting K. O. Morgan's assertion that the New Liberalism did not affect Wales in a significant way.[17]

Further, Parry demonstrates that not only were the local unions dominated by the Liberals, but the Labour leadership within Wales were either former Liberals or adhered to the same nonconformist radical tradition. They believed in gradual change rather than the instant change of revolution.[18] In the end, it was the Independent Labour Party (ILP) that began to make some inroads into the area; however, the First World War wiped out any progress that the ILP made. The remnants of the ILP formed the backbone of the Labour Party associations that began to appear after the war. Parry argued that this was coupled with the opening of Gwynedd society to more English influences, mostly from those who had served in the forces during the First World War and had gained an understanding of socialism from their peers.[19] This hastened the end of Liberal dominance in Gwynedd.

Considering the number of articles that focus on the Liberal decline in the 1920s, it is quite odd that it took until 2014 for a full history of the party to be published. Russell Deacon's book reiterated that the history of the LPW and its later incarnations was an important part of Welsh history, even during its 'lean years' following the Second World War. It showed that the LPW had many challenging years, but that once a capable and charismatic leader took over, the party was able to rebuild itself in the 1960s and 1970s. Deacon's arguments on the decline of the LPW are further expanded upon by his articles on the subject.[20]

Deacon has termed the period between 1906 and 1979 as the 'slow death of Liberal Wales'. These seventy-three years encompassed the 1906 Liberal general election 'landslide' and ended with the 1979 loss of Emlyn Hooson's seat, the final seat to have been held continuously by a Liberal since the Liberal heyday of the nineteenth century. Deacon's thesis rests on identifying the causes of the 'slow death' and, apart from the rise of Plaid Cymru in the late 1960s, he shows that the other causes lie in the period up until the late 1950s. As such, he named four main reasons for the 'slow death':[21]

1. The end of the electoral pact with Labour.
2. The First World War and the inability of the Welsh Liberals to adjust to socialism.

3. The splits within the Liberal Party and the failure of the Welsh party machine.
4. The arrival of Plaid Cymru and the withering away of the remaining Welsh Liberals.

This thesis is important, as it is one of the few[22] that attempt to show the causation of the decline in Wales from the Liberal point of view and place it into a larger picture of the party after the Second World War. Deacon found that many of the arguments that had been put forward for the Liberal decline in the rest of the UK (that is, England) crossed over to the Welsh context. For example, these included the departure of pacifists and others from the LPW following the illiberal actions of the Liberal/Conservative wartime coalition,[23] most notably the Defence of the Realm Act and conscription. However, there were differences in the Welsh context compared with the rest of Britain, albeit minor at first glance, but indicative of the LPW's hold on Welsh politics. The major differences included Labour's more drawn-out usurpation of the Liberals' position as the alternative to the Conservatives, which took longer than in the rest of the UK. Also important to the party's longevity was the LPW becoming the third-placed party in 1931, comparable with the 1924 results at the UK level.

Moreover, Deacon argues that the Liberal schism between Asquith and Lloyd George 'did not cause much of a problem in Wales',[24] and focuses more on the 1931 three-way split in the Liberal Party. There is little doubt that the 1931 split was more damaging to Welsh Liberalism in the long term. Once the Lloyd George faction realigned with the Liberal Party in time for the 1935 general election, there remained two parties with the Liberal name in Wales. Yet, there can be no doubt that the actions of Lloyd George during the 1918–22 period had a dramatic effect on the Asquithian Liberal wing in Wales. The vindictiveness that Lloyd George displayed in denying the 'coupon' to those who had opposed him or the coalition created a bitterness that was never fully resolved, despite the 1923 reunification. Within Wales, the Liberal in-fighting and denial of the 'coupon' had seen many of those who identified with the Asquith wing either lose their seats or choose not to stand at all. The hatred felt by the Asquithian Liberals towards Lloyd George culminated in the February 1921 'Liberal versus Liberal' Cardiganshire by-election. Although comfortably won by Lloyd George's coalition candidate, it opened a fissure that saw the Liberals engage in open civil war. The two separate Liberal associations in the county would contest the next two general elections against each other.[25] In the 1923 general election, the seat was taken by Rhys Hopkin Morris, the anti-Lloyd George candidate. Hopkin Morris opposed Lloyd George and the use of his 'political fund', which gave Lloyd George financial control over the Liberal Party. It was a contentious issue, with many opposing Lloyd George because of the influence it gave him. Hopkin Morris would represent the seat until 1932 and then Carmarthenshire from 1945 until he died in 1957.

Other arguments that were more directly linked to the Welsh context include the state of the internal organisation of the LPW, the defections to Labour in the 1950s (in particular, of Megan Lloyd George), and the rise of Plaid Cymru. The latter two points will be examined later, but it is right that we examine the state of the LPW, both electorally and internally.

THE WELSH LIBERAL DECLINE

It is essential to realise that after 1918 the Liberals, of both persuasions, lost support to Labour in the south and north east of Wales, whilst local associations in the south began to fold or suffer from inactivity.[26] In purely electoral terms, the by-elections that were held in the 1918–22 parliament give a stark indication of the challenge facing the Liberals in the south. Other than the Cardiganshire by-election, eight others were held, all in the industrial south. The Liberal coalition candidates stood in five of them and an Asquithian Liberal contested just one – the famous October 1922 Newport by-election that brought down the coalition government and led to Lloyd George's resignation. Despite a spirited challenge by the Liberals, the six seats that Labour retained during these by-elections show how embedded the party had become in the south. The November 1922 general election shows a starker picture. After the collapse of the coalition, there was a noticeable decline in the Lloyd George faction, with its share of the vote dropping by almost thirteen per cent, and losing a net total of ten seats when compared with the 1918 result.[27] Although the Asquithian Liberals were barely troubled by the decline in Liberal fortunes in Wales, having just the two seats, it was a blow to Lloyd George's hegemony over the country. One could point to the 1922 general election as the turning point in Welsh politics where, for the first time, Labour's votes and its share of the seats outstripped those of both Liberal factions.

However, Wales was much kinder than the rest of Britain to the Liberals during the 1920s, particularly after reunification in 1923. The BLP may have had an artificial boost at the 1923 general election, but it was followed by a dramatic decline in 1924. Yet, the situation with the Liberals in Wales was markedly different. At the 1923 general election, the reunified LPW attained a third of the vote in Wales, totalling almost the combined vote of the Asquith and Lloyd George factions in 1922. The LPW retained that position for the next three general elections, despite the rise in the electorate, Labour's assault on the southern mining constituencies and the number of three-cornered contests taking place. Liberals still enjoyed a sizeable amount of popularity within their traditional, rural heartlands, a popularity that Labour was finding hard to penetrate, let alone destroy. Duncan Tanner points out that despite being particularly strong in the industrial areas of south Wales, Labour had found it difficult during the 1920s to, at least, contest the rural seats where there was little to no Labour organisation. Also, Labour could not bridge the gap in rural seats with small industrial areas, finding it difficult to appeal to both sections of the constituency at election time. Equally, Labour also found it difficult to appeal to the middle classes or the Welsh-speaking intelligentsia in the rural areas. This was primarily due to Labour's weak organisation, particularly in north Wales.[28]

Yet, despite Labour's difficulties in the Liberal heartlands,[29] both Deacon and Morgan have stated that the Liberals were ill-equipped to deal with the onslaught of Labour during this period. Morgan points out that by the 1920s, the Liberals had begun to lose the 'working man'. A lack of understanding and the societal bonds that had kept the Liberals tied to the nonconformist movement had now been lost to Labour within south Wales.[30] Deacon points to the appeal that Labour's revolutionary 'quick fix' had on the incomers from England who settled in the south and north-east of Wales. These settlers had little affiliation with Wales, the language, or the nonconformist tradition.[31]

It was not until the general elections of 1931 and 1935 that the vulnerability of these Liberal heartlands was fully exposed and, ironically, the Conservatives would be the beneficiaries. By exploiting a Liberal Party that had been split three ways in 1931, the Conservatives were able to gain a foothold in these 'small c' conservative areas. In Wales, the Conservatives had polled more votes in 1931 than the combined total of the three Liberal factions, effectively putting the LPW into third place. It was just a matter of time before the Conservatives consolidated their support and turned it into seats, which was achieved with the aid of the Liberal Nationals. Following the 1931 general election, the Liberal Nationals were becoming increasingly linked with the Conservatives, and from the 1935 general election onwards they were seen as indistinguishable from each other. Liberal Nationals generally did not face a Conservative opponent and often stood with Conservative backing; at subsequent general elections, it was felt that having two major parties with the Liberal name aided the Liberal National candidates. Following the reunification of the 'Samuelites' with the Lloyd George faction, both sets of 'Liberals' engaged in very public arguments, particularly during the 1935 general election. These hostilities would carry on until the 1960s, becoming a thorny issue for the LPW, as there was a belief in Liberal circles that the continued existence of the Liberal Nationals caused confusion for the voters. The Conservatives were happy to indulge the ambiguity.[32]

THE INTERNAL STATE OF THE LPW

This electoral challenge was worsened by the internal state of the LPW. Following the 1931 split, Lloyd George effectively retreated from the front line of Liberal politics. He had stopped funding the Liberal general election campaigns after 1929, a decision that would disproportionately affect the LPW. This disproportionality was not an unusual situation for Lloyd George because where he had been seen as a New Liberal reformer[33] on the national stage, he had long treated Wales in a more parochial fashion.[34] The decline in the LPW had its roots in Lloyd George's funding of the wider party and his attitude to any reform of the Welsh party structure.

The electoral challenge and the internal organisational difficulties were not related to each other but go some way in understanding the state that the party found itself in before 1945. They highlight Lloyd George's neglect of the BLP and the LPW and, conversely, show his need to dominate both organisations. The first reveals his desire to gain and wrest control of the BLP from Asquith; the other, which happened almost thirty years before, was an example of his ability to cut his losses and change his mind on a political issue. Each had implications for the LPW and affected it in different ways.

During the 1924 general election, Lloyd George used his 'Political Fund'[35] to blackmail the Asquithian Liberals by refusing to fund constituencies that he considered to be 'hopeless seats'. As such, the BLP contested just over half the seats in Britain and left a third of seats in Wales, mainly in the south, uncontested.[36] Nationally, the lack of general election candidates made the Liberals look like a party with no intention of forming a government. More seriously, at a crucial juncture in Wales, Lloyd George had committed an act of self-harm that effectively abandoned south Wales. Lloyd George may have been right in his assessment, as south Wales had become Labour territory. Yet, abandoning these areas right at the point when he identified the Liberals needed to regain the support of the working classes was an act of sabotage that was repeated in 1931 when Lloyd George split from the Liberal Party, refusing to allow the Liberals to use his fund. In this sense, 1924 is the point when the Liberals abandoned south Wales for the best part of fifty years, while 1931 was the point when the Liberals abandoned any pretence of wanting to win a general election in Wales or the UK. In Wales, 1929 was the final year that Lloyd George funded a general election campaign, and it was the last time that the LPW contested thirty-five of the thirty-six seats in Wales. In 1931, due to the split, all three Liberal groupings contested a total of nineteen seats; in 1935, the reunified LPW (minus the Liberal Nationals) contested just eleven seats. It would take until the October 1974 general election before the WLP was able to contest every seat in Wales again.[37]

However, the most significant organisational mistake that Lloyd George made was his failure to reform the Party structure. In 1896, through his leadership of the Cymru Fydd (Young Wales) movement, there was a stated aim to further the cause of Home Rule for Wales. To do this, Lloyd George attempted to form a Liberal Party of Wales, which was to be separate from the wider BLP, by merging the Northern Welsh National Federation with the South Wales Liberal Federation (SWLF). The leaders of the SWLF (in particular, D. A. Thomas)[38] were very vocal opponents of a merger and it failed, due to their opposition. In part, this opposition was due to the cultural divide that existed in Wales.

The south feared domination by a Welsh-speaking, nationalist intelligentsia, whilst the north feared an anglicised dominance from the south. The fear of the anglicisation of Wales was not without evidence, as the influx of inward migrants from England was beginning to have a notable consequence on Welsh culture and the language. Combine this with the Education Act of 1870 and the Commissioners of Enquiry report, and it is understandable that a divide existed.. Yet, the failure was also linked to personal animosity towards Lloyd George, as many within the LPW were unhappy with what they believed to be his personal 'ambitions'.[39]

Following the failure to enact the merger, Cymru Fydd folded. Lloyd George would come to reject the idea of Home Rule in Wales and, by extension, reform of the LPW. The reasoning was that the more prosperous and anglicised south would dominate any future Welsh parliament to the detriment of the Welsh-speaking north.[40] For the next sixty years, the LPW would remain divided along these lines and exist as two autonomous federations, nominally under the umbrella of the LPW and a wider member of the BLP. When the local associations paid them, affiliation fees would be sent to the BLP. The lack of a coherent policy framework between the two Welsh federations would be reflected in the Liberal manifestos. Devolution and Federalism were the only mentions that Wales received in most of the post-1931 manifestos.

The loss of Lloyd George and his political fund during the 1930s meant that the LPW was left in an indeterminate state. The new leadership of the BLP were largely unconcerned with Wales and, as Jones points out, by 1945, the British Liberal Party organisation had 'ground to a halt during the war, finances were low and the party was racked by dissension over the number of candidates which it should put up'.[41] Despite suffering a decline in its organisation and membership, it is a little ironic that, to the BLP, the LPW was seen as something of a beacon for a potential Liberal revival. Rural Wales remained one of the Liberal strongholds in 1945, and it is this image that fed into the complacency of the leadership, particularly that of Clement Davies.

THE RISE OF EMLYN HOOSON, 1945–62

Although the withdrawal of Lloyd George's funding severely wounded the LPW, it was the immediate leadership failures after the Second World War that would bring Welsh Liberalism to the brink of extinction. The newly appointed chairman of the parliamentary party, Clement Davies,[42] has been credited for keeping the BLP together in the decade after the war. His refusal to accept a cabinet post from Churchill in 1951 (thus avoiding the fate of the National Liberals, who were later subsumed into the Conservative Party), has been rightly lauded as one of the chief reasons for the Liberals' survival as a political party. Deacon stated, 'As well as being the most important act by any Welsh Liberal to determine the party's future, it was also perhaps the greatest act undertaken by any Liberal.'[43] Davies had the unenviable task of becoming the leader of a political party that had, by 1945, shrunk to just twelve MPs. This was right at the point when the BLP needed a charismatic and able figurehead. Davies's sacrifice of a ministerial post went some way to addressing that.

Following the 1945 general election, the BLP was quite a polarised entity. The left wing of the party included prominent Welsh Liberals, such as Megan Lloyd George and Emrys Roberts, who would openly support the Labour government. They were matched to the right by figures such as Lady Violet Bonham-Carter, Asquith's daughter, and Rhys Hopkin Morris, both of whom were generally favourable to the Conservatives. This might not have been such an issue in a larger political party, but to have a divergence of opinion in a small grouping of powerful personalities would have severe consequences for the Welsh Liberals. Despite the criticism of him being an ineffectual leader of the Liberal Party and his assessment of his leadership style as being one of 'almost supine weakness',[44] the fact remains that Davies acted as a counterpoint to the extreme wings of the BLP. Although to the right of his party, Davies became adept at appeasing both factions, and it was a testament to him as a leader that he handed over to Jo Grimond a BLP which, although it may have reached its nadir, had pretty much remained intact.[45]

Yet, the same could not be said of the Liberal Party of Wales, whose own nadir had yet to occur. As Emlyn Hooson would later state:

> there was no real leadership for the Welsh Liberals in the decade after 1945 . . . It is my belief, as I look back, that not one of the Liberal members of the 1945 vintage up to 1962 believed in their hearts that there was a future for Liberals as a Party standing on its own feet.[46]

The problem within Wales after 1945 was that despite Davies being Welsh and caring deeply about the country,[47] he could not be all things to all people. For the Liberal Party to survive in Britain, any meaningful reforms to the LPW had to be ignored.[48] Of course, the primary reform that was sorely needed was an amalgamation or abolition of the federations. The animosity between the northern and southern federations had continued, with both factions mistrusting the other. Neither was prepared to engage in formulating either a joint policy or electoral strategy. For example, the SWLF tended to allow only members of its executive Committee to stand in general elections (if they fielded any candidates at all), on the pretence that they could not find other suitable candidates. This meant that large sections of south Wales would see little or no Liberal activity until 1970. As Hooson later remarked, if you wanted to ruin a political party in Wales, 'then set up a North and South Wales Federation!'[49]

When Davies took over the leadership of the BLP in 1945, the party had been subjected to an electoral drubbing that would enhance the status of the Welsh Liberals. The LPW, between 1945 and 1955, was the glue that held the BLP together, with the majority of Liberal MPs emanating from Wales (see tables 1 and 2).

Table 1: BLP – British general election results, 1945–59

General election year	Seats	Votes	Percentage of votes
1945	12	2,252,430	9%
1950	9	2,621,487	9.1%
1951	6	730,546	2.6%
1955	6	722,402	2.7%
1959	6	1,640,760	5.9%

Table 2: LPW – General election results in Wales, 1945–59[50]

General election year	Seats	Votes	Percentage of votes
1945	7	203,792	15.2%
1950	5	193,090	12.6%
1951	3	116,821	7.7%
1955	3	104,095	7.3%
1959	2	78,951	5.3%

It is unsurprising that Deacon would state that the 1951 general election results confirmed that the 'Welsh party had become, in effect, the British Liberal Party'.[51] However, he may well be inadvertently damning the LPW with faint praise, as there were significant signs that Liberalism within Wales was experiencing a downward trajectory throughout the 1950s. By the 1959 general election, the LPW appeared to be teetering on the brink of disaster. The reason for this is that from 1951, the LPW contested the seats that it felt had a chance of winning, roughly a third. This aided the Conservatives, as Liberal voters would tend to give their vote to a Conservative candidate in the absence of a Liberal.[52] By the mid-1950s, the LPW at the local association level was exceptionally weak, with the SWLF reporting some activity, but places such as Swansea had been lost to the Liberal Nationals, informing the LPW that 'there is no longer Liberal support there'.[53] Clearly, the SWLF was being neglected whilst Clement Davies focused on the survival of the wider parliamentary Liberal Party and the organisation in England.

The lack of leadership was also in evidence when one tries to locate the BLP on the political spectrum. As Deacon points out, during this period, the policy of the BLP swung from left to right, with many feeling that the party was firmly on the right during Clement Davies's stewardship.[54] This shift to the right was reflected in the 1951 and 1955 general elections, where all three of the successful LPW candidates (Davies, Bowen and Hopkin Morris) were to the party's right, faced no Conservative opponent and were returned as MPs. However, those on the left, namely Lloyd George and Emrys Roberts, did face strong Tory opposition and, due to a split in the anti-socialist vote, were both defeated, albeit by Labour candidates.[55] Part of the reason that they faced a Conservative opponent was that they were seen as being too close to the Labour Party.

There were several reasons why those on the right did not face a Conservative opponent. Most notable was Churchill's desire to bring the Liberals into a closer working position with his party in 1951. On a more tactical level, all three of these MPs faced a Labour opponent and, if the Conservatives had stood, it might have split the anti-socialist vote. This was especially so in Clement Davies's seat. Between 1951 and 1955, the Conservatives were worried that if they opposed Davies, the Liberals would target Tory marginal seats, thereby splitting the vote and letting Labour in.[56] Also, from 1951, all three of these MPs had supported the Conservative policy agenda in Parliament.[57] As Jones points out, Lloyd George, in particular, had become a victim of the sharp upsurge in the Conservative vote that was being seen throughout Britain.[58] It would also be remiss not to mention that since 1918, the Liberals were particularly vulnerable if they faced more than one opponent. Depending on the political composition of the constituency, a Liberal who faced both larger parties and, later, Plaid Cymru would struggle to hold on to the seat. For example, Clement Davies's Montgomery seat was a conservative, rural and anti-socialist seat. When he faced just a Labour candidate, he enjoyed a healthy lead, but, as in 1959, Davies's lead was severely cut when the Conservatives stood in the seat (see table 3).

Table 3: Montgomery general election results, 1950–9[59]

General election	Liberal votes – %	Labour votes – %	Conservative votes – %	Total votes cast
1950	14,401 – 51.3%	6,070 – 21.6%	7,621 – 27.1%	28,092
1951	17,075 – 69.2%	7,584 – 30.8%	N/A	24,659
1955	16,021 – 68.1%	7,521 – 31.9%	N/A	23,542
1959	10,970 – 42.1%	6,950 – 26.6%	8,176 – 31.3%	26,096

On this note, one of the more straightforward reasons for the decline concerns 1951 and the loss of the higher profile 'radical' left wing of the LPW. As Butt Philip comments, until 1951, the Liberals 'were still very much the expression of the Welsh radical tradition and Welsh nonconformity'.[60] Both Emrys Roberts and Megan Lloyd George lost their seats[61] in this general election, leaving the Liberals in Wales without its standard-bearers for the more traditionally radical and Welsh-focused section of the party. As an example of their radicalism, both members had been instrumental in the Parliament for Wales campaign, to which the rest of the Welsh Liberal MPs gave only scant support, if they supported it at all.[62] So, with the loss of these two members, the Liberals' interest in the campaign petered out, and so would the LPW's claim to be institutionally interested in the subject for the rest of the decade.

In 1956, Clement Davies's health began to decline and he was persuaded to resign the leadership of the Liberal Party in favour of Jo Grimond, the Scottish Liberal leader. Following the 1959 general election, Davies began to court Hooson as the successor to his Montgomery seat, aiming to resign in 1962. However, Davies died in 1962 and did not get the chance to retire.

It was in this situation that Emlyn Hooson would emerge as the successor to Clement Davies in Wales. It would be Hooson who not only recognised the inherent failings of the LPW, but also had a remedy for its ailments.

HOOSON'S BACKGROUND

Emlyn Hooson, the son of a farming couple from Denbigh, came from a family that were great admirers of Lloyd George[63] and were Liberal supporting nonconformists.[64] Hooson had been in the Royal Navy during the Second World War and, following the end of hostilities, returned to the University College of Wales, Aberystwyth, to finish his Law degree. Whilst at Aberystwyth, he led the university's Liberal society, gaining a name for himself within Liberal circles as the editor of the *New Radical* publication. Upon leaving Aberystwyth, he was called to the bar in 1949 and, in 1960, became one of the youngest QCs at the age of 35. Hooson was also a fluent Welsh speaker and committed federalist, but could countenance devolution.

Lloyd George and his policy documents, particularly the 'Yellow Book', were an influence on Hooson and something he looked to emulate. It is indicative of his admiration for Lloyd George that whenever historians write about Hooson, they never fail to mention the link, with good reason. In some autobiographical notes, Hooson offered an insight into Lloyd

George's effect on him when, as a 14-year-old, he heard him speak at the 1939 National Eisteddfod in Denbigh. The speech was followed by an encounter with Lloyd George (who patted Hooson on the head), which held some personal significance for Hooson. Hooson remembered the 'Welsh Wizard' describing the effects and possible aftermath of the coming war:

> I remember his vivid imagery, his comparing the destructive impact of war with the destructive impact of massive storms on forests; and remember how, in an extended smile, he went on to say that after the storm abated the outdated rotten trees would give people the opportunity to garner kindling to warm their hearths, and that the people also would see signs of fresh green growth between the trees which had survived.[65]

The influence of Lloyd George on Hooson's politics was not lost on his friends either, one of whom recounts that in a passionate discussion of a Liberal revival, his friend's father remarked to Hooson: 'And, do you know, you look like Lloyd George when he was a young man' – a remark that Hooson took very seriously.[66] In 1947, Hooson was also chosen to contest Lloyd George's Caernarvon Borough constituency, although, due to boundary changes, it was renamed Conway by the time of the 1950 general election. He also contested the seat at the 1951 general election, losing both times, to Labour and the Tories, respectively.

THE LPW AND HOOSON

Although there was no joint policymaking, it would be incorrect to say that the Liberals were devoid of policies for Wales, but they were somewhat limited. As Emrys Roberts, soon to be MP for Merioneth, stated just before the 1945 general election:

> I am seriously concerned that the Liberal Party should include in its Election Programme a proposal in regard to Wales. Its Welsh Members and candidates do advocate the recognition of the special interests of Wales in post-war reconstruction, the need for the treatment of Wales as a whole, and in particular the establishment of a Secretary of State and a Welsh National Development Council. It is essential for the official Liberal programme to back these demands.[67]

The 1945 general election Liberal Party manifesto called only for 'suitable measures of Devolution', using depopulation from Welsh areas to English towns and cities as a reason for the policy.[68] This lack of a serious policy platform for the LPW meant that Wales was something of an afterthought when it came to the wider BLP. Throughout the 1950s and into the 1960s, the BLP manifestos all contained similar wording and nothing further. This was a situation that Hooson was determined to tackle.

Speaking in 1948, Hooson voiced similar concerns to Roberts when he is reported to have said that the 'Liberal Party had side-tracked the issue of a definite Liberal Policy for Wales long enough, and if it could not face up to it, they might as well give up'.[69] The lack of a policy for Wales did not mean that there were no ideas being expressed. At public meetings during this period, Hooson was fleshing out policy positions that he would back for most of his political career. For example, he made the case that 'electricity produced in Wales ... [should] be used for the welfare of Wales'. Additionally, Hooson would hark back to Liberal policies that Lloyd George had made famous, most notably in the 1920s, when he stated that the agricultural '"Owner-occupier" was the Liberal Party's aim and ideal'.[70] He had even begun preparations on a 'Welsh Yellow Book',[71] an idea that would continue to be considered up until 1965. It is safe to assume that Hooson's planned 'Yellow Book' would have included his own five-point plan for Wales from 1948:

[1.] a Welsh Economic Corporation based on the Tennessee Valley Association for co-ordinating all industries to benefit the whole community;
[2.] a North to South Wales road, essential both for Welsh industry and culture;
[3.] a Welsh B.B.C. to develop the art and culture of Wales;
[4.] self-government within a federal State;
[5.] a national body to control the use of land.[72]

All these ideas, in one form or another, would be incorporated into Hooson's vision for a separate Welsh Liberal Party and would later form the backbone of the 1970 general election manifesto.

It was the second-to-last of these proposals that occupied Hooson the most and would be the mainstay of his political career. From that one policy point sprang all his other positions regarding Wales. Hooson would never have considered himself as a Welsh nationalist in the Plaid Cymru mould, as he was too much of an internationalist and viewed them as isolationists. Yet, he was acutely aware that he travelled the same path as them, even sharing a platform during the Parliament for Wales campaign in the early 1950s. Still, he deviated from them on the issue of full independence. His language, as reported, often spoke about Wales being a separate country. It is in this respect that we see Hooson setting out his stall for Wales, as he was reported as saying that 'as a separate nation Wales had her own problems on which the Welsh people should have power to decide. On questions of foreign policy and many other matters, Wales should co-operate with England.'[73]

Hooson would not contest either the 1955 or 1959 general elections, due to his burgeoning legal career, though his growing influence within the LPW was felt at the 1959 general election. One of the earliest signifiers of how different a Hooson-led LPW would be when compared with it under Clement Davies's leadership was the contents of the 1959 LPW general election manifesto, 'A New Deal for Wales'. This manifesto, written by Hooson and Glyn Tegai Hughes,[74] has been described by Deacon as being 'as Welsh Nationalist as any produced by Plaid Cymru'.[75] It pinpointed the direction that Hooson wanted the LPW to take in the coming years and assembled his policy ideas into one document. The manifesto called for:

1. A domestic parliament and a Secretary of State for Wales.
2. A Welsh-language television channel, greater support for the professionalisation of the arts and support for Welsh-medium books; Welsh-language secondary and grammar schools to be established.
3. Quarrymen to be given compensation for pneumoconiosis.
4. A Welsh Water Board to be established; major road developments to take place; support for Welsh ports.
5. Agricultural support for hill farmers, cooperatives and small-scale farmers.
6. Support for rural unemployment.[76]

This document formally set out Hooson's stall and was intended as a rebuttal to Plaid Cymru. Plaid had begun to worry the LPW, as it had started to gain a great deal of publicity during the 1950s. By sharing a platform with prominent Welsh Liberal and Welsh Labour members during the Parliament for Wales campaign, Plaid were provided a modicum of political respectability. Plaid had begun to steer their limited financial resources towards by-elections, turning the contests into spectacles, thereby gaining further publicity. By-elections were important to the party as they were cheaper than general election campaigns and, of the ten by-elections held between 1945 and 1959, Plaid contested seven. The LPW contested just one, the 1957 Carmarthen by-election. This was the seat that had been held by the Liberal Rhys Hopkin Morris, who had recently died, and which the Liberals had hoped to keep. However, it was taken by the former deputy leader of the BLP, Megan Lloyd George, who had recently defected to the Labour Party. This was a crushing blow to the LPW, and it was felt that they might have kept the seat if Plaid had not split the vote.

Plaid then took a prominent position in opposing the flooding of the Tryweryn valley. This valley included the Welsh-speaking village of Capel Celyn and was being flooded to provide water to Liverpool. Plaid opposed this, on the basis that the small Welsh-speaking community needed to be protected. This provided Plaid with a significant amount of media coverage during the mid to late 1950s, which continued into the 1960s. There has been much debate about how far Plaid's opposition to the flooding of the valley benefited the party, as the 1959 general election results were considered disappointing for them. However, Plaid had stood in seven of the eight seats that the LPW contested, coming close to matching the LPW's overall share of the Welsh vote, with just 1,380 votes between the parties.[77]

The electoral challenge posed by Plaid Cymru had begun to disturb those within the LPW, so much so that there were calls to enter some sort of electoral pact, but these were not heeded and it did not come to fruition.[78] It was the loss of the LPW's radical wing, coupled with a more emboldened Plaid Cymru, entering more and more candidates at by-elections and general elections, that threatened the existence of the LPW in this period. The nationalists could appeal more naturally to the same Welsh-speaking, nonconformist communities as the Liberals without the threat of being seen as a socialist political party. At this stage, Plaid was viewed as a more eclectic political grouping, much like the Liberal Party of Wales had been in its heyday. Couple the existential threat that an organised Plaid Cymru was posing in the rural areas, with the disorganised state of the LPW during the mid to late 1950s, and it is easy to see why the Liberals feared that they could be squeezed electorally.

1962 – A YEAR OF CHANGE

Yet there were signs of change following the 1959 general election. Whereas the LPW had previously shied away from standing in by-elections (largely due to cost), it did contest the three that were held in Wales between 1960 and 1963. Two were in the south (Ebbw Vale in 1960 and Swansea in 1963), and the other was in mid-Wales (Montgomery in 1962). This change in strategy had a lot to do with a shift in influence within the LPW. The older and more right-wing generation, figures such as Davies and Bowen, were giving way to a younger generation, of whom Hooson and Glyn Tegai Hughes were the most prominent, with both recognising the threat posed by the nationalists.[79]

Additionally, under Grimond's leadership, the BLP had seen a refocusing of energy. Grimond had proven himself an effective leader during the Suez crisis, holding the Conservative Government to account. His leadership had attracted new members and the party had begun to see a revival in its local associations, something which had been teetering on the brink of collapse by the mid-1950s. Grimond had begun to overhaul the BLP's policies and the policymaking process; however, his methods were controversial as he used his leadership status to bypass the established structures within the party.[80] Despite this, the reinvigoration of the BLP started to pay dividends in the 1959 to 1964 parliament, especially in terms of by-election successes and near misses.

The first significant by-election win came in 1958 when Mark Bonham-Carter took Torrington. However, the BLP's most sensational success was the March 1962 Orpington by-election win, where Eric Lubbock, the Liberal candidate forever associated with 'Orpington Man',[81] gained the seat with a 26.8% swing from the Conservatives to the Liberals.[82] This was an unexpected triumph for the Liberals and is generally regarded as the start of or, at least, the confirmation that a mini-revival was underway in the BLP's electoral fortunes. All eyes turned to the LPW for another crucial by-election in Montgomery, which had been called following the death of Clement Davies, just a few days after the Orpington win. The local association had selected Hooson the previous year to succeed Davies to face the electorate on 15 May 1962. It was feared that Montgomery would fall if Hooson faced all three main parties.

This fear was not unfounded. Davies had gained the seat in 1929 and contested it at the next seven general elections. He had left the BLP to join the Liberal Nationals and, as such, faced no opposition at both the 1931 and 1935 general elections.[83] In 1945 he was comfortably returned, having faced just a Conservative opponent. However, by 1959, all three of the main parties contested the seat, reducing Davies's share of the vote to 42.1% from a high of 68.1% in 1955.[84] Admittedly, in 1955, Davies faced just a sole Labour candidate, but the 1959 result indicated that the seat had become more marginal. Additionally, there had long been a suggestion that Davies benefited from a personal vote, where the incumbent had generated enough goodwill to almost guarantee his success, no matter how marginal the seat became. The Liberals were worried that this goodwill would not be passed on to Emlyn Hooson.[85]

There was every reason to be nervous, especially considering the result in Orpington and a near miss in Blackpool North, the day before. It meant that there was a significant amount of expectation being focused on this by-election. In terms of newspaper coverage, the announcement that Plaid would put up a candidate was seen as something of a game-changer, but it was also felt that the Conservatives could be the beneficiary of a split vote. The *Sunday Telegraph*, using patronising and clichéd language such as 'the mist-shrouded village' and describing the LPW as 'the party of his [Hooson's] fathers', believed that the result did not matter and a by-election 'mishap' could act as a balance to Liberal over-confidence. The journalist points out that the Liberals were aware that a few thousand votes to Plaid could put them in second or third place, and that Hooson behaved 'far too much like a Macleod Tory', by being unsure as to whether he should 'mix the old faith with the new fervour'.[86]

Conversely, the *Coventry Evening Telegraph* felt that the most significant threat came from the Conservative candidate, as he was well known and came from the constituency. However, the paper commented that Hooson needed to do more than just retain the seat; he needed to increase the majority to gain a vote of confidence.[87] This was typical of the press coverage, and the sense of apprehension within the LPW was fuelled by the buoyancy of the local Conservative Party, which had seen the reform of several previously derelict associations.[88]

Although the apprehension was understandable, the result was a revelation and further confirmed that Orpington was no fluke or one-off victory. As table 4 shows, the turnout for the by-election was 85.1% and Hooson took a 51.3% share of the vote.

Table 4: Montgomery by-election result, 15 May 1962[89]

Candidate	Party	Number of votes	Percentage of vote
Emlyn Hooson	Liberal Party	13,181	51.3%
R. H. Dawson	Conservative	5,632	21.9%
T. Davies	Labour	5,299	20.6%
Islwyn Ffowc Elis	Plaid Cymru	1,594	6.2%
Total		25,706	

The coverage of the by-election win ranged from begrudging respect[90] to an acknowledgement that the Liberal victory had 'plunged the Tories into even deeper gloom'. It was feared that the upcoming by-elections in Derbyshire West and Middlesbrough West would see the Conservatives 'lose both of them to either Labour or to the Liberals'.[91] In the wake of the Orpington win and the popular image of 'Orpington Man', many historians forget about the significance of the Montgomery by-election win and how remarkable it was.

The 1959 general election had reduced the LPW to two MPs and had continued the downward electoral trend. This was the trajectory that the 1959 result indicated the Welsh Liberals were facing and it would have been entirely possible that, in a 'small c' conservative seat like Montgomery, the LPW could be left with just one MP. Hooson not only benefited from being anointed as Davies's chosen successor, but also proved that the former leader's vote was not a personal one.

The result also gave the party hope that the LPW had turned a corner and that the Liberal revival would benefit them. It also showed that the Liberals could hold a seat in the face of an onslaught from the other three parties.

THE CHANGING FACE OF WELSH POLITICS

The rise of Plaid Cymru, or at least its perceived threat to the established political parties, put the constitutional status of Wales on the political agenda. Voices from all political parties had begun to assert the right of Wales to define itself as a nation and a political entity in the immediate post-war period. Within government, there had been moves to recognise Wales and attempt to stave off the nationalist threat. The list of concessions that were extracted in a relatively short space of time, from both Labour and Conservative governments, is impressive.

The greatest visible sign of the elevation of Wales in the eyes of the government was Cardiff becoming the capital city in 1955. The status had been bestowed upon the city in response to a written question in Parliament and was deliberately kept low-key.[92] This had been preceded in 1941 by the Welsh Courts Act, which gave the Welsh language equal status with English within the legal system in Wales. This was followed in 1944 by the inauguration of a 'Welsh Day' in the Commons, when a whole day of parliamentary business was set aside for issues about Wales.[93] Welsh interests were further represented by the 1949 establishment of the Council for Wales and Monmouthshire, an appointed body that would advise the government on Welsh matters. This was followed by the appointment of a Minister of Welsh Affairs in 1951,[94] whose office was situated in Cardiff. These were concessions that further legitimised the role of Cardiff as a capital city and Wales as a country.

The Conservative government's decision to quietly declare Cardiff the Welsh capital city was designed to not increase demands for either Welsh independence or the establishment of a Secretary of State for Wales.[95] Yet, it was the Labour Party, as the party that now defined Wales politically, that had the most to lose from a nationalist revival. Although Plaid's organisation during the 1950s was rudimentary, the fact that they were fighting by-elections and could place twenty candidates into a general election, whilst making some impressive headway,[96] certainly influenced Labour's pledge at the 1959 general election to back the creation of a Secretary of State for Wales.[97] It was a belated acknowledgement that Welsh interests should be taken seriously by the government.[98] Further, as Davies argues, the disintegration of community institutions was incorporated into the functions of the Welfare State, and this was a significant factor in the rise of the nationalist movement. By agreeing to separate administrative and institutional provisions for Wales, partly based on a cultural distinctiveness, the state helped to build the nationalist case for a degree of political autonomy for Wales.[99]

In addition to the changes in political status, Wales was going through a cultural reassessment linked to the status of the Welsh language and the displacement of Welsh-speaking communities. The aforementioned flooding of the village of Capel Celyn was a defining moment within the post-war nationalist movement. The flooding and construction of a dam at the site were the triggers for a militant nationalist campaign. It began with an act of sabotage in 1962 and continued throughout the rest of the decade, including a bombing campaign targeting the investiture of Prince Charles.[100] Similarly, the Welsh Language Society/Cymdeithas yr Iaith Gymraeg (WLS), was founded in 1962 following a radio broadcast by the former Plaid Cymru President, Saunders Lewis.[101] Lewis called for more direct methods to safeguard the language, arguing that 'Success is only possible through revolutionary methods.'[102] In a quest to gain equal status for the language, the WLS became a disruptive element to government agencies through its largely non-violent actions. The early years of the WLS were initially treated as a 'futile joke',[103] and their demands were only taken seriously once nationalist activities escalated and the bombings began.[104]

However, the flooding of Tryweryn and the fight for Welsh-language rights are now viewed quite differently by historians, with Edwards pointing out that the 'writing of a Welsh nationalist history by activists and supporters of nationalism has generated myths that cloud a more balanced history of the nationalist movement generally and Plaid Cymru specifically'.[105] To a different degree, Johnes points to the nationalist mythmaking that surrounds incidents such as Tryweryn by showing that not all the villagers agreed with the nationalists. Some of them felt that their cause had been infiltrated by the nationalists, who had then taken over the campaign. Johnes argues that most of the villagers were happy to move to brand-new homes three and a half miles away.[106] Regardless of whether these events have been the subject of myths, Plaid did not gain any immediate electoral advantage from its support for the villagers or the language. Yet, both historians concede that Wales and Plaid did see benefits from such campaigns, with Johnes noting that it had the effect of encouraging both major parties to take Welsh issues seriously.[107] Edwards notes that events such as Tryweryn were contributing factors in Plaid Cymru's electoral successes in 1974.[108]

Despite the later mythmaking, at the time these events were of specific importance to politicians within Wales. For Hooson, who fought against the proposed flooding of the Dulas valley in his constituency,[109] Welsh culture, Welsh natural resources, the language, farming, rural depopulation and devolution were all very relevant issues to Wales and the Liberals. These were policy areas that he was eager to foster within the LPW, as was the re-emergence of a Welsh Liberal form of nationalism that had originally been at the forefront of Lloyd George's politics in the late nineteenth and early twentieth centuries. For Hooson, Liberal radicalism, or perhaps more specifically, Liberal nationalism, could challenge Plaid's brand of nationalism.

THE BLP AND PLAID CYMRU

The threat from Plaid Cymru was becoming clearer to Hooson and those within the LPW, but Hooson had also identified a more imminent threat to Welsh Liberalism, the BLP itself. The structure of the LPW was such that any association fees were passed on to the BLP, and the larger organisation would dictate how much funding went back to the LPW. Additionally, the election manifestos barely mentioned Wales, and the 1959 LPW manifesto was more of a statement, as it did not make its way into the BLP manifesto.

However, quite aside from the lack of an autonomous and centralised separate party, for Hooson the biggest threat to the Welsh Liberals was the stated intentions of Jo Grimond and his aim of a 'Realignment of the Left'. Grimond had hoped to appeal to the more moderate members of the Labour Party, emphasising that, following the success in Torrington and Orpington, the centre ground was with the Liberals. In truth, Grimond had hoped to entice members of the social democratic wing of the Labour Party (and reform-minded Conservatives) into a new grouping, essentially a non-socialist alternative to the Conservative Party.[110] His offer of a realignment would later morph into a more direct appeal for a Liberal-Labour pact.[111] It was a policy that appealed to many Liberal activists and some MPs, although, Hooson was vehemently opposed[112] stating that the 'only course open to the Liberal Party . . . to soldier on in complete independence of any agreement with the Conservatives or Labour and press for the politics in which we believe'.[113] Jones states that this represented the 'nub' of Hooson's political beliefs,[114] effectively reasserting that the Liberals were not a middle way between Labour and the Conservatives, but a political creed of their own. Hooson's hostility towards Labour was rooted in a distrust of socialism, but also in the belief that to align the BLP with either the Conservatives or Labour would do a great deal of harm to the electoral fortunes of the Liberals in Wales.[115] There is no clearer indication of Hooson's animosity to Grimond's aim than his mini manifesto for the 1967 Liberal leadership contest:

> First, the Liberal Party must maintain absolute independence of the Labour and Conservative parties.
> Secondly, we Liberals must never allow our policies and our attitudes to change in the hope of small, short-term gains.
> Thirdly, we Liberals must reaffirm strongly our beliefs that human progress comes largely through individual efforts.[116]

If there was a point when we could say Hooson decided that the time was right for the LPW to change direction, then it was surely the combination of Grimond's desire for a realignment and the results of the 1966 general election.

1966 GENERAL ELECTION

For the LPW, the 1966 general election was an opportunity dressed up as a disaster. In terms of the disaster, the campaign would end with the loss of Roderic Bowen's seat in Cardigan. The opportunity was that Hooson, now the undeniable leader and only MP, was able to undertake a root and branch reform of the LPW.

The unexpected death, in 1965, of the Commons Speaker, Harry Hylton-Foster, would provide the Labour government with a serious dilemma. Hylton-Foster was a Conservative and his party let it be known that they would not nominate another Tory to the position, in the hope that Labour would be forced to fill the vacancy. The 1964 general election had provided the Labour Party with a slim Commons majority of just two seats[117] and to fill the role, which was a non-voting position, would reduce that to just one seat. Hylton-Foster had two deputies, one Conservative and one Labour.

The Prime Minister, Harold Wilson, approached Bowen and asked if he would be willing to accept one of the deputy roles. The offer was vehemently opposed by most of the Liberal MPs, not least because it severely hampered Grimond's ambition of a pact with Labour, which would have been more likely if its majority had been further reduced.[118] Despite the nearly unanimous opposition within his own party, Bowen accepted the role of deputy chairman of Ways and Means, seeing it as a step toward the Speaker's role. It was also, like the Speaker, a non-voting position and it kept the Labour Party majority intact. However, unlike the Speaker, who would generally face no opposition by the main political parties at a general election, there was no custom of this for the deputy role. As such, Labour campaigned vigorously for the Cardiganshire seat at the 1966 general election. Deacon points out that Bowen had a belief that he was in a secure Liberal seat and barely mounted a campaign,[119] whereas Jones points out that Bowen understood his image as an absentee MP and the deputy speaker issue had allowed Labour to capitalise on his failings. In the end, Jones argues, it was the superior electioneering of the Labour Party that outflanked the Cardiganshire Liberals, and Bowen lost the seat to Labour by a mere 523 votes.[120] Although Bowen's dogged ambition to become deputy speaker meant he had become something of a pariah within the BLP, the loss of his seat was acutely felt within the LPW. Hooson had become the last remaining Liberal MP in Wales and was keen to ensure that Bowen did not disappear from the Liberal ranks. In a letter to Bowen, Hooson stated that he hoped he would 'fight again' and should 'arrange an Adoption Meeting as soon as possible and before the enthusiasm that you have engendered dies down. This is vitally important.'[121]

Yet, this was not the only disappointment for the LPW, as the results of the 1966 general election were generally disastrous. In 1964, the LPW had twelve candidates and took a healthy 106,114 votes on a 7.3% share of the vote, whereas in 1966, this had dropped to 89,108 votes on a 6.3% share.[122] Labour had taken thirty-two seats in Wales, the party's largest number to that point.

Following the general election, recriminations for the Liberals' poor performance were received by Hooson. It was felt that the BLP manifesto commitment to a 'Council for Wales' whilst advocating an 'elected Scottish Parliament', which had been BLP policy in 1964 and 1966,[123] was ambiguous. The executive of the Denbigh Association wanted it to be clarified that the 'party advocates a nationally-elected Council for Wales as the first step towards the creation of a Welsh Parliament'.[124] Hooson was asked to endorse this resolution but refused, because he had 'always believed that the powers to be granted [to] the Council for Wales were to be identical . . . to a Parliament for Scotland' and that the 'reason why the Welsh legislature was called a Council was to distinguish our policy from that of the Welsh Nationalist Party'.[125] The possibility of association with Plaid's call for Welsh independence had led to an ambiguous situation in the areas where the LPW were vulnerable to the nationalists.

Added to this threat was the result of the 1966 Carmarthen by-election, a loss that stung the LPW on two fronts. The first was that this seat had previously been Liberal before Lady Megan Lloyd George took the seat for Labour in 1957. At the

1959, 1964 and 1966 general elections, the LPW were in a strong second place. Naturally, the death of Lloyd George had raised the hopes of the LPW, who campaigned vigorously for the seat. The second was that the LPW took third place behind Labour, and it was Plaid's president, Gwynfor Evans, who became the MP. Evans had previously placed third at the previous two general elections, behind Labour and the LPW.

The result for Plaid came after a turbulent few years for the party. The relatively poor result at the 1959 general election, where the party had contested twenty seats to the LPW's eight, had affected morale. They had hoped for an electoral upswing based on its opposition to the flooding of the Tryweryn valley and the media coverage it had garnered. This was then exacerbated by a string of poor by-election results between 1960 and 1963. Yet, the 1964 general election was a turning point for Plaid, with the leadership recognising the need for organisational change. Following an internal report that placed a focus on the party workers and the constituencies themselves, a more modern political outfit began to emerge in 1965.[126]

Plaid's organisation needed to modernise and appeal to areas outside of its traditional Welsh-speaking heartlands, including the enforcement of bilingual meetings in the south. In addition, the party adopted a more 'communitarian' approach and, like Labour, they recognised that the north-west Wales tradition of political parties staying out of local politics had to come to an end. The party activists were instructed to make Plaid Cymru a force within local politics.[127] The approach began to have an evidential effect on the number of members, with Plaid claiming a membership of 3,475 in the 1964–5 period, which would rise to over 16,000 in the 1965–6 period.[128] This reorganisation had paid dividends and it only heightened the sense that something significant needed to change within the LPW. This was an area in which the LPW had yet to make any headway, and even up until the 1969 council elections many of those who were known to be Liberal members would stand as independents. This was true not just in the northern seats, but also in southern seats, such as Brecon and Radnor.[129]

Although Labour was the dominant force within Wales, the immediate threat to the existence of Welsh Liberalism came from Plaid Cymru. Hooson understood that the policies he wished to pursue could blur the boundaries with Plaid. His policies were Welsh nationalist in nature – a Welsh Parliament, a Welsh Water Board, a Secretary of State for Wales – but it was on economic independence that he differed from Plaid. Hooson put it succinctly to Lord Ogmore, the former President of the Liberal Party, following the formation of the WLP:

> We are opposed to economic independence on the grounds that we do not like to see economic barriers raised between nations. We are in favour of political union in Europe, but we think that Wales, like Scotland, should have a very large measure of control over her own affairs. Hence our policy for a domestic parliament for Wales.[130]

Hooson fully understood the history of the LPW and knew that to be a true Liberal within Wales meant the party had to reassert its Welshness. Advocating policies that were aimed at treating Wales as a separate entity to England meant that the LPW/WLP could not only reassert its Welsh credentials, but could potentially undermine Plaid.

LPW: THE ORGANISATION AND FINANCIAL SITUATION

A large part of the impetus may have come from outside the LPW, but this did not change the fact that it was an organisation in need of reform. After all, as previously mentioned, the LPW had long been a party of two halves, with neither particularly engaging with the other on policy or electoral strategy. This lack of communication, coupled with the neglect of the LPW by successive leaders of the BLP, was among the factors that led to the sharp decline of the Liberals within Wales. Between 1945 and 1966, the LPW had gone from being the BLP's perceived biggest hope for a Liberal revival to the brink of extinction within Wales. Yet, to understand the reason for this neglect of the LPW, one must look to the role of the federations within the BLP and the autonomy they were granted.

Outside of its internal organisation, the BLP devolved responsibility for the constituency organisation within England to ten area federations. As Rasmussen notes, the Liberal distrust of centralised coordination and power meant that a substantial amount of decentralisation occurred within the BLP. This gave the federations greater power over the BLP at the association level than their corresponding counterparts within the Conservative or Labour parties, particularly when it came to finances. Further, the BLP constitution made the associations (the tier below the federations), responsible for their own 'organisation, working arrangements and finance'. This meant that regional professional staff, such as an organiser, were responsible to their regional association rather than to the BLP, making coordination by the parent organisation that much more difficult.[131]

The decentralised nature of the BLP structure was meant to 'facilitate administrative decentralisation and to provide more immediate assistance to the constituency associations than national headquarters can achieve'.[132] Yet, when compared with the English structure there was an extra organisational body, the LPW itself. The Liberal Party of Wales has been described as maintaining a 'modicum of separate organization';[133] however, this description of the LPW belied the true nature of the Welsh party. It was not the LPW that held this autonomy, but the two federations. The truth is the Welsh federations were the constitutional bodies of the LPW[134] and often acted as though it was free of any constraints that the BLP might have otherwise imposed. The LPW was effectively an umbrella organisation for the North and South Wales Liberal Federations, both of which held jurisdiction over the constituency associations within their areas. They also had responsibility for the affiliated groups, such as the Young Liberals. The federations would keep their finances secret from the LPW (believing that the local level was best placed to decide how to spend the money),[135] despite that body having responsibility for the coordination of these resources.[136] This attitude was also prevalent at the constituency association level, where many of the officers of the SWLF also held positions.

The true power of the federations and constituencies, within the BLP structure, was related to the control of the financial resources, although, within the LPW, there was another added dimension that had more to do with the cultural divide within Wales. This cultural divide within the LPW had progressed to the point that there was no effective dialogue or policy coordination between the federations.[137] When seats were contested, particularly in the 1950s and 1960s, it was the executive members of the federation who tended to stand.[138] In addition to the cultural animosity between the two federations, there was considerable personal animosity within the SWLF and it was felt this was impeding the Liberals in south Wales, with Lord Ogmore[139] stating: 'It is infuriating with so many winnable seats in South Wales that we should be held up over the silly personal differences of some of the people down here.'[140]

These personal differences were exacerbated by the power wielded by the executive of the SWLF, a clique-ridden organisation embodied by the secretary of the SWLF, John Gibbs, and his wife, Jennie, both from the Maesteg/Ogmore constituency association. They were viewed as a formidable team and not adverse to causing trouble. Jennie had been described in the press as '[d]iminutive' but 'a live-wire of the newly-formed Maesteg Liberal Party'.[141] Martin Thomas, alluding to this clique, pointed out that 'To the outsider, it [the SWLF] resembles a loose scrum between the Lions and the All Blacks: a static heaving mass with most of the action taking place in the middle out of the referee's eye.'[142]

However, for every grouping that appeared to be holding the SWLF back, there were figures, such as the Pontypridd councillor Mary Murphy, who were creating opportunities for Welsh Liberalism. Murphy's grouping was leading a campaign in Pontypridd which would challenge Labour's hegemony in the area during the 1960s.[143]

In comparison with the SWLF, Deacon notes that the NWLF was much better organised and was able to afford paid agents, albeit on a small salary.[144] This contrasts with Martin Thomas's contemporaneous assertion that 'Internally, the North Wales Federation is practically functionless. For advice one simply has to look to London.'[145] What can be said is that the real difference lay in the financial situation of the NWLF. This was due to the relative strength of the Liberal vote and its demographic – mid and north Wales had higher proportions of Welsh speakers and still had residual areas of nonconformist voters who supported Liberalism. The party had held on much longer in these areas than in the south, as there was a traditional animosity towards the Conservatives and a distrust of Labour.

As an indicator of the organisational and financial issues that the LPW faced in the early 1960s, out of the thirty-six constituencies in Wales, just fifteen had affiliated with the BLP.[146] This might seem like a startlingly low number of constituencies, but it is more a reflection of the state of the LPW at this time. Especially when one considers that, in the 1964 general election, the LPW would contest just twelve seats. This does not mean that just fifteen, or even twelve, constituencies had some type of organisation in place at this point, as even these constituencies were teetering on the brink of collapse, but it does highlight that the LPW was facing a crisis; a crisis that was largely centred on south Wales.

This crisis had been exacerbated by the addition of a chief organiser for south Wales, who had been appointed in 1962. The BLP had decided to provide funding of £1,000[147] for up to two organisers, one for the north and the other in the south. As

Patrick Kemmis, the head of the LPO, pointed out in a letter to the SWLF's Madoc Jones:

> the impression I gain is that the organisation has gone ahead well in North Wales, but that very little planned development has taken place in South Wales . . . but all reports reaching me do suggest that Mr Lance is not really well fitted for the task given him, certainly not in the absence of positive control from the LPW which it has not apparently been possible to provide.[148]

Although Kemmis had heard that the organiser was not suited to the role, there was more to it than that. A condition of the initial funding was that the 'person appointed would have adequate financial support for expenses, adequate facilities such as offices or secretarial assistance where appropriate',[149] yet this was impossible in the SWLF, which had accumulated a £300 debt.[150] This meant that the organiser was unable to reach remote constituencies and, no matter how essential the post was, it proved to be unaffordable.[151]

Financially, the LPW as an organisation was in dire straits. Between July 1965 and 31 August 1966,[152] the total income was £198 11s.,[153] and the amount in the LPW accounts before the transfer to the WLP was £123 1s. 6d[154] – whereas the Scottish Liberal Party (SLP)[155] had an income of £6,000 annually.[156]

FORMATION OF THE WLP

'The tradition is dead: it is time for a new inspiration'[157]
(Martin Thomas, Liberal PPC, 1966).

The loss of Cardigan and, later, the failure to gain Carmarthen added pressure on Hooson to facilitate a change in the organisational structure of the LPW. It was Hooson's belief in the 'second coming' of the Welsh Liberals, as the radical non-socialist party in Wales, which drove his ambition to reform the party. These plans were first mooted in 1965 and looked to change the organisation of the LPW, whilst bringing in new people to the party who would be internally elected and far removed 'from the factions of intrigue which have so bedevilled the Liberal Party of Wales and the South Wales Liberal Federation over the past few years'.[158] A year later, Hooson began to implement his plans; he was determined to tackle the dominance of the federations and unite the LPW by abolishing the old structure and forming the Welsh Liberal Party.

In correspondence with Bowen,[159] following the 1966 general election, Hooson stated that he proposed a root-and-branch reorganisation of the LPW. Hooson began by pointing out that the organisation in Wales 'has left much to be desired'. It was from the SLP model that Hooson sought inspiration, stating that:

> We have no comparable central strategic direction as that exercised by the small executive of the Scottish Liberal Party. No one wields the same authority in Wales as does the Chairman of the Liberal Party (George Mackie) in Scotland . . . Their executive meets regularly, they are not troubled with federations, and they have an annual conference as a separate Liberal Party. They send delegates – fraternal delegates – to the Liberal Assembly and their aims and objects are to organise Scotland so as to return as many Members of Parliament as possible to join the Liberal Parliamentary Party.

What Hooson was proposing was that the constitution of the LPW

> should be scrapped, the North & South Wales Federation should be scrapped and should be replaced by a Welsh

Liberal Party with a similar constitution as that of Scotland. Additionally, Wales should be divided into areas, as is done in Scotland, which can be carefully worked together.[160]

The new WLP would be federated to the BLP but would enjoy a greater deal of autonomy and with 'a novel *centralised* organisation modelled on the Scottish Liberal Party'.[161] This is an interesting point because it was a marked departure from the traditional British Liberal Party model, described above, that allowed for greater decentralisation of the federations. By having no federations (which were replaced by area committees), the WLP was the governing body and this, in theory, would allow the WLP to exert greater control over the constituency associations.

It is interesting to note that barely thirteen days before writing to Bowen, Hooson received a letter from O. Glyn Williams that argued for a reorganisation of the LPW. Williams proposed:

a. The Welsh Candidates Association should be reinforced as an organ of the LPW.
b. The LPW should be set up as Bureaux e.g. Transport Bureau, Mining Bureau, Ports Bureau, Agricultural Bureau or whatever.
c. There should be Official Spokesmen of LPW in various fields charged with the task of making official statements frequently and ostentatiously.
d. Candidates should be made official spokesmen. They would then acquire added status as such, with appropriate National prestige.
e. The chairman of the LPW should hold office for at least the next three years continuously.
f. S. Wales Liberal Federation should be immediately reconstituted so that it no longer exists as a querulous cantankerous self-alienating 'rump'.

g. An Action Committee of LPW should be set up with emergency plenary powers. It should meet at least once a month and consist of no more than half a dozen members.
h. The Welsh Radical Group should be merged into a renovated and effective LPW.
i. Welsh Liberal News should be further encouraged and expanded.[162]

As several of Williams's points would make it into the later proposals put to the NWLF and SWLF in June 1966, Hooson's reply to Williams that these 'were extremely helpful'[163] seems an understatement. Further, it is unlikely that it was a coincidence that Hooson replied to Williams on the same day that he wrote to Bowen. It suggests that Hooson was encouraged that there were people that held similar views and the remedy needed to help the ailing LPW. Hooson's plan, as put to the Extraordinary Meeting of the LPW on June 4, 1966, certainly had similarities to those proposed by Williams. Hooson's plan was as follows:

i. to translate the Liberal Party of Wales into an independent Welsh Liberal Party with a constitution similar to Scotland.
ii. to abolish the federations and set up Area Groups of constituencies e.g. North East Wales (West and East Flint, Denbigh and Wrexham).
iii. To initiate a three-year plan for organising all constituencies possible and finding candidates to fight the next election.
iv. to commence the campaign at a National Assembly at Llanidloes on 10th September next.
v. to revive the Welsh candidates' association, merging with the Welsh Radical Group to initiate a Welsh policy of economic and social development.
vi. to set up a financial appeal organisation.

vii. to appoint a full-time directing secretary for the Welsh Liberal Party with central offices and secretarial assistance.[164]

These plans, when they were initially announced, created a heated debate within Welsh Liberalism, particularly within the South Wales Federation. John Gibbs reacted to the news by stating that Hooson's plans of 'a radical reorganisation of the Liberal Party's structure in Wales' had caused 'considerable annoyance'.[165]

It is not difficult to see why the proposals garnered such a reaction, especially when the wording of the motion passed by the executive spoke of being 'independent':

> The Executive Committee of the Liberal Party of Wales . . . recommends to the Annual General Meeting of the Party that the name of the Liberal Party of Wales be changed to that of the Welsh Liberal Party and adopt a constitution similar to that of the Scottish Liberal Party; that is, an independent Liberal Party, sending fraternal delegates to the Liberal Party conference in England. Its object would be to send Liberal members to represent Wales and to join the Parliamentary Liberal Party.[166]

Although this motion was accepted by the majority of the delegates of the LPW at an extraordinary meeting of the executive on 11 June 1966, including members of the SWLF, John Gibbs started a campaign against the plans once the initial motion had been released. The Gibbs group's opposition towards the plans was carried in a resolution that was to be put to the SWLF's executive AGM, expressing their intention to remain 'a Federation of the Liberal Party and reaffirm[s] its satisfaction with the aims and ideals of that Party as led by Mr Grimond'.[167] This was an understandable position to take, as even the LPO agreed that Hooson's proposals would 'translate the Liberal Party of Wales into an *independent* Welsh Liberal Party with a constitution similar to Scotland'.[168] However, the Gibbs group were unwilling to acknowledge that an independent WLP would be no different from the SLP, which was also federated with the BLP, and had sent Jo Grimond to Westminster.

John Gibbs stoked the animosity further by leaking to the press that there was opposition to the plans, although it was becoming more like the Ogmore Association's opposition. Gibbs even contacted the press, masquerading as an anonymous member of the BLP's executive, and then denied having done so to Hooson, even though he had already admitted it to Pratap Chitnis, the chief press officer at the LPO.[169]

Gibbs and his allies were also worried about Hooson's intentions, noting that the NWLF had already discussed the plans before the meeting.[170] This added fuel to the notion that Hooson, Welsh-speaking and from Denbigh, was in league with the NWLF to take over the LPW. This fear of the WLP being ruled by north Wales is given further credence by Gibbs writing to the press stating that he hoped 'a substantial number of associations will affiliate to the Liberal Party' and that what was on offer was 'no more than a plan for a Welsh parliament with built-in minority rule by the West and North'.[171]

Moreover, in the letter that carried Gibbs's proposed SWLF resolution, Gibbs pointed out that they were worried about the implications of Hooson's plan 'that the Welsh Candidates Association should merge its activities with the Welsh Radical Group'. Gibbs highlighted that the secretary of the Welsh Radical Group described it thus: 'Whilst many members are Liberals, the Group has no official connection with the party itself and hopes to attract members from all parties.'[172] This quote originally came from the back page of Hooson's 1965 policy document *The Heartland*, a document that he hoped would attract wider political support. Such a move would bring an already proven research body into the new party structure. However, the suggestion that the LPW/WLP would court members of other political parties just added fuel to the Gibbses' fire.

Opposition to the plans was not limited to Gibbs and certain members of the SWLF, as letters were received that questioned the reasoning for the change. One correspondent wrote: 'The Liberal Party was all right as it was, why isolate it, we are all British. For the first time in 40 years, I have a doubt in my mind that it is worthwhile voting Liberal'.[173]

Deacon does not comment on the resistance to Hooson's plan in his book, whilst John Graham Jones states that 'rumours of a serious split within the party had proved totally unfounded'.[174] However, this was not entirely true, as this was quite a concerted campaign, playing out in the press and on TV.[175] It is obvious from the number of letters in the archive relating to the issue that it was a source of embarrassment for Hooson and the other officers.[176]

The campaign by John Gibbs and his Ogmore Association came to an end in March 1967,[177] with the group affiliating with the WLP. This about-face was due in part to a personal appeal by Lord Ogmore to raise funds to clear a debt that had been accrued by Jennie Gibbs.[178] The circumstances of the debt related to the 1964 local elections, where Jennie Gibbs had stood in the Maesteg seat and lost by just three votes. She was advised to challenge the result, and when this failed, she owed a substantial amount in court costs to the County Clerk. The couple were facing bankruptcy, but the LPW did not acknowledge the debt and individuals within the party denied making assurances that the Gibbs would not be financially liable.[179] Although it would be unfair to state that the LPW and its officers had abandoned the Gibbses financially,[180] this affair created a large amount of animosity between the LPW leadership and the Gibbses, no doubt adding fuel to their opposition to the new political party. Although, by their admission, the Gibbses were hostile towards the founding of the new party, by the end of 1966 they had decided that 'The Welsh Liberal Party is a fact of life by now' and that they were 'quite prepared to accept its existence'.[181] It would be churlish to suggest that the opposition was just related to the Gibbses' financial issues, as there was genuine support within the SWLF for the stance taken. However, once the Gibbses accepted defeat, the rest of the opposition slipped away.

THE STRUCTURE OF THE WLP

Despite the animosity, the WLP was officially formed at the LPW's 1966 annual conference, held in Llanidloes. Figure 1 shows the organisation of the Welsh Liberal Party.

Figure 1: The organisation of the Welsh Liberal Party

The organisation of the WLP was a streamlined version of the BLP, using the Scottish Liberal Party as its model, with the WLP's constitution setting out the role of each committee:

a) The annual conference

The WLP annual conference was the voice of the wider WLP and would consist of all members of the general council, the executive committee, prospective parliamentary candidates (PPC) and five from each affiliated organisation and association. It could only be convened on the advice of the executive to the secretary of the Party. The conference would consider accounts, elect the officers of the Party and the executive and consider resolutions on public policy. As with the BLP, there was nothing in the WLP constitution that specifically stated that the MPs were bound by the policy decisions made at the conference. Similarly, the resolutions passed at the WLP annual conference were not binding on the MPs of the WLP. This omission was, almost certainly, deliberate. As Rasmussen points out, the BLP's original 1936 draft constitution makes it clear that the Liberal Parliamentary Party would not be bound by the proclamations of the assembly or the council.[182]

b) The general council

The council would meet three times a year and would consist of the officers of the Party, the executive committee, two representatives from each affiliated association and organisation and all Welsh Liberal MPs and peers, plus PPCs. The duties of the council were subject to the authority of the Annual Conference and were the equivalent of the LPO and the BLP's own council, in that it had responsibility for the finances of the WLP, to maintain the WLP headquarters and staff, pass resolutions on current political issues and to 'stimulate militant Liberalism in every part of the country'.[183] In light of the rise of militant Welsh nationalism (and the Liberals' opposition to it) in this period, one wonders if this was an advisable object to put into the constitution, bearing in mind that the WLP sought to highlight its peaceful nationalist credentials. However, in later years, the word 'militant' was left out of the re-drafts of the constitution.

c) The executive committee

The executive consisted of the officers and nine conference members, from affiliated associations/organisations, which were voted in at the annual conference. Although the council had oversight of the executive committee, it was, in effect, the executive that dealt with the day-to-day running of the Party, with the constitution stating that the 'Functions of the General Council shall, subject to the authority of the General Council, be within the powers of the Executive Committee'.[184] The executive had the power to appoint staff, including the general secretary, set up sub-committees, act as the disciplinary body of the Party, and would nominate the officers of the Party, including the president and chairman, for consideration at the annual conference.

d) Affiliated associations and organisations

These included the constituency associations, groups such as the Welsh Young Liberals and the Welsh Women's Liberal Federation and the Association of Liberal Trade Unionists in Wales, amongst others.

e) Officers

The officers of the Party would include the President, ten Vice-Presidents, Chairman, Vice Chairman, Treasurer and Secretary, all of whom were subject to annual re-election at the conference and would serve no more than three years at a time, with a three-year break before they could seek re-election.

WHY SO LONG?

It is something of a curiosity as to why it took so long for Hooson to change the LPW's organisation. Since the Cymru Fydd era there had long been an acknowledgement that the organisation was not fit for purpose. What had changed was the leadership of the LPW and, by 1966, the party had been reduced to just one MP.

The 1962 Montgomery by-election result gave Hooson a clear vote of confidence from the electorate. It was also a metaphorical handing of the Welsh leadership baton from Clement Davies to Emlyn Hooson. Roderic Bowen was initially too engaged in his legal career to have any particular interest in reforming the party. This disinterest was further exacerbated by his desire to take on the deputy speaker role at Westminster. Although he could be effective when he wanted to be, Bowen's time as an MP was largely unremarkable. He was to the right of the party and took very little interest in campaigns such as the 1950s Parliament for Wales group or in party reform.

Although Hooson, like Bowen, was a barrister, that is where the similarity ends. In contrast to Bowen, even before becoming an MP, Hooson was an active member of the party. After Bowen lost the Cardiganshire seat, he returned to his legal career and had minimal interaction with the Welsh Liberals after this. Hooson had been part of the Parliament for Wales campaign and even though he did not stand for parliament in 1955 or 1959, was still very much involved in the LPW.

A famous quote by Charles Masterman stated that 'when Lloyd George came back to the party, ideas came back to the party',[185] and the same could be said of Hooson. Hooson understood the issues facing the LPW and Wales. The 1959 manifesto was a statement that Liberalism in Wales could still be relevant if it focused on what it could provide to the people. Although it will be explored later, the 1965 policy document *The Heartland* was a reaction to the depopulation crisis in mid-Wales and it further indicated that Hooson understood and wanted to address the issues of contemporary Wales.

No ordinary or executive member of the party would have been able to push through the reforms, especially if the political will was not there from the MPs. Additionally, there were too many vested interests in retaining the status quo, especially in south Wales, which feared a move away from the close cooperation with the BLP. However, the psychological impact of the only Liberal MP left in Wales suggesting a change to the SLP model, coupled with its association with Jo Grimond, held a certain amount of sway.

The influence of the SLP on the BLP had increased throughout the 1950s, spurred on by Jo Grimond's leadership; there was little doubt that the SLP had begun to prosper whilst the LPW was in danger of extinction. Table 5 highlights the speed with which the SLP replaced the LPW in the UK party:

Table 5: SLP, LPW and BLP elected MPs, 1955–64[186]

General election year	Scottish Liberal Party	Liberal Party of Wales	British Liberal Party[187] (UK result)
1955	1	3	6
1959	1	2	6
1964	4	2	9
1966	5	1	12

Although the SLP had not become the great hope for the Liberal Party that the LPW had been in the early 1950s,[188] its numerical strength had relegated the LPW to a minor section of the British Liberal Party during the 1960s. By undertaking a root-and-branch reorganisation of the LPW, the new party, it was hoped, would be in a better position to challenge Plaid and save Welsh

Liberalism from extinction. It should be noted that from the point of separation, the BLP did not seek to interfere in the day-to-day running of the WLP and left it to its own devices. The exceptions were when the WLP requested financial assistance or during major campaigns, such as the EEC referendum, the BLP would offer guidance, but the WLP was free to ignore the intervention.

CONCLUSION

Whereas the BLP had a sharp electoral decline following the First World War, the decline of the LPW was a long, drawn-out affair. The fact that the leadership, particularly after 1945, viewed the Welsh section of the party as holding the Liberal flame aloft, whilst the rest of British Liberalism slipped into a deep slumber, was a double-edged sword. The need for organisational reform within the LPW was neglected because the leadership were concentrating on rebuilding elsewhere in England and Scotland.

Lloyd George recognised that organisational reform was needed as far back as the late nineteenth century and his plans included making the LPW an independent party within Wales. However, the opposition to his plans meant that they were abandoned and Wales was viewed as the poor cousin to the English section of the party. It would take the near wipeout of the Welsh Liberals for the necessary reforms to take place. Emlyn Hooson, the charismatic leader who understood Liberalism's unique historical attachment to Wales, was the driving force behind the reforms and the founding of the independent Welsh Liberal Party. It was a project seventy years in the making and fulfilled Lloyd George's original plan for the party.

The next chapter will focus on the organisation and finances of the WLP and will cover the period 1966 to 1979. It will seek to chart the progress of the party, how and why it changed. It will seek to show that for the first few years, Hooson was at the forefront of the new party, but this began to change. The chapter will examine the reasons why and the consequences for the WLP.

Notes

1. Kenneth O. Morgan, 'The new Liberalism and the challenge of Labour, 1885–1929', *Welsh History Review*, 6/3 (June 1973), 290.
2. Kenneth O. Morgan, *Rebirth of a Nation: Wales 1880–1980* (Oxford, 1990), p. 52.
3. R. Merfyn Jones,, 'Beyond Identity? The Reconstruction of the Welsh', *Journal of British Studies*, 31/4 (October 1992), 342.
4. Jones, 'Beyond Identity?', 342. Jones points out that the Liberals based their sense of identity on religion, language, temperance and community interests between the *gwerin* (meaning either 'the people in general without reference to social class . . . or else the common people in contradistinction to the gentry'), whilst Labour added the working-class base to Welsh identity. Both of these left out sections of the community, such as Anglicans and the middle and upper classes.
5. 'Table 13.11 – Religion Census of 1851, summary table for Wales (1)'. Available at: *https://webarchive.nationalarchives.gov.uk/ukgwa/20150402173126/http:/gov. wales/statistics-and-research/digest-welsh-historical-statistics/?lang=en#/statistics-and-research/digest-welsh-historical-statistics/?tab=previous&lang=en* (accessed 5 March 2025). This table gives the reported number of attendants in Wales for Sunday 30 March 1851 at the morning, afternoon and evening worship for each denomination. The total number of attendants on the day for the Church of England was 189,706, whilst non-conformists had 777,315 attendees. The tables do not specify whether some of the people attended all three sittings or not. Yet, even with that caveat, the population numbering 1,163,139 at the time of the census ('Table 1.1a Total population and intercensal changes by sex, Wales 1801–1971', same website), it is not difficult to see how the nonconformists held sway with the largest political party in Wales.
6. Russell Deacon, *The Welsh Liberals: The History of the Liberal and Liberal Democratic Parties in Wales* (Cardiff, 2014), p. 40.
7. Cyril Parry, *The Radical Tradition in Welsh Politics: A Study of Liberal and Labour Politics in Gwynedd 1900–1920* (Hull, 1970), p. 71.
8. *Reports of the Commissioners of Inquiry into the State of Education in Wales* (London, 1947). Available at: *https://viewer.library.wales/4753689#?c=&m=&s =&cv=&manifest=https%3A%2F%2Fdamsssl.llgc.org.uk%2Fiiif% 2F2.0%2F4753689%2Fmanifest.json&xywh=-1412%2C-1%2C5839%2C4742* (accessed 5 March 2025). For example, the authors call the Welsh language 'evil' and state that 'there is no Welsh literature worthy of the name', p. 66.

9   For example, see *London Daily News*, 25 November 1847, 3. The article damns the Welsh with faint praise when it mentions that 'the Welsh are singularly quick and acute by nature', but then goes on to say that 'They [the commissioners] are . . . equally correct in lamenting their marked inferiority to the English in honesty and veracity and the almost universal propensity to drunkenness among the men and to want of chastity among the women.'
10 John Davies, *A History of Wales* (London, 1994), p. 436. The 1870 Act was seen as driving the Welsh language out of schools; but this had begun at least a decade earlier, certainly in 1861, with the introduction of tests that sought to assess the student's ability to read and write in English.
11 The 1902 Act was an attempt to safeguard the financial future of the Anglican schools in Wales, by providing all denominations with funding from the rates. This was highly unpopular because in many areas the local school was Anglican but most of the children were chapelgoers. David Lloyd George led a rebellion in Wales that eventually meant that no Welsh county council implemented the Act, thereby provoking the Conservative government to pass the Education (Local Authority Default) Act, commonly known as the 'Coercion of Wales Act'. If it were not for the fall of the Conservative government in 1905, this Act would have allowed the government to withhold grants and funding from Welsh local authorities.
12 See later in the chapter for an explanation.
13 The 'Coupon Election' was named after the piece of paper that endorsed the recognised government candidates during the 1918 general election. Bonar Law and Lloyd George signed these. Many within the Asquith camp were denied the coupon and were either opposed by an 'official' candidate or did not stand.
14 The Labour government collapsed due to high unemployment and a budget that was seen as unworkable by economists, the Liberals and the Conservatives. A committee, led by Sir George May, was set up to scrutinise the budget and recommended massive cuts to public spending. Some within the government were unable to accept this, and MacDonald resigned as Prime Minister and set up the National government.
15 Plaid Cymru polled third at the 1970 and 2001 general elections.
16 Parry, *The Radical Tradition*, p. 72.
17 Kenneth O. Morgan, *Modern Wales: Politics, Places and People* (Cardiff, 1995), p. 65.
18 Parry, *The Radical Tradition*, pp. 73–4.
19 Parry, *The Radical Tradition*, p. 76.
20 In particular, Russell Deacon, 'The Slow Death of Liberal Wales, 1906–1979', *Journal of Liberal History*, 49 (Winter 2005–6). For the post-war period, Deacon, 'The Steady Tapping Breaks the Rock', *Journal of Liberal History*, 22 (Spring 1999), 14–17.
21 Deacon, 'The Slow Death', 15–19.
22 Deacon, 'The Slow Death', 12–23. See also John Graham Jones, *David Lloyd George and Welsh Liberalism* (Llandysul, 2010), pp. 479–508. Also, David Roberts, 'The Strange Death of Liberal Wales', in John Osmond, *The National Question*

THE FALL AND RISE OF THE WELSH LIBERALS, 1918–1966   81

     Again: Welsh Political Identity in the 1980s (Llandysul, 1985), pp. 75–98. I have used Deacon's work as it is the most up to date and references the other two works.
23 Deacon, 'The Slow Death', 15.
24 Deacon, 'The Slow Death', 18.
25 Deacon, *Welsh Liberals*, p. 76.
26 C. P. Cook, 'Wales and the General Election of 1923', *Welsh History Review*, 4/2 (1968), 392.
27 Beti Jones, *Welsh Elections 1885–1997* (Talybont, 1999), pp. 59 and 63.
28 Duncan Tanner, 'The Pattern of Labour Politics 1918–1939', in Duncan Tanner, Chris Williams and Deian Hopkin (eds), *The Labour Party in Wales 1900–2000 (*Cardiff, 2000), pp. 126–8.
29 The heartlands can be defined as the rural, Welsh language-speaking and nonconformist/chapel-going populations of mid- and north Wales.
30 Morgan, *Rebirth of a Nation*, p. 193.
31 Deacon, 'The Slow Death', 17.
32 Deacon, *Welsh Liberals*, p. 130.
33 For example, his introduction of the old age pension in 1911 and the policy documents of the 1920s.
34 Morgan, *Modern Wales*, p. 71. As Morgan points out, he was a 'New Liberal in England and Old Liberal in Wales'.
35 Lloyd George had amassed a small fortune, primarily from the sale of peerages whilst prime minister and the generosity of rich business associates. In addition, in 1912, he had also purchased shares in a Marconi subsidiary that indicated he had used government knowledge of a lucrative contract being awarded to the company. Many within the Liberal Party objected to the fund and the nefarious way he obtained the money.
36 Deacon, *Welsh Liberals*, p. 85.
37 Colin Rallings and Michael Thrasher (eds), *British Electoral Facts 1832–1999* (Aldershot, 2000), pp. 31–55.
38 D. A. Thomas was an MP for Merthyr Tydfil (1888 to January 1910) and Cardiff (January to December 1910). Ivor Thomas Rees, *Welsh Hustings 1885–2004* (Llandybie, 2005), p. 285, describes Thomas as 'The colossus of the South Wales economy in his day'.
39 Roy Hattersley, *David Lloyd George* (London, 2010), pp. 83–4. Although he denied them, there were rumours that Lloyd George wished to abandon Caernarvon Boroughs for a Cardiff seat.
40 Deacon, *Welsh Liberals*, pp. 40–1.
41 Jones, *David Lloyd George*, p. 481.
42 Deacon, *Welsh Liberals*, p. 127. Deacon points out that Davies's appointment was to be a temporary position until Archibald Sinclair could return to the Commons, having lost his seat in 1945, and lead the parliamentary Liberal Party. Sinclair remained leader outside of the Commons, and his failure to get re-elected meant Davies would be accepted as the leader by 1950.
43 Deacon, *Welsh Liberals*, p. 138.

44 Alun Wyburn-Powell, *Clement Davies: Liberal Leader* (London, 2003), p. xi.
45 Lord Emlyn Hooson, 'Foreword', in Wyburn-Powell, *Clement Davies*, p. xi.
46 Lord Emlyn Hooson, *Rebirth or Death?* (Aberystwyth, 1994), p. 3.
47 See, for example, Emlyn Hooson, 'Clement Davies: An Underestimated Welshman and Politician', *Journal of Liberal Democrat History*, 24 (Autumn 1999), 10: 'Clement Davies' concern for Wales and its people runs like a golden thread through his career.'
48 See, for example, John Graham Jones, 'Emlyn Hooson as a Politician', in Derec Llwyd Morgan (ed.), *Emlyn Hooson: Essays and Reminiscences* (Llandysul, 2014), p. 97.
49 Hooson, *Rebirth or Death?*, p. 5.
50 Jones, *Welsh Elections*, pp. 87–103, for both tables 6 and 7.
51 Deacon, *Welsh Liberals*, p. 138.
52 Deacon, *Welsh Liberals*, p. 136.
53 Deacon, *Welsh Liberals*, p. 144. This was a memorandum from Major J. Parry Brown, who had been chairman of the LPW.
54 Deacon, *Welsh Liberals*, p. 129.
55 Jones, *Welsh Elections*, pp. 96–102.
56 Sam Blaxland, *The Conservative Party in Wales, 1945–1997* (Cardiff, 2024), p. 132. This is a good explanation as to why Davies faced no opponent in 1955, when he was BLP leader, but faced a targeted attack by the Tories in 1959, when he was no longer leader.
57 Deacon, *Welsh Liberals*, p. 135.
58 Jones, *David Lloyd George*, pp. 531–2.
59 Jones, *Welsh Elections*, pp. 94–106.
60 Alan Butt Philip, *The Welsh Question: Nationalism in Welsh Politics 1945–1970* (Cardiff, 1975), p. 305.
61 Merioneth and Anglesey, respectively. Throughout this book, I will refer to the constituencies as they were listed at the time of the general election. This means that Welsh names will become more prevalent as of the 1974 general election, following the boundary changes.
62 Jones, *David Lloyd George*, p. 493. Clement Davies gave it his nominal support but was more involved in reviving the Liberals nationally. Roderic Bowen and Rhys Hopkin Morris were quite opposed to it.
63 Deacon, *Welsh Liberals*, p. 156.
64 Emlyn Hooson, 'A Snatch at an Autobiography', in Derec Llwyd Morgan (ed.), *Emlyn Hooson: Essays and Reminiscences* (Llandysul, 2014), p. 15. Hooson's mother was a devoted Calvinist, whose theological views he did not share.
65 Emlyn Hooson, 'A Snatch at an Autobiography', p. 19. It was a speech Lloyd George had delivered many times since the First World War, and there is a different version in Hattersley, *David Lloyd George*, pp. 266–7.
66 Eifion Roberts, 'Emlyn in the Law', in Derec Llwyd Morgan (ed.), *Emlyn Hooson: Essays and Reminiscences* (Llandysul, 2014), p. 33.
67 NLW, Clement Davies Papers D1/35: Confidential memorandum by Emrys O. Roberts, 23 April 1945. As quoted in Jones, *Lloyd George* (2010), p. 481.

68 Iain Dale (ed.), *Liberal Party General Election Manifestos, 1900–1997* (London, 2000), p. 67.
69 *The North Wales Weekly News*, 25 March 1948, 4.
70 *The North Wales Weekly News*, 1 September 1949, 7.
71 Liberal Party National Executive Minutes, 14 December 1956, p. 9. Available at: *https://microform.digital/boa/collections/81/volumes/585/grimond-and-thorpes-liberal-revival-1954–1976(microform.digital)* (accessed 5 March 2025). This, of course, was a reference to Lloyd George's own *Britain's Industrial Future* policy document from 1928, often termed the 'Yellow Book' from the colour of its cover.
72 *The Western Mail and South Wales News*, 26 January 1948, 1.
73 *The North Wales Weekly News*, 2 February 1950, 7.
74 Glyn Tegai Hughes (1923–2017) was an LPW candidate in the 1950, 1955 and 1959 general elections and was also the vice president in 1959. He was a celebrated Welsh literary critic and was chairman of the Broadcasting Council for Wales, 1971–9. Meic Stephens, 'Glyn Tegai Hughes, obituary: esteemed literary critic who championed Welsh writing', *Independent*, 12 September 2017. Available at: *https://www.independent.co.uk/news/obituaries/glyn-tegai-hughes-obituary-literary-critic-who-championed-welsh-writing-a7748841.html* (accessed 1 August 2024).
75 Deacon, *Welsh Liberals*, p. 148.
76 Deacon, *Welsh Liberals*, p. 148.
77 Jones, *Welsh Elections*, pp. 103–6. The LPW took 5.3% of the vote (78,951 votes), to Plaid's 5.2% (77,571 votes).
78 Butt Philip, *The Welsh Question*, p. 306. Hooson and other senior Liberals did meet with Plaid Cymru in the late 1960s to talk about an electoral pact, but they found they were ideologically different.
79 Butt Philip, *The Welsh Question*, p. 306.
80 Robert Ingham, 'Liberal Revival (1956–1974)', in Robert Ingham and Duncan Brack (eds), *Peace, Reform and Liberation: A History of Liberal Politics in Britain, 1679–2011* (London, 2011), pp. 244–6.
81 '"Orpington Man" was coined by the press to identify a new type of voter, young, white-collar, skilled, well-educated and upwardly mobile socially and economically, a social group supposedly rejecting an old-fashioned and out-of-touch Tory party but not attracted to a cloth-cap, Clause IV Labour Party either.' Emily Robinson, 'Whatever happened to Orpington Man? Report of a Liberal Democrat History Group meeting at the National Liberal Club, 23 January 2012, with Dr Mark Egan and Professor Dennis Kavanagh. Chair, Duncan Brack', *Journal of Liberal History*, 74 (Spring 2012). Available at: *https://liberalhistory.org.uk/events/whatever-happened-to-orpington-man/* (accessed 1 August 2024).
82 Rallings and Thrasher, *British Electoral Facts*, p. 168.
83 Jones, *Welsh Elections*, pp. 82, 85.
84 Jones, *Welsh Elections*, pp. 101, 106.

85 J. Graham Jones, 'Emlyn Hooson and Montgomeryshire Politics 1962–79', *The Montgomeryshire Collections*, 97 (2009), 171.
86 *Sunday Telegraph*, 13 May 1962, 21.
87 *Coventry Evening Telegraph*, 11 May 1962, 18.
88 Jones, 'Emlyn Hooson and Montgomeryshire Politics', 169.
89 Jones, *Welsh Elections*, p. 106.
90 *The Daily Telegraph*, 17 May 1962, 1. The paper noted that 'The Liberal bandwagon rolls triumphantly on with another victory . . . the Conservative and Labour parties are left to wonder just how and when it is going to be stopped.'
91 *Daily Mirror*, 17 May 1962, 5.
92 Martin Johnes, *Wales Since 1939* (Manchester, 2012), p. 190.
93 Deacon, *Welsh Liberals*, p. 111. Deacon points out that these were successes brought about by the Welsh Liberals, headed by Henry Morris-Jones and Megan Lloyd George, respectively.
94 The minister was part of the Home Office and not a separate minister.
95 Johnes, *Wales*, p. 190.
96 Morgan, *Rebirth*, p. 381.
97 Labour's deputy leader, Jim Griffiths, was an ardent supporter of a Secretary of State and was instrumental in changing the policy within the party. Other Welsh Labour MPs, particularly in the south, were against devolution, including Aneurin Bevan.
98 Johnes, *Wales*, p. 218.
99 Davies, *Welsh Nationalism*, p. 84.
100 For more on this campaign see Wyn Thomas, *Hands Off Wales: Nationhood and Militancy* (Llandysul, 2013). The first act was an attempt to blow up a transformer at Tryweryn by releasing a thousand gallons of oil to disrupt the electricity supply to the dam (p. 33).
101 The broadcast was entitled *Tynged yr Iaith* (The Fate of the Language) and aired on the BBC on 13 February 1962.
102 Morgan, *Rebirth*, pp. 382–3.
103 Correspondence between the author and John Summers, former Daily Telegraph columnist, March 2006.
104 Thomas, *Hands Off Wales*, p. 270. Although nine members of the Free Wales Army (FWA) were imprisoned for their activities, it was the more clandestine MAC or Mudiad Amddiffyn Cymru (Movement for the Defence of Wales), who were responsible for the campaign. The FWA's claims of involvement in the bombings were never really taken too seriously by the media or the authorities. The trial of the FWA was seen to be based on hearsay rather than an 'astute police investigation'.
105 Andrew Edwards, *Labour's Crisis: Plaid Cymru, The Conservatives and the Decline of the Labour Party in North-West Wales, 1960–74* (Cardiff, 2011), p. 268.
106 Johnes, *Wales*, pp. 215–16.
107 Johnes, *Wales*, p. 218.
108 Edwards, *Labour's Crisis*, p. 268.

109 Gareth Morgan, 'A Montgomeryshire Valley Under Threat', in Morgan, *Emlyn Hooson*, p. 125.
110 Peter Joyce, *Realignment of the Left?* (Basingstoke, 1999), p. 130.
111 Joyce, *Realignment*, p. 136.
112 Ingham, 'Liberal Revival', p. 255.
113 Jones, *David Lloyd George*, p. 498.
114 Jones, *David Lloyd George*, p. 499. Jones cites Hooson's opposition to the nationalisation of the steel industry in 1965 as the effective end of Grimond's policy.
115 Roberts, 'The Strange Death', p. 88.
116 Russell Deacon and Alex Carlile, 'Politician and Lawyer', in Morgan, *Emlyn Hooson*, p. 159.
117 Rallings and Thrasher, *British Electoral Facts*, p. 49. There was already a Labour MP serving as the deputy speaker, a non-voting position, which meant the effective majority was two.
118 Deacon, *Welsh Liberals*, p. 164.
119 Deacon, *Welsh Liberals*, pp. 164–5.
120 J. Graham Jones, 'The Cardiganshire Election of 1966', *Llafur: Journal of Welsh People's History*, 9/1 (2004), 103–4.
121 NLW, Lord Hooson Papers, Box 79, Letter from Hooson to Roderic Bowen, 20 April 1966.
122 Jones, *Welsh Elections*, pp. 107 and 111.
123 Rallings and Thrasher, *British Electoral Facts*, pp. 111 and 125.
124 NLW, Lord Hooson Papers, Box 42, Letter and Memorandum from Roger Taylor of Llandudno Junction to Hooson, 29 April 1966.
125 NLW, Lord Hooson Papers, Box 42, Reply to Roger Taylor from Hooson, 6 May 1966.
126 Edwards, *Labour's Crisis*, pp. 113–15.
127 Edwards, *Labour's Crisis*, p. 116.
128 Butt Philip, *The Welsh Question*, p. 175.
129 Deacon, *Welsh Liberals*, p. 175.
130 NLW, Lord Ogmore Papers, File 4, Letter from Hooson to Lord Ogmore, 13 April 1967. Hooson's commitment to Europe would soon change.
131 Jorgen Scott Rasmussen, *The Liberal Party* (London, 1965), pp. 86–8.
132 Rasmussen, *Liberal Party*, p. 87.
133 Rasmussen, *Liberal Party*, p. 87n. In his study of the Liberal Party, Rasmussen gives both the LPW and Scottish Liberal Party short shrift.
134 NLW, Lord Hooson Papers, Box 42, Letter to Elfyn Lloyd Morris from Gruffydd Evans, Chairman of the Liberal Party Executive, 5 July 1966.
135 Deacon, *Welsh Liberals*, p. 160. Most of the constituencies withheld their £100 affiliation fee for this reason.
136 Deacon, *Welsh Liberals*, p. 169.
137 Hooson, *Rebirth or Death?*, p. 5.
138 Deacon, *Welsh Liberals*, p. 162.

139 In 1959, Ogmore had left the Labour Party to join the Liberals, due to his disillusionment with Labour's nationalisation plans, believing that a strong anti-socialist alternative would also help defeat the Conservatives.
140 NLW, Lord Hooson Papers, Letter from Lord Ogmore to Hooson, 4 August 1962.
141 *Glamorgan Advertiser*, 24 November 1961, 1.
142 NLW, Lord Hooson Papers, Box 42, Memorandum by Martin Thomas to All Members of the Executive, 28 July 1966.
143 See Steve Belzak, 'Swinging in the '60s to the Liberals: Mary Murphy and Pontypridd Urban District Council', *Journal of Liberal History*, 68 (Autumn 2010), 26–33.
144 Deacon, *Welsh Liberals*, p. 160.
145 NLW, Lord Hooson Papers, Box 42, Memorandum by Martin Thomas to All Members of the Executive, 28 July 1966.
146 Deacon, *Welsh Liberals*, p. 158.
147 Adjusted to 2023 levels, £17,862.58 at 4.8% inflation p/a.
148 NLW, Lord Ogmore Papers, File 3, Letter from Patrick Kemmis to G. M. Madoc Jones, 7 May 1963.
149 NLW, Lord Ogmore Papers, File 3, Letter from Patrick Kemmis to G. M. Madoc Jones, 7 May 1963. The original proposal stipulated that the 'person appointed would have adequate financial support for expenses, adequate facilities such as offices or secretarial assistance where appropriate'.
150 Adjusted to 2023 levels, £5,244.10 at 4.9% inflation p/a.
151 Jones, *David Lloyd George*, p. 497.
152 NLW, Lord Hooson Papers, Box 42, Accounts of the Welsh Liberal Party for the period 31 July 1965 to 31 August 1966, dated 8 September 1966.
153 Adjusted to 2023 levels, £3,097.83 at 4.9% inflation p/a.
154 Adjusted to 2023 levels, £1,914.74 at 4.9% inflation p/a.
155 NLW, Lord Hooson Papers, Box 42, Letter from Arthur Burden, Secretary and Chief Agent of the SLP, undated but probably mid-1966.
156 Adjusted to 2023 levels, £93,402.04 at 4.9% inflation p/a.
157 NLW, Lord Hooson Papers, Box 42, Memorandum by Martin Thomas to All Members of the Executive, 28 July 1966.
158 Jones, 'Emlyn Hooson and Montgomeryshire Politics', 180.
159 NLW, Lord Hooson Papers, Box 79, Letter from Hooson to Roderic Bowen, 20 April 1966.
160 NLW, Lord Hooson Papers, Box 79, Letter from Hooson to Roderic Bowen, 20 April 1966.
161 Jones, 'Emlyn Hooson and Montgomeryshire Politics', 184. My italics.
162 NLW, Lord Hooson Papers, Box 79, Letter from O. Glyn Williams to Hooson, 7 April 1966.
163 NLW, Lord Hooson Papers, Box 79, Letter from Hooson to O. Glyn Williams, 20 April 1966.
164 Minutes of the LPO Executive Committee, 29 July 1966, p. 3. Available at: https://britishonlinearchives.com/collections/81/volumes/585/grimond-

and-thorpes-liberal-revival-1954-1976?filters[query]=&filters[className]=d
ocument – *Image 512*.
165 NLW, Lord Hooson Papers, Letter from John Gibbs to Hooson, 24 April 1966.
166 NLW, Lord Hooson Papers, Box 42, Memo from Martin Thomas to All Members of the Executive, 28 July 1966. This motion was passed by the executive on 4 June 1966, put to a vote of the NWLF and SWLF delegates on 11 June 1966, and ratified at the LPW annual conference on 10 September 1966.
167 NLW, Lord Hooson Papers, Circular letter to the SWLF from John Gibbs, 5 June 1966.
168 Minutes of the LPO Executive Committee, 29 July 1966, p. 3. My italics. Available at: https://britishonlinearchives.com/collections/81/volumes/585/grimond-and-thorpes-liberal-revival-1954-1976?filters[query]=&filters[className]=document (accessed 5 March 2025).
169 NLW, Lord Hooson Papers, Letter from Hooson to Major Parry Brown of Newport, 10 June 1966.
170 NLW, Lord Hooson Papers, Circular letter to the SWLF from John Gibbs, 5 June 1966.
171 NLW, Lord Hooson Papers, Letter from T. R. Jones, a Liberal supporter, to Hooson. Letter and paper cuttings were undated, but Hooson's reply was sent on 8 December 1966.
172 NLW, Lord Hooson Papers, Circular letter to the SWLF from John Gibbs, 5 June 1966.
173 NLW, Lord Hooson Papers, Letter from T. R. Jones, undated but copied verbatim.
174 Deacon, *Welsh Liberals*, p. 170, mentions that members of the LPO released a statement in support of the new party. Jones, 'Emlyn Hooson and Montgomeryshire Politics', 184.
175 NLW, Lord Hooson Papers, Letter to John Gibbs from Hooson, 14 June 1966. This letter was never sent, probably due to the angry tone. At the end of the letter is a transcript from a 'News of Wales' broadcast on the establishment of the new political party which alludes to the ongoing arguments.
176 NLW, Lord Hooson Papers, Letter to T. R. Jones from Hooson, 8 December 1966. Hooson mentions that 'these bickerings also make me very sick'.
177 By this point, the SWLF had been disbanded and it was just Gibbs's group that had been unwilling to affiliate.
178 NLW, Lord Hooson Papers, Letter from Michael Meadowcroft to Hooson, 22 March 1967. The debt, at this point, was around £295 and the appeal had raised £40.
179 NLW, Lord Ogmore Papers, File 4, Letter from Michael Meadowcroft to Rhys Gerran Lloyd, 11 January 1967.
180 NLW, Lord Hooson Papers, Letter from Hooson to Lord Ogmore, 25 November 1966. On the part of some of the LPW leaders, there was an intention to save the Gibbs from bankruptcy. Hooson noted that, despite the

Gibbses' lack of 'gratitude or appreciation', a barrister from his chambers worked pro bono to contest the bankruptcy.
181 NLW, Lord Ogmore Papers, File 4, Letter from Jennie Gibbs to Michael Meadowcroft, 11 December 1966.
182 Rasmussen, *Liberal Party*, p. 64. 'The assembly and the council shall have no power to control or dictate to the Liberal Parliamentary Party who must be responsible under the guidance of their leader for defining the attitude to be adopted in regard to current problems as they arise.' This was left out of the 1936 constitution, as the 'party had no right to treat the LPP as delegates'.
183 NLW, Merfyn Jones Papers, Box 35, The Constitution of the Welsh Liberal Party, undated, but probably 1966, clause 9b. The initial constitution is undated but, as it refers to the 'Welsh Young Liberal Movement being in a state of flux' when it came to affiliating, this dates it to the setting up of the WLP.
184 NLW, Merfyn Jones Papers, Box 35, The Constitution of the Welsh Liberal Party, undated, but probably 1966, clause 12.
185 David Dutton, 'Personality Politics and the Break Up of the Party (1914–1929)', in Robert Ingham and Duncan Brack, *Peace, Reform and Liberation: A History of Liberal Politics in Britain, 1679–2011* (London, 2011), p. 192.
186 Rallings and Thrasher, *British Electoral Facts*, pp. 220–2.
187 Rallings and Thrasher, *British Electoral Facts*, pp. 46–51
188 Deacon, *Welsh Liberals*, p. 134.

2

THE ORGANISATION AND FINANCES
OF THE WELSH LIBERAL PARTY, 1967–1979

INTRODUCTION

The previous chapter assessed how and why Hooson dismantled the LPW and formed the WLP. This chapter will assess the organisation and financial position of the newly formed WLP. As such, it will be divided under those two headings. The first part of the chapter will discuss and analyse the organisation, pointing out the main actors and the effect that they had. It is not the intention for this chapter to go into any detail on the inner workings of the separate committees; it will focus on the upper echelons of the WLP, namely the headquarters. It will touch upon the aspects of the separate committees, when required, but the focus of the chapter is on how the organisation changed and who changed it. The second part of the chapter will assess the financial position of the WLP, how it was financed, and the role of undeclared donations that kept the party's finances afloat.

This chapter fits into the historiography of Wales, as it provides a fuller picture of the WLP during this pivotal decade in Welsh politics. It follows in the footsteps of works such as Laura McAllister's *Plaid Cymru: The Emergence of a Political Party* (2001) and Andrew Edwards's *Labour's Crisis* (2011), both of which went into detail about the reorganisation of both parties, but of Plaid in particular. In terms of this book, organisational and financial triumphs and disappointments were pivotal to the success of the party in the 1970s. We should not forget that the WLP were, in terms of votes, the third-largest political party in Wales, with Plaid Cymru a distant fourth.

The chapter will begin by assessing Hooson's role within the new organisation, what he wanted to achieve and the sacrifices that he was prepared to make. Hooson purposely ensured not only that he was the 'face' of the party, as its only MP, but also that he maintained some form of direction over the party. It will be argued that, particularly in its early years, Hooson was very much in control of the WLP and it took up a significant amount of his time. His interest in safeguarding Liberalism extended to working with other parties. However, it will be shown that following the 1970 general election, Hooson had become preoccupied with his Westminster role, the Jeremy Thorpe issue, Europe, the Lib-Lab Pact and devolution, quietly becoming the figurehead of the party and leaving its day-to-day running to others.

After assessing Hooson's role, the organisation of the WLP will then be assessed. It is important to understand that the WLP, during the period examined, was almost entirely staffed by volunteers. Every person on the council, executive and other committees was there as a volunteer. There were exceptions to this, namely the WLP office staff and the general secretary and organisers, who were employed. However, as will be explored below, these volunteer and paid roles could be a double-edged sword for the party.

The role of the general secretary will be examined and the chapter will argue that, contrary to popular opinion, Mary Murphy, the councillor for Pontypridd, was the first general secretary of the WLP. It will be shown that she had a brief, but successful, tenure. Yet, she was forced out by the attitudes of members of the executive. Not only will the chapter place Murphy in her correct historical position, but it will also re-examine the role of her successor, Emlyn Thomas. Long regarded as the man who almost bankrupted the WLP, the chapter will argue that this is unfair and that the executive bore as much blame as he did, perhaps more so.

Following the departure of Emlyn Thomas and the disappointing results of the 1970 general election, it will be argued that two people took over the day-to-day running of the WLP – Rhys Gerran Lloyd, the honorary treasurer of the WLP, and Winifred 'Freddie' Whitaker – and steered the party into its most successful phase. Rhys Gerran Lloyd's role was largely organisational and he delegated much of his work to 'Freddie' Whitaker. It will be shown that she was more responsible for resurrecting the local associations than almost any other figure.

Finally, following the departure of Lloyd and Whitaker in 1974, the executive was then tasked with the organisation and finances of the WLP. It will be argued that following the success of 1974, the WLP was scuppered by the lack of organisation at the top of the party. This section will assess the financial situation of the WLP and will argue that without the organisational skills of Lloyd and Whitaker, the WLP began a gradual decline that nearly ended in bankruptcy. It will be shown that the measures that the executive tried to put into place were often thwarted by a lack of funding and the ego and/or indifference of Geraint Howells.

It should be noted at the start that the only 'budget' that existed was for the running of the WLP office, whether that was in Aberystwyth or, from 1970, Cardiff. It would be misleading to state that the running of the WLP was budgeted – it would be better to say that it was an expenditure that changed each year.

HOOSON'S ROLE

Following the September 1966 creation of the WLP, a steering committee was set up to implement the new processes and positions. Being the only Welsh Liberal MP, there was an expectation that Hooson would take an active role in the new organisation. He had already declined the role of chairman of the party because he did not want to be 'involved in the cross currents and rows . . .which shake the Party up in Wales, and I would like to avoid this if humanly possible!' Hooson wanted the role of president of the WLP, so he could give it a political direction.[1] However, the role would eventually be taken by the former Labour MP and previous president of the BLP, Lord Ogmore. The matter of the presidency did arise again in 1970, with Ogmore seeking to relinquish the role, becoming the 'Sole Patron of the Party'; Hooson's ambition was thwarted by the prospective parliamentary candidate (PPC) for Brecon (and future MP) Geraint Howells. Hooson advised Ogmore that:

> when I discussed this point with Geraint Howells on the telephone on Sunday, he expressed violent opposition and thought that we should retain the same officers in the same positions until after the general Election . . . He was of the view that our political opponents would try to make as much of any changes as they could. I thought that I should mention this matter to you as he is a shrewd observer.

At the bottom of the letter, Ogmore made a note that he had replied 'not agreeing'.[2] As it would come to pass, Howells would become the president of the WLP between 1974 and 1977, and would assume the leadership of the party when Hooson lost his seat in 1979.

Hooson had to be content with the role of leader of the WLP, which meant that he would leave the overall organisational direction to the committees, intervening only when necessary. However, the policy direction of the WLP still interested him and he sat as the chair of the policy committee, overseeing the publication of documents such as *Life to a Nation: An Economic Policy for Wales* and producing papers on other areas that mattered to Wales. Hooson was also instrumental in proposing the Government of Wales Bill to parliament in 1967, seconded by the President of Plaid Cymru, Gwynfor Evans.[3]

The 1970 general election was a disappointment for Welsh Liberalism (as it was for the wider BLP), especially as it was the first general election of the newly founded party. In the four years that followed that election, Hooson appears to have been content, whether through necessity or otherwise, to be the figurehead of the WLP. His parliamentary position had expanded and in 1973, Jeremy Thorpe, the leader of the BLP, had given Hooson several substantial spokesperson portfolios, namely those of Agriculture, the Law and Wales. Added to this was his ongoing legal career, which included high-profile cases for the likes of the Ministry of Defence. There were also his campaign against joining the European Economic Community (EEC), the Jeremy Thorpe scandal, the Lib-Lab Pact and the campaign for devolution, all of which limited his time with the WLP.

Although he left the day-to-day running of the party to the committees and staff of the WLP, most notably Rhys Gerran Lloyd and Winifred Whitaker, he kept a close eye on the financial situation and the decisions that were being made. He was once again instrumental in the further reorganisation of the WLP in 1972, following the Conservative government's local government restructuring of Wales into eight counties and thirty-seven districts. It was Hooson who proposed that the WLP should be reformed into eight federations, with two members of the federation being able to attend executive meetings on behalf of their areas, with full voting rights.[4] Following this intervention, it would be the October 1973 publication of the findings of the Royal Commission on the Constitution that allowed Hooson to refocus his attention on devolution and the WLP, although his involvement was more to do with policy and campaigning for the creation of an elected Welsh Assembly.

Following the 1974 general elections, the upper echelons of the WLP changed dramatically. The organisation and finances of the party began to decline, with Hooson offering no real organisational direction to the party and the newly elected MP for Cardigan, Geraint Howells, taking on more of the leadership role.

GENERAL SECRETARIES AND ORGANISERS, 1967–74

Mary Murphy

Initially, the WLP was entrusted to a steering committee with Mary Murphy (the councillor from Pontypridd who led a band of energetic councillors, posing a serious threat to Labour in the constituency) now elected as the first chair of the party. In early October 1966, Hooson wrote to Murphy stating that he was 'delighted' that she was taking on the role of general secretary, thereby further cementing her position as the most senior woman in Welsh Liberalism since Megan Lloyd George.[5] Further, in December 1966, Hooson confidentially informed a student of the Oxford University Liberal Club, that Murphy will be appointed to the role of '*full-time* General Secretary of the Party' on 1 January 1967.[6] Yet, Murphy's initial appointment as chair of the steering committee has created a narrative amongst historians that Emlyn Thomas was the first general secretary. Jones keeps Murphy in the chair rather than acknowledging her promotion,[7] whilst Deacon states that her role was 'Secretary of the WLP' and that she ran the WLP from her home. Without being given an office, as Thomas would be, there is an underlying suggestion or belief that Murphy was appointed in something of a caretaker position, with Emlyn Thomas being appointed as the 'permanent General Secretary'.[8]

The confusion as to Murphy's actual role has not been limited to historians, as she was criticised during her tenure by members of the party. In particular, the conference secretary, Leslie Jones, criticised her for going on holiday and not helping to co-ordinate the annual conference.[9] Concerning this, Murphy was subjected to a 'gossip' campaign between members of the steering committee and other committees. Murphy felt that any criticism of her role should have been 'made at the Steering Committee – and there only' whilst those criticising her contribution to the annual conference did not explain or realise that 'I hadn't been appointed Conference Sec[retary]'.[10] Murphy initially resigned in July 1967,[11] yet she carried on with the role until June 1968. However, it was obvious that by the end of her tenure Murphy was still facing criticism, stating that 'I've had the impression that as long as people feel I'm getting the cash, I can do without the thanks. Well, the little cash I get after all my expenses is just not worth the heartbreak.'[12] The gossiping and outright targeting of certain, particularly female, high-profile members of the WLP would become a common feature of the internal politics of the party. As will be shown, it led to the resignation of some very capable and dedicated people, leaving the party poorer in the process.

Despite the gossip campaign, Murphy was a very capable general secretary and, by the time she had provided her initial resignation, there were some very positive signs of Welsh Liberal activity (see table 6, below). Additionally, her correspondence shows that she was travelling around Wales, meeting prospective candidates[13] and providing some type of order to the party. For example, she wrote to Lord Ogmore:

> Everyone was thrilled with Sat.'s meeting – all are agreed that there has never been such a splendid spirit prevailing in Liberal meetings. You have no idea the sort of meetings we used to have – not just petty bickering – tho' there was plenty of that, but, often we verged on brawling and the City of Cardiff Liberal meetings were very often almost stand-up fights.

The letter continues, 'I [Murphy] don't feel the same sense of impotence that I might have done a year back – I'm beginning to feel – not just hope – that things can be done'. She credits Ogmore with this, but the point should be made that these constituencies were no longer being left to their own devices and they were starting to have contact with the leaders of the party. The lack of leadership was being addressed, and the 'weirdies at the helm'[14] of the constituencies were being challenged.

However, there was a large amount of ambiguity as to Murphy's actual job description. For example, Murphy believed her role was largely organisational and that 'candidates are not my particular province',[15] even though she found herself involved in these matters. Yet, this blurring of the lines and lack of detail about each officer's role would cause considerable trouble for the WLP. Even the party's constitution set out the titles of the officers but did not provide a role description.[16] This would become more noticeable with the next general secretary, Emlyn Thomas, but the party did not learn this lesson.

Emlyn Thomas

Emlyn Thomas, the former general secretary of the Farmers' Union of Wales, was appointed by the executive as the general secretary in June 1968, with a generous salary of £1,800 and £600 expenses.[17] These were paid from funds that had been raised by Hooson and Rhys Gerran Lloyd from some wealthy friends.[18] The headquarters were moved to Aberystwyth, largely due to this being close to Thomas's home, but also because Cardigan was a target seat for the WLP.[19] Many generally agreed that Thomas, in March 1970, left his position under a cloud of financial incompetence, severely hampering the financial situation of the party in the immediate period before the 1970 general election.[20] It would be remiss not to assess his impact at this crucial point in the WLPs existence. It must be stated that Thomas's role was vague,[21] but his activities show that he was expected to strengthen the local constituency associations and attract revenue for the party. One of the unusual aspects of his employment (like that of the local organisers employed in this period) was that the revenue he was to generate would, in part, pay for his role after the first year.[22]

One of the priorities for Thomas was the reactivation of the constituency associations. This was a process that had begun under Murphy and, although not fully addressed under Thomas, it would give the party a base to work from in subsequent elections. The plan was for regional organisers to be employed by the constituencies (something that some areas had done in the past); they would increase membership levels, which, in turn, would pay for their salaries. In May 1969, having been in the position for eleven months, Thomas reported that there were five organisers, three in the south and two in the north; however, one of these was off sick and another had resigned shortly before taking their post.[23] Thomas was damning of constituency organisations, stating that 'Constituency Associations are rather reluctant to adopt new ideas and that very often they fail to appreciate that elections are won through detailed planning right down to street group levels'.[24] Although this points to the constituencies being in a rather mixed state, Thomas was at pains to point out that there had been 'progress in the . . . re-organisation of the Mid-Wales constituencies' and that the full-time organisers, particularly in Brecon and Radnor, 'were having extremely good results . . . bringing in some £85'.[25] Table 6 illustrates how far the organisation of the WLP was progressing under Thomas when compared with the first eighteen months of the party under Murphy, although her run was remarkable enough.

There is little doubt that Thomas was beginning to have a positive effect on the organisation and despite the derelict constituencies, all of which were in the south, the party had adopted twenty candidates at this point, although only nineteen would eventually contest the 1970 general election. This was a remarkable feat, considering that at the previous general election the LPW fielded just eleven candidates.

Table 6: State of WLP constituencies

General secretary	Organiser in place	Candidate adopted	Active (e.g. executive in place and fundraising)	Lacklustre constituency (some activity)	Derelict constituencies (no activity)
M. Murphy[26]	N/A	9[27]	10	15	11[28]
E. Thomas[29]	5	20	17	8	9

However, as already noted, it was financially where the role of the general secretary was reaching the limits of an unclear remit. An unfair amount of criticism has been levelled at Thomas, but ominous signs were appearing for at least a year before his resignation. Thomas was expected to run the Aberystwyth headquarters, deal with the headquarters' finances and reactivate the associations – a daunting task for anyone. As such, Thomas had written to the treasurer, Rhys Gerran Lloyd, expressing how worried he was about the scale of the role. Lloyd, despite cataloguing what he saw as the state of the Aberystwyth office and what needed to be done to bring more money in, also attempted to give words of encouragement, stating that Thomas was 'making magnificent efforts to building up an excellent organisation'. Yet, he forwarded a copy of the letter to Hooson with a handwritten note expressing that 'I am a little worried'.[30]

In March 1970, Thomas resigned from his post, with the executive being critical of his efforts and claiming that he had done a poor job, leaving the state of the party's finances unclear.[31] The state of the WLP's finances may not have been totally clear but it would be true to say that the party was almost bankrupted by Thomas's financial accounting.[32] Yet, the burden of strengthening a complex organisation, whilst raising funds for his role and the party, had not gone unnoticed during Thomas's tenure. Members of the Council commented in August 1969 that 'far too heavy a burden was being placed on the General Secretary in the field of raising money', whereupon it was proposed that a financing or fundraising committee be established.[33] No committee was created at this point, but Thomas was to be held up as a scapegoat by the party for the financial issues that the WLP faced before the 1970 general election. Whilst it is true that many debts went unpaid by Thomas, a great deal of blame should be shared by the executive and individual members, especially by the treasurer, who was diverting money from the WLP's other accounts, so Thomas could keep the Aberystwyth HQ financially stable, despite the latter not generating much income.[34] Additionally, there was an opportunity by Hooson and Lloyd to relieve Thomas of his position, but it was felt they 'should maintain the status quo for the time being!' Quite why they chose to carry on is not properly explained, but Lloyd hinted that Thomas's 'Banker's Orders operation seems to be gathering momentum'.[35]

One of the major issues that some members of the party had with Thomas, especially Lloyd and Ogmore, was his insistence that the party headquarters remained in Aberystwyth. Lloyd opined that 'Emlyn Thomas pitched us into a three-year lease at Aberystwyth without consulting me. He knows I would myself have bought some premises so that HQ could be free of rent.'[36] This is an issue that became a tug of war between certain factions of the party, with Lloyd later pointing out that 'My offer to supply premises was made some weeks ago after I had ascertained that all officers were in favour of the proposal, but there seems to have been some change of mind'.[37] The reason that Lloyd and others wanted the office moved was because of the transport links to Cardiff and the proximity of the press. This was a contentious issue, possibly because Aberystwyth was in a central location. It would not be solved until Thomas's departure.

In addition to the finances, it was clear that Thomas had not been able to properly manage the scale of the role. For example, before Thomas's appointment, the party had made some inroads into the southern constituencies,[38] but these were not maintained or expanded upon by Thomas, as he had emphasised the targeting of north and mid-Wales.[39] This was possibly due to an understanding that the party needed to strengthen the organisation in the traditional heartlands before attempting anything in the south. As Deacon points out, the role was vague, and the WLP executive was 'uncertain about what he was actually doing, if anything'.[40] This was coupled with a lack of help and oversight by the WLP executive and treasurer which, perhaps more so than Thomas's incompetence, were to blame for his failure as general secretary.[41] As has been demonstrated, there were ample opportunities for the officers of the party to intervene, although Lloyd felt that his hands had been tied on the matter by the executive, stating that 'I do blame myself for not bringing to an end before the divided responsibility for finance. But members of the Executive always thought I was too tough as it was!'[42]

The state of the finances may not have been fully understood, but there was an acknowledgement that something was wrong. Perhaps the most telling example came in February 1969, with Lloyd stating that:

> Our central funds have been subsidising HQ at the rate of £300 or more a month. The bare minimum for running HQ at Aberystwyth allowing a small amount for stationary is £350[43] a month . . . Subscriptions to HQ have been much, much lower than Emlyn Thomas' estimates. Geraint Howells gave me a warning about this at the London dinner.[44]

The fact that the party was aware of the situation almost a year before Thomas's resignation shows that there was culpability on all sides that has never been fully acknowledged. Culpability should be shared by Thomas, the executive, the leader (Hooson) and the treasurer (Lloyd).

CARDIFF HEADQUARTERS

Winifred 'Freddie' Whitaker

Following Thomas's resignation, the post of general secretary remained vacant (despite attempts to get some form of political director in place[45]), and the party moved its headquarters to St Mary's Street in Cardiff from May 1970. This made a lot more sense as, arguably, the remoteness of the Aberystwyth office, especially from the Cardiff media, meant that publicity for the party was harder to generate.[46] The move to Cardiff not only aided the accessibility of the WLP to the media, but also allowed the party to attempt a regrouping exercise after the Emlyn Thomas years.

Again, financial insecurity meant that the running of the party headquarters and organisation of the WLP were entrusted to a small number of employees, namely Rhys Gerran Lloyd and his secretary, Winifred 'Freddie' Whitaker. However, this pairing was quite an active and effective force within the WLP and would carry on the work that had begun under Murphy and Thomas. In truth, it was Whitaker who ran the office and liaised with the local associations, helped them to identify potential candidates, and was the administrative point of contact for the party. Lloyd, on the other hand, oversaw the work but was more concerned with the financial situation of the WLP, as he still held the role of treasurer. For his part, Lloyd and his family were the leaseholders of the Cardiff HQ and had furnished the office, allowing him a form of indispensability to the WLP.[47] Notwithstanding this, a lot of the archival correspondence between Whitaker and Lloyd shows that the secretary was the driving force behind the new headquarters.[48]

Following the move to Cardiff in 1970, Whitaker stayed with the party until the middle of 1974. In that time, she had been instrumental in the expansion of the WLP, to the point that the party was able to contest thirty-one of the thirty-four Westminster seats. This was the first time since 1929 that the Liberals had contested the majority of seats in Wales. The true impact of Freddie Whitaker was through 'building up local associations . . . Great credit is due to Mrs Whitaker for her persistent efforts in encouraging constituency workers, often in places where no Liberal candidate had been adopted for forty years.'[49] It was not a lone effort, as there were some remarkable PPCs who worked with their association to build up the organisation.[50] Yet, it was Whitaker's work in reactivating the constituencies that led to this success. In 1972, Lloyd had charged Whitaker with the following tasks concerning her work on the constituencies:

> You should continue your excellent tactful work in encouraging and activating constituencies throughout Wales . . . You should persuade constituencies to pay AFFILIATION FEES, adopt prospective candidates as soon as possible and prepare for the 1973 local elections . . . You should give every assistance to winnable seats.[51]

Having said this, it would be wrong to give the impression that, even by 1974, every constituency was in great shape and ready to take on the opposition, because many just had the PPC and little else. For example, as late as December 1973, eleven constituencies were still described as being without an organisation or only having a partial organisation in place. Couple this with the realisation that the WLP had selected a total of only twenty-one candidates, although this was two more than stood in 1970, and it is easy to see the mountain that Whitaker had to climb.[52] As Lloyd pointed out, it was Whitaker's 'work in fostering constituency organisations' that was the main factor in getting so many candidates by the time of the general election.[53] Even hitherto derelict constituencies, such as Caerphilly,[54] Merthyr Tydfil, Aberdare and Neath, were re-forming and placing a candidate at one or both 1974 general elections. Without a full-time general secretary or an organiser, it would have been difficult for the party to manage this feat without someone like Whitaker coordinating the operation and ensuring that Liberalism would be represented at the ballot box.[55]

Yet, Whitaker and Lloyd's time at the forefront of the WLP was not without its controversies, most notably when the Cardiff office mistakenly sent out several fundraising letters to deceased donors. This issue showed that the WLP was woefully understaffed, as there was no up-to-date record of donors and the list used was comprised of names Whitaker 'found in old letters and files'.[56] This incident also allowed criticism of Whitaker and Lloyd to increase, with some members of the executive misunderstanding Whitaker's role and trying to tell her what she should be doing.[57]

However, this criticism highlights a familiar thread running through the WLP operation, and that was concerning the payment to its female staff and the treatment they experienced. It should be noted that Whitaker was vastly underpaid for her role: she was officially employed part-time but worked full-time. Her starting wage was £3 a week in 1970 and only rose to £16 before her resignation in 1974.[58] 'As a good Liberal' Whitaker viewed the paltry wages as 'my contribution to the Welsh Liberal Party'. Despite the pay, she knew her worth to the WLP and half-joked that the press described her role as a 'general factotum', or a person who takes on many roles, and indicated that she was expected to be a 'press officer/researcher, secretary and field officer'.[59] It was in this description of the roles she was carrying out and the aforementioned criticism levelled at her by some members of the executive, which shows the WLP had not learnt any lessons from the Thomas affair. There was no consensus on what her role should be and, apart from Lloyd, no executive committee oversight of her employment. The criticism that she faced was mostly unwarranted and had its roots in the inability of the WLP to properly state the functions of its staff. Whitaker left the WLP due in part to this criticism and being 'overworked'.[60]

Her departure was preceded by that of Lloyd, who had grown unhappy with the criticism.

Despite this, Whitaker can be praised for leaving an organisation that, with the right stewardship, could have built on her success. This success was most notable with the adoption of thirty-four candidates at the October 1974 general election and the retention of both MPs, Hooson and Howells. As will be shown, the WLP failed to build on the success of 1974.

THE NEW EXECUTIVE

Following the resignation of Lloyd and Whitaker, the party experienced something of an organisational drift away from the founders of the WLP. Although the day-to-day running of the WLP was technically controlled by the executive, as we have seen, organisational matters had mostly been entrusted to other members of the party. Since the transition to the WLP had taken place, Lloyd, in his capacity as honorary treasurer, had overseen the running of the organisation, first with Emlyn Thomas and then with Freddie Whitaker. The loss of Lloyd and Whitaker had meant that two important functions, those of treasurer and secretary/organiser, would become more entwined with the executive.

Once Lloyd had left, he relinquished the office lease and it passed to officers of the party, including Hooson and Howells. It was obvious that Hooson was worried about the direction the party would now take; he asked for a complete review of staffing at the Cardiff office, questioning 'Exactly how is the Party to be run?'[61] This was not an abstract musing: the running of the office was vital to the organisation of the WLP. John Morgan, the chairman of the executive, also recommended that the executive committee should become 'much more divorced from party politics and should become the business of the party. The Executive should have control of the Cardiff Office, its staffing and the day-to-day running . . . insofar as all business functions of the party are concerned.'⁶²

This idea that the executive become the business end of the party began to be reflected in the way the executive worked. The party advertised for an organising secretary, as the role had now become known, and Gwyneth Ashford was employed. She was paid considerably more than Freddie Whitaker (see the following section, on finances), but Ashford's role was governed by the executive, whereas Lloyd managed Whitaker. Lloyd's greater autonomy is best illustrated in Whitaker's salary, however woefully underpaid she was during her time with the WLP. Whitaker's initial salary was set by the executive but, towards the end of their tenure, Lloyd gave her a pay rise that does not appear to have gone through the executive.[63] This autonomy appears to have been a situation that the executive wanted to change. With everything that had preceded Ashford, namely the lack of knowledge as to what their employees were doing, it was commendable that the executive was taking more of an interest. Ashford certainly experienced tighter control by the executive,[64] but she was treated as expendable and a luxury that the WLP could ill afford (see below). Also, her role and duties remained unclear, and in 1977 she requested 'clarification of her duties and a more precise allocation of her workload'.[65]

This greater sense of control over staff coincided with some major changes in the executive. Not only had the party employed Ashford, but it had seen a 'change in the composition of the Executive'.[66] By early 1975, just a cursory scan of the officers of the party showed that the makeup of the executive had changed.[67] High-profile members such as Martin Thomas,[68] Mary Murphy, Lloyd and the Gibbses were no longer regular officers or members of the executive. They had been replaced by members who would come to dominate the WLP in the following decades, including the future Police and Crime Commissioner Winston Roddick, and the future Brecon and Radnor MP Richard Livsey. Geraint Howells, now MP and President of the

WLP, was more involved with the organisation, especially once Hooson took on more responsibility in parliament and focused his energies on the campaign for a Welsh Assembly.

Yet, despite the success of the 1974 general elections, in terms of those elected and the number of candidates put forward, the WLP was seeking some sort of direction. A review of the constitution took place in 1975 and the position of the executive was strengthened. In the original constitution, the WLP council had oversight of the executive, but that body, it was felt, had become little more than a 'talking shop'. The executive was given the express right to provide the administrative and financial functions of the party: it would be responsible for drafting party policy, publicity and publications. Also, it would be responsible for ensuring that candidates were adopted.[69] All of these were previously under the remit of the council and were delegated to the executive.[70] John Roberts, reflecting on the period between 1974 and 1976, pointed out that, despite these changes in the organisation, there was 'a great feeling of apathy . . . even antagonism towards the organization of the Party' and that this stemmed from a lack of communication between the Party and the constituencies.[71] The antagonism and apathy were reflected in the wider structure of the WLP. The press attention towards Plaid Cymru during the general election had overshadowed the WLP's successes.

As Deacon points out, by June 1975, every constituency in Wales had a secretary, something which had not occurred since the mid-1960s. Whilst some were more active than others, south Wales was once again being targeted.[72] However, within a year, the WLP was reporting a noticeable drop in active constituencies and secretaries.[73] Added to this state of affairs was the resignation of Jeremy Thorpe and the ensuing scandal, which affected Liberal morale. The WLP recognised this fact and there were moves to reinvigorate the party by re-establishing the policy committee, which had not properly met for a few years (examined in the next chapter). There was also the establishment of the candidates' committee, and the post of honorary secretary was re-established.

However, whilst being positive moves in themselves, the power grab of the council's responsibilities by the executive had occurred without much thought and without defining the roles of the officers. Additionally, some of the issues that would be experienced between 1975 and 1979, particularly in terms of finance, could be traced to this reorganisation and the lack of defined roles. Also, an all-powerful executive that had no oversight from the council was not the way to gain the trust of the constituencies. The reorganisation would not be enough to hold back the internal and external forces that would rock the WLP in the coming years.

The seemingly buoyant nature of the constituencies, following the 1974 general election, would be almost undone by the time of the 1979 general election. As Deacon points out, the unpopularity of the Lib-Lab Pact, coupled with the Jeremy Thorpe scandal and the WLP's prominent role in the devolution campaign, made it difficult to attract prospective candidates. Of the twenty-eight seats the WLP contested, sixteen would lose their deposits.[74] Following the general election, the WLP was in mixed spirits, having lost Montgomery to the Conservatives and being left with just one MP, and this was reflected in the responses to a questionnaire sent out by the executive to the constituencies (table 7). Although just seven out of thirty-six constituencies replied, the responses do give a good indication as to the state of the WLP.

Table 7: Constituency questionnaire response[75]

Constituency	PPC	Councillors	Organiser	Membership	Finances
Caerphilly	Not given	Not given	Not given	Not given	Not given
Denbigh	Not given	12	1	500	Not given
Montgomery	Not given	4	Not given	Not given	Not given
Newport	Not given	Not given	Not given	100	Not given
Ogmore	Not given	3	Not given	20	Not given
Pembroke	Not given	Not given	Not given	33	£1,000 p/a[76]
Wrexham	Not given	2	Not given	39	Precarious

An internal report went further and stated that in seventeen constituencies the 'associations are so poor that I doubt they fulfil the minimum constitutional requirements,' with a further three constituencies experiencing a 'serious lack of local organisation'.[77] In addition, during the 1979 general election, twelve constituencies were awarded grants and deposit guarantees from the LPO and WLP, totalling £2,108.[78] The level of help highlights how far the constituencies had been neglected. The arduous work that was put in by Whitaker had not been maintained, and it had been exacerbated by the financial issues of the WLP, meaning the organising secretary and the organiser, who had been employed in 1978, were both unable to fully commit to their roles. Internally, the issue of the party's finances and near bankruptcy affected the running of the WLP.

WLP FINANCES

Upon the formation of the WLP, Hooson and Rhys Gerran Lloyd were especially keen to establish what finances were available to them. This was an urgent requirement, as the final balance sheet provided by the LPW treasurer had stated that the new party had about £123 1s. 6d in the bank account and a total income of £198 11s for the previous year.[79] The initial aim was to transfer the monies from the federations' accounts to the WLP, yet this proved a lot more difficult than it should have been and there was evidence of a reluctance to relinquish the money. For example, the North Wales Liberal Federation had £47 9s. 4d in funds but the Federation's executive gave £35 to the honorary secretary 'for services rendered', with most of the balance being sent to the WLP.[80] Others, such as the treasurer of the moribund Welsh Radical Group, were reluctant to send their money to the WLP. He believed that the group was not part of the WLP and that the funds should be left alone, in case there was a need to reconvene the group.[81] It was also alleged that the Tenby Association had around £12,000 of funds but would not confirm the amount with Hooson.[82]

In addition to the request for the disbanded federations and moribund groups to surrender their funds to the WLP, the party had also gradually sought to centralise the income that had generally been the preserve of the local associations. When the WLP initially formed, the steering committee set the affiliation fee at '£30 for the first two hundred members and an additional £10 for every additional Council member'.[83] However, very few associations paid the affiliation fee, either in full or part. So, in 1969, the WLP decided to abolish the affiliation fee and centralise the membership subscriptions, which would have initially been paid directly to the association by its members. The idea was that the constituencies would not have to pay the affiliation fee, provided that the standing orders from the constituency members totalled at least the affiliation amount. If not, they would have to pay the affiliation fee.[84] The centralisation of the membership subscriptions gave the WLP, in theory, more control of the organisation's finances.

This marked a change of direction for the WLP: the local association finances were traditionally decentralised and it would have been up to the association to decide how the finances were deployed. Initially, the scheme did not appear to be popular and there was a mixed reaction, with some associations sending sums as large as £458 11s. 6d whilst others sent as little as £1 1s., or nothing.[85] The constituencies that initially embraced the scheme included Carmarthen, where sixty members paid subscriptions directly to the WLP in 1969. Yet almost a third were not renewed in 1970, a pattern that was replicated in Montgomery and Pembroke.[86] Of course, this could reflect that 1970 was a general election year and the constituencies were expected to finance their campaigns, with little help from the WLP, so they might have kept hold of the funds rather than allowing them to be diverted to the WLP.

In terms of overall income, as table 8 shows, the first four years of operation did show some steady financial growth. The first seven months of the party's existence generated a healthy amount of income, but this would have been due to the party attracting some goodwill because, as well as the balance transfers from the federations, the bulk of the income came from donations and subscriptions. Contrast this with the previous year, where there were no donations and the affiliation fees that had been received were minimal. Interestingly, in the final statement for 1968 the honorary treasurer, Lloyd, stated that the expenditure figures 'do not include expenses paid for directly by Officers of the Party and Members of the Executive', which he estimated as totalling a further £1,000.[87] This strongly suggests that the WLP was surviving on the generosity of those who ran the party, rather than generating its own income. This would be a mainstay of the WLP finances throughout Lloyd's time as treasurer.

Table 8: Income and expenditure of the WLP, 1966–70

Period	Income	Expenditure	Balance brought forward	Totals
31 July 1965– 8 September 1966[88]	£198 11s.	£136 18s. 10d	£61 9s. 4d	£123 1s. 6d
September 1966–3 March 1967[89]	£1,019 0s. 1d	£255 13s. 10d	£122 1s. 6d	£886 7s. 9d
31 August 1967–29 May 1968[90]	£1,727 6s.	£1,606 11s. 5d	N/A	£120 14s. 7d
2 August 1969[91]	£2,000	£1,550	N/A	£450
1 April 1969–31 March 1970[92]	£2,504 6s. 9d	£2,186 9s. 2d	N/A	£317 7s. 7d

Lloyd also instigated some novel fundraising appeals, with the most successful being his loan scheme. The scheme was designed so that members could donate a sum to the WLP, preferably over £100, allowing the party to get eight per cent interest on the loans from the bank. The person who loaned the money would get an undated cheque that they could use to withdraw the money at any point.[93] By January 1968, Lloyd wrote to Lord Ogmore stating that 'the loan scheme should have £12,000 in by the end of the week. I have been bringing pressure to bear on the Lloyd family.'[94] This is interesting because, as previously noted, Lloyd's family became quite intertwined with the finances of the WLP. He would often mention that he and his family were contributing to the running of the party.[95] Although an undoubted success,[96] the loan scheme became something of an albatross around Lloyd's neck. In 1972, the novel nature of the loan scheme meant that the Inland Revenue was 'at a loss as to understand how this operation can be described as a loan scheme' and did not think the party was assessable on the amount.[97] By this point, many of the people who joined the scheme had withdrawn their money and there were only six left, with a balance of £6,500 in the account.[98] The issue would rumble on until Lloyd left his post and the scheme was wound up, with the WLP owing £800 in corporation tax.[99]

The biggest financial issue faced in the early 1970s was the costs incurred following the resignation of Emlyn Thomas and the folding of the Aberystwyth office. The final column in table 8 shows that the WLP had a balance remaining just short of £318,[100] once all the bills from the Aberystwyth office had been paid. This had depleted the financial reserves of the party, but it was a lesson that the party needed to heed, although financial issues would blight the WLP by the mid-1970s.

In March 1971, Lloyd wrote to Lord Ogmore with news that the WLP funds were now in credit, with £5,300 in the bank.[101] However, as treasurer, Lloyd was aware of the precarious position that the WLP was in financially, and he was not averse to pointing out the rights of the party to a share of the BLP's funding:

> At the business meeting . . . it was disclosed that English constituencies contribute about £7,000. The Party expects to get an income of £80,000 . . . In a federal Liberal Party, it seems to me wrong that all money for the Liberal Party should go to the English constituencies. I feel we are entitled to a maximum of 10%.[102]

Although the WLP was a federal member of the British Liberal Party, it is difficult to ascertain how much funding came directly from the LPO. On this matter, the BLP's financial reports omitted the contributions the LPO made to the Scottish and Welsh parties, although Pinto-Duschinsky has estimated that the services of the LPO probably covered only five per cent of activities in Scotland and twenty per cent within Wales.[103] This does raise the question of how much money was allocated to the WLP during the 1970s. In 1972, the financial report shows that £500 was received from the LPO,[104] but Lloyd continued to ask for further funding from the BLP. Such funding was forthcoming, with Lloyd remarking in 1974 that he continued 'to press hard for contributions from the LPO . . . It is particularly clear that without LPO subsidy WLP will be quite unable to fight many seats at an election'.[105]

Regarding election funding, the subsidies that Lloyd was talking about probably included funds that were donated by anonymous organisations or people, to be used by Hooson and the WLP. One such 'election aid', as Hooson described it, was for the sum of £3,850 which was passed via the 'medium of the Treasurer of the L.P.O. from one donor on certain trusts, of which he acquainted me'.[106] The existence of this money caused some issues within the constituencies, and Lloyd had written to Hooson to say 'Your distribution of wealth particularly to derelict seats is causing me trouble with the harder workers! Do keep these gifts very confidential.'[107] Mindful that these payments could open the party up to criticism about how the organisation was funded, Hooson felt that all contributions to the party should be disclosed,[108] although there is no evidence that this happened.

However, the main issue for the WLP in this period was its lacklustre income from the affiliation fees. As table 9 shows, these remained relatively static between 1971 and 1973 when both Lloyd and Whitaker, respectively, left their positions. Table 10 shows the income and expenditure for the WLP in 1972 and 1973.[109]

Table 9: Affiliation fees and subscriptions received by the WLP, 1971–3

Year	Number of constituencies paying (out of 36)	Amounts received
1971	10	£320[110]
1972	13	£258[111]
1973	10[112]	£335[113]

Table 10: WLP income and expenditure, 1972–3

Year	Income	Expenditure	+/-
1972[114]	£2,154.53	£2,808.88	-£654.45
1973[115]	£2,047.71	£2,781.19	-£733.48

The above two tables show that the WLP headquarters were operating at a substantial loss, according to Lloyd's figures. Interestingly, Lloyd's financial reports did not always show the full picture, partly because the true running costs were unknown (see below) but, also because he was fixated on building up the WLP's reserves. For example, the 1973 accounts mention affiliation fees received (around £335[116]), yet they do not mention the receipt of any subscriptions or banker's orders. The reason for this is because Lloyd placed them in a separate account and, according to a financial statement by John Morgan following Lloyd's 1974 resignation, these totalled almost £2,000.[117] It is unknown whether Lloyd used these funds unofficially to prop up the WLP. Morgan goes on to state that, despite the estimated deficit of £1,000 for the 1974 period, there was £3,000 of cash available and 'we can jog along comfortably for a couple of years'.[118] This is remarkable, as the WLP kept posting an operational loss during Lloyd's tenure when it could have shown itself to be in a better financial position. Cash reserves matter, but this meant that the WLP always appeared more financially stretched.

A further reason for casting doubt on Lloyd's accounting is that the published accounts do not reflect the true running costs of the WLP. Lloyd tended to comment in every financial report from 1969 onwards that the officers and others within the WLP provided 'informal and generous contributions' to the party, paying various expenses.[119] However, this state of affairs did not go unnoticed by the executive, and in 1974 the chairman pointed out that it 'has come to a point where the Executive itself, through its members, have had to pay for almost every function including hire of the room in which it meets'.[120] Although Lloyd was not always personally responsible for these unofficial payments (although he certainly provided money to the party[121]), the fact that he allowed the practice to continue meant that the true running cost of the WLP was unknown.

Lord Lloyd (as Rhys Gerran Lloyd became in 1973) had sought to build up the cash reserves of the WLP, whilst officers of the WLP continued to pay the running expenses of the party. As such, it seems a tad naive for John Morgan to believe that the estimated £1,000 yearly deficit would mean that the WLP could survive on the £3,000 cash reserves. For example, following Lloyd's resignation, the accounts of the WLP no longer mentioned the informal payments by the officers of the party, although it is unclear as to whether they continued, because the account refers only to 'private donations'.[122]

This way of separating funds was not just peculiar to the WLP; it was common practice within the LPO. As Pinto-Duschinsky points out, the LPO's secret funds (raised and administered by the party's 'Direct Aid Committee') were not published or disclosed to Lord Houghton's Committee on Financial Aid to Political Parties, reporting in 1975, which looked at and recommended state funding for political parties. Pinto-Duschinsky believes that the Liberal case for state subsidies 'must have been helped by the artificially low figures of Liberal central income and spending'.[123] This can equally apply to the WLP which, for example, and as we have noted in table 10, had an income of £2,154.53 in 1972 and £2,047.71 in 1973. However, the WLP informed the Houghton committee that the party's income totalled £1,500 and £1,800, respectively.[124] The WLP deliberately left out any donations and grants it received, despite being asked for such details. This was repeated in all the accounts submitted to the Houghton Committee that covered the period between 1970 and 1976.[125]

Following Lloyd's departure, the WLP experienced a fiscal crisis that almost bankrupted the party. Chris Davies, Lloyd's replacement as treasurer, informed the executive that the WLP had around eighteen months' 'worth of ready cash available',[126] largely due to the cash reserves that Lloyd had built up in a separate account.[127] Despite these reserves, it was clear from the estimated yearly deficit that the WLP could not survive without depleting these cash reserves. As it was, the WLP began to see a sizeable deficit within the 1975/6 financial period and, as the published accounts (see table 11) show, this morphed into quite a substantial revenue deficit that occurred between 1975 and 1978. There were several reasons for this, for example, the rising inflation that was being experienced in the mid-1970s. This undoubtedly affected the running costs of the WLP, particularly in terms of the rental of the Cardiff offices,[128] which increased from £219 in 1976/7 to £398 in 1977/8.[129] This was coupled with a rising salary bill (see below) and an income that for two financial periods had failed to cover even that expenditure.[130] There were also the costs involved with fighting two successive general elections in 1974 and the 1975 EEC referendum. Table 12 shows the decline of the WLP's bank balance; both tables are from accounts between 1975/6 and 1977/9.

Table 11: Income and expenditure, 1975–9

Financial year	Income	Expenditure	Revenue surplus or deficit
1975/6[131]	£4,541	£4,950	-£409
1976/7[132]	£2,285	£4,058	-£1,773
1977/8[133]	£3,972	£6,281	-£2,309
1978/9[134]	£8,240	£7,056	+£1,184

Table 12: Bank balance, 1975–9

Financial year	Balance
1975/6[135]	£4,241
1976/7[136]	£2,497
1977/8	£754
1978/9[137]	£1,227

Part of the reason for this decline was that, following Lloyd's resignation, the role of honorary treasurer was ill-defined. Whereas Lloyd had been able to approach wealthy friends or would actively send out letters to raise funds, the new treasurer pointed out that they had 'not agreed to serve as a fundraiser, and that the raising of funds independently from the constituencies was not now being undertaken'. There was even trepidation about the possibility of raising the affiliation fee, as the constituencies had to feel 'like they were getting something in return from the WLP organization, which in turn could not be effective if it was not adequately financed'.[138]

It would take until 1978 for the WLP to raise the affiliation fees to £100,[139] the first such rise in nearly a decade. As table 13 shows, when compared with the early 1970s, more of the constituencies decided to pay something towards the affiliation fees, partly because it worked out cheaper than relinquishing the membership fees or banker's orders from their members. Others just sent in small amounts, and this caused some issues with underfunded local associations. For example, the Montgomeryshire Liberal Association's honorary treasurer, Colin A. Smith, enclosed a cheque for £25 in part payment of the affiliation fee. Smith complained that his association should not be singled out for a delay in payment. He argued that the association was 'in a similar position to the Party. We have a similar income, and we have a full-time professional employee. We have no surplus money and at certain times of the year, money does tend to run short'.[140]

Table 13: Affiliation fees, 1976-9

Financial year	Number of constituencies paying (out of 37)	Affiliation fees received
1976/77[141]	28[142]	£951
1977/78	23[143]	£1,077
1978/79[144]	23[145]	£1,645

Although the affiliation receipts may have superficially increased, as pointed out by John Roberts in 1976, before the rise, 'with an affiliation fee of £40, if every constituency in Wales affiliated it would give us an income of less than £1,500.00. What exactly are we supposed to organize with that?'[146] The reality is that, following the rise, the total amounts received were roughly the same as if every constituency affiliated at the former rate. Before the affiliation rate rise, the WLP had adopted the expectation that the constituencies would pay the affiliation fee, whilst the party would also receive the subscriptions from new members. An ongoing issue was that several constituencies objected to this practice, especially if they were paying more than others, and withheld affiliation fees from the party. Brecon and Radnor complained that any banker's orders had been for the sole use of Geraint Howells's 1970 general election fund when he stood in the constituency. The WLP had continued to collect these funds for its use but could see the case for refunding the money and collecting just the affiliation fee.[147]

There was a dawning realisation that the WLP was facing severe financial issues in the mid-1970s. This became clear when we consider how the party treated the organising secretary. Following the resignation of Lloyd and Whitaker, staffing at the HQ would remain an issue throughout the rest of the 1970s. The appointment of Gwyneth Ashford to the role of full-time organising secretary, in October 1974, was a large undertaking for a party that had just fought two general elections at a considerable cost. Having said this, there may well have been a false sense of security in terms of the party's financial position because, after all, Lloyd had left the party with some cash reserves.

However, employing Ashford at a considerably higher rate of pay than Whitaker's, which, including expenses, was set at £1,750,[148] compared with Whitaker's maximum annual pay having risen to only £1,092,[149] without a proper plan as to how the role would be financed in the long term, was foolhardy. Additionally, Ashford was employed on a full-time basis, whereas Whitaker had been employed part-time, but her workload meant that she was working full-time. As table 14 shows, the cost of employing Ashford rose quite considerably during her time with the WLP.

Table 14: Financial cost of the organising secretary[150]

Financial year	Salary	Expenses
1974 (W. Whitaker)	£832 (£6,369.93)	£260 (£1,990.60)
1974 (G. Ashford)	£1,250 (£9,570)	£500 (£3,828.08)
1975/6[151]	£2,380 (£12,951.07)	Not given
1976/7[152]	£2,039 (£9,674.21)	Not given
1977/8	£3,647 (£16,095.06)	Not given
1978/9[153]	£4,466 (£17,757.56)	Not given

As the above table shows, when compared with table 11, the income generated by the WLP was barely covering the cost of Ashford, let alone the rest of the expenditure. It would be a case of déjà vu for the Cardiff office, because over the next five years, and despite this higher rate of pay, the party would cut her salary. Contractually, her remuneration was in line with the above, but such was the financial position of the WLP, Ashford was working part-time between August 1977 and March 1978. Although her workload did not shrink, she was still working on a full-time basis without recompense.[154]

JOHN SPILLER, ORGANISER

A further strain on the finances of the WLP came in 1978, right in the middle of the party's looming financial crisis. It had long been recognised that if the WLP was to have any hope of survival, then the headquarters should continue supporting the constituencies. Hooson had suggested the appointment of a political director in 1972 but the idea had been shelved, due to the amount of travelling the appointee would need to undertake. Additionally, this was also dependent on receiving money from the LPO for such a post.[155] The idea cropped up time and again, but it was in 1976 that the executive was to begin the process of looking for an organiser, stating that the appointee had:

> To be a professional and to be offered a salary and appointed in clearly defined terms. He/she would generate money to pay for his/her salary and expenses. Guarantors could be available for the first year . . . it should be possible to get 1,000 people to contribute.[156]

This would have been the WLP's ideal circumstances for employing someone, but it was not the reality. The executive formally decided in February 1977 that they would seek to employ an organiser, yet it would take until April 1978 for John Spiller to be appointed. This was due to the funding not being in place for such a costly role, and the executive turned to Geraint Howells to raise the estimated £5,000 needed.[157] This appears to have been initially promised by Howells, but he continually ignored the request for the money, ostensibly because he was no longer president. Howells had to step down from the presidency, as his term of office was over, and this appears to have irked him somewhat. The executive expressed 'serious concern . . . regarding Geraint Howells' attitude to the appointment of an organiser'.[158] The appointment of an organiser took well over fourteen months and was only secured when Howells eventually pledged £1,500.[159] Spiller commenced employment on 1 April 1978 on a part-time, self-employed contract of a minimum of forty-two days. Spiller had requested that he had the status of an employee, but the WLP were prepared to offer only a self-employed contract. They were worried about being liable for unfair dismissal if they had to terminate the employment without notice.[160]

At the start of his employment, Spiller visited several constituencies and detected 'a looseness and lack of direction and coordination in (the) W.L.P.'.[161] However, when his work had barely begun, the executive realised the financial crisis the party was facing and asked Spiller 'whether there might be an external source of funds to support his work . . . after the election'.[162] Spiller was not open to the idea of having to seek his own funding and let it be known that 'no funds would be coming from outside sources, and that any money necessary to employ him would have to be raised in Wales'.[163] Spiller was concerned that the WLP's 'relationship with him (should) be placed on a firm and continuing financial basis'.[164] Spiller left the role in January 1979, as the WLP were unable to secure his appointment due to a lack of funds, even though Howells had stated that he would need until March 1979 to secure further funding.[165] Spiller had accomplished little in terms of organisational reform.

Funding had been a major issue with the WLP and it reflected poorly on the party that it was unable to secure finance for such a pivotal role. Additionally, the executive still expected the employee to secure the funding, or to raise the funds from subscriptions, for their continued employment. This shows that the WLP had not learnt any lessons from its dealings with Emlyn Thomas, and this severely hampered the WLP at the constituency level.

That Spiller's employment began just as the WLP had cut Ashford's hours, suggests not only that they were seeking to save some money by cutting her role, but that the party saw more worth in Spiller. However, by September 1978 there came an acknowledgement that the WLP was facing a deeply disturbing financial problem. The treasurer declared that 'the office account would, at best, only survive until December'. Having already cut Ashford's hours, the initial reaction was 'not to economise further but to secure more income' via a fundraising committee.[166] To turn the financial fortunes of the party around, Norman Lewis, the honorary treasurer, sought to rein in all unnecessary expenditure. Although Ashford would resume full-time hours in April 1978,[167] by February 1979 the WLP were advising that there would not be enough to pay her salary and that an overdraft should be sought.[168] Despite Deacon stating that Ashford was laid off due to the rising debt in the party,[169] it can now be established that Ashford decided to go of her own volition. In June 1979, having asked for a pay rise and refusing to take unpaid leave for the following two months,[170] she then asked to be laid off,[171] eventually being made redundant at the end of March 1980.[172]

Other methods were sought to bring the party back to solvency. Initially, there was a suggestion that the party should try to secure a £600 loan,[173] which Lewis later declined in favour of maintaining 'a holding operation' and trying to increase the income through fundraising.[174] It would take until November 1979, well after that year's general election, before Norman Lewis was able to declare the WLP finances as 'healthy'.[175] Following the departure of Ashford, it would be several years before the Cardiff office was adequately staffed again.[176] Yet, both Ashford's and Spiller's resignations alleviated the burden on the WLP's finances, and it is little wonder that the party came back into solvency.

CONCLUSION

The first twelve years of the WLP's existence were something of a haphazard affair. Following its inception, the organisation was hampered by the lack of direction and oversight given to the general secretaries, which almost bankrupted the party. It was only following the departure of Emlyn Thomas, along with the headquarters being moved to Cardiff, that we see a more stable organisation begin to emerge. Freddie Whitaker must be given credit for the success in establishing the local associations and encouraging candidates to stand in time for the February 1974 general election. It is testament to her work, under the guidance of Rhys Gerran Lloyd, that upon their resignation the organisation began to falter.

The chapter has also shown that financially, the WLP was fighting a battle with the local associations to collect the affiliation fees. The centralisation of the fees was seen as a step too far by the local associations, who believed they were best placed to spend the money. However, the treasurer, Rhys Gerran Lloyd, was able to use creative means to swell the WLP's coffers, which involved a loan scheme and relying on donations from his own family and members of the executive to keep the party afloat. These creative measures severely hampered the WLP when Lloyd left the role, and the financial issues affected the organisation.

The next chapter will address the policy process of the WLP. It will focus on Hooson's plan to re-energise policymaking within the WLP and the emphasis placed on promoting its Welshness. It will show that the WLP was a vibrant and ideas-led political party with something distinctive to offer to Wales.

Notes

1   NLW, Lord Hooson Papers, Box 42, Letter from Hooson to Elfyn Lloyd Morris declining the offer of Chairman of the WLP, 1 July 1966.
2   NLW, Lord Ogmore Papers, File 6, Letter from Hooson to Ogmore, 17 April 1970.
3   The issue of the WLP and devolution will be examined in chapter five.
4   NLW, Lord Hooson Papers, Report on the Welsh Liberal Party Council Meeting, Llandrindod Wells, 22 July 1972. Plans were approved at the AGM in October 1972.
5   NLW, Lord Hooson Papers, Box 42, letter from Hooson to Murphy, 13 October 1966.
6   NLW, Lord Hooson Papers, Letter from Hooson to Peter J. Ellis, 16 December 1966. My italics.
7   J. Graham Jones, 'Emlyn Hooson and Montgomeryshire Politics, 1962–79', *Montgomeryshire Collections*, 97 (2009), 191. 'Emlyn Thomas . . . had been appointed to the *newly* created position of general secretary' (my italics).
8   Russell Deacon, *The Welsh Liberals: The History of the Liberal and Liberal Democratic Parties in Wales* (Cardiff, 2014), p. 177.
9   NLW, Lord Hooson Papers, Box 42, letter from Leslie Jones to Emlyn Hooson, 2 July 1967. Because of the lack of help with the conference role, amongst other concerns, Jones resigned as conference secretary.

10 NLW, Lord Hooson Papers, Letter from Murphy to Martin Thomas, 12 July 1967.
11 NLW, Lord Hooson Papers, Letter from Murphy to Martin Thomas, 12 July 1967.
12 NLW, Lord Ogmore Papers, File 4, Letter from Murphy to The Hon. Edward Davies, 5 February 1968.
13 For example, NLW, Lord Ogmore Papers, File 4, Letter from Murphy to The Hon. Edward Davies, 5 February 1968.
14 NLW, Lord Ogmore Papers, File 4, Letter from Murphy to Ogmore, 25 October 1967.
15 NLW, Lord Hooson Papers, Letter from Murphy to Martin Thomas, 12 July 1967.
16 NLW, Merfyn Jones Papers, Box 35, *The Constitution of the Welsh Liberal Party*, undated (1975), Clause 23.
17 Adjusted to 2023 levels, £26,345.66 and £8,781.89, respectively, at 5% inflation a year.
18 Deacon, *Welsh Liberals*, p. 177.
19 Deacon, *Welsh Liberals*, p. 177.
20 Deacon, *Welsh Liberals*, pp. 177–8.
21 Deacon, *Welsh Liberals*, p. 177.
22 NLW, Lord Hooson Papers, Box 45, Letter from Rhys Gerran Lloyd to Emlyn Thomas, 11 February 1969. Lloyd states: 'You have always maintained you could cover your own fees.'
23 NLW, Merfyn Jones Papers, File 34, Minutes of the Council of the Welsh Liberal Party, 24 May 1969, Item 4, General Secretary's Report.
24 NLW, Lord Ogmore Papers, File 4, Letter from Emlyn Thomas to Lord Ogmore, 21 May 1969.
25 NLW, Lord Ogmore Papers, File 4, Letter from Emlyn Thomas to Lord Ogmore, 21 May 1969. Adjusted to 2023 levels, £1,181.99 at 5% inflation p/a.
26 NLW, Merfyn Jones Papers, File 34, Secretary's Report by Mary Murphy, undated but probably around June 1967, from the mention of the county council elections.
27 There were five candidates adopted, but another four constituencies were negotiating with prospective candidates.
28 Murphy states that two of these were currently forming an association, but as they were not in existence, they have been placed in this category.
29 NLW, Merfyn Jones Papers, File 34, Minutes of the Council of the Welsh Liberal Party, 24 May 1969, Item 4, General Secretary's Report.
30 NLW, Lord Hooson Papers, Box 45, Letter to Emlyn Thomas from Rhys Gerran Lloyd, 11 February 1969.
31 Deacon, *Welsh Liberals*, p. 177. Deacon states that 'Emlyn Thomas left his post', indicating that as he was still allowed to fight the Merioneth seat for the WLP, which continued to be a target seat in 1970, it was a resignation rather than a termination of employment.

32 NLW, Merfyn Jones Papers, File 34, Report by Hon. Treasurer to Annual Conference, May 1970. The party was left with around £318 (2023 equivalent £4,174.22, inflation 5% p/a).
33 NLW, Merfyn Jones Papers, File 34, Minutes of the Council of the Welsh Liberal Party, 2 August 1969, Item 5 'Finances'.
34 NLW, Lord Hooson Papers, Box 45, Letter to Emlyn Thomas from Rhys Gerran Lloyd, 11 February 1969.
35 NLW, Lord Ogmore Papers, File 4, Letter from Rhys Gerran Lloyd to Lord Ogmore, 6 August 1969. The banker's orders were paid directly to the WLP, bypassing the local constituency association.
36 NLW, Lord Ogmore Papers, File 4, Letter from Rhys Gerran Lloyd to Lord Ogmore, 12 February 1969.
37 NLW, Lord Ogmore Papers, File 4, Letter from Lloyd to Lord Ogmore, 6 August 1969.
38 Deacon, *Welsh Liberals*, p. 171. Lord Ogmore had tried to set up a Cardiff West association, but this was short-lived.
39 NLW, Lord Hooson Papers, Box 44, Letter to Jennie Gibbs from Hooson, 29 July 1970. 'It is my strong feeling that . . . Cardiff and the surrounding areas are fought in local government elections. I feel that the North and Mid-Wales constituencies now need regular bulletins but do not need the kind of special attention which was given by Emlyn Thomas.'
40 Deacon, *Welsh Liberals*, p. 177.
41 As a side note, when Thomas resigned, he fought the Meirionnydd constituency for the WLP at the 1970 general election. However, by the time of the 1979 general election he had become a Conservative and fought Geraint Howells's Ceredigion seat, coming second behind Howells.
42 NLW, Lord Ogmore Papers, File 6, Letter from Lloyd to Geraint Howells, 27 April 1970.
43 Adjusted to 2023 levels, £4,171.73 and £4,867.01, respectively, at 5% inflation p/a.
44 NLW, Lord Ogmore Papers, File 4, Letter from Lloyd to Lord Ogmore, 12 February 1969.
45 NLW, Lord Hooson Papers, Letter to Hooson from Rhys Gerran Lloyd, 3 August 1972. These attempts generally failed for lack of finances and because the scale of the role would be too much for one person. As Lloyd put it 'We just do not want another grand seigneur, partly office bound and partly travelling huge distances.'
46 Despite the move, the WLP would still sometimes hold its executive meetings in Llandrindod Wells and, later, Cardiff.
47 NLW, Lord Hooson Papers, Letter from Lord Lloyd to John Morgan, 24 April 1974. However, the furniture now belonged to the WLP.
48 For example, NLW, Welsh Liberal Party Papers, Letter from Lloyd to the Welsh Liberal Party, undated but after the February 1974 general election. 'The amount of work in the office increased immensely during 1973 and Mrs Whitaker has dealt valiantly with it all.'

49 NLW, Welsh Liberal Party Papers, Letter from Lloyd to the Welsh Liberal Party, undated but after the February 1974 general election.
50 Russell Deacon, 'Interview with Lord Geraint of Ponterwyd', *Journal of Liberal History*, 44 (Autumn 2004), 22. Howells mentioned how, when standing in Brecon and Radnor, he 'helped build up the constituency'.
51 NLW, Lord Hooson Papers, Report on the Welsh Liberal Party Council Meeting, Llandrindod Wells 22 July 1972.
52 NLW, Lord Hooson Papers, Letter from John Morgan to Hooson, 5 December 1973.
53 NLW, Welsh Liberal Party Papers, Financial Report by the Lord Lloyd of Kilgerran for the period 1973 to February 1974 general election. Undated but 1974.
54 NLW, Lord Hooson Papers, Letter/Memo from Winifred Whitaker, undated but late 1973 or early 1974.
55 NLW, Lord Hooson Papers, Letter from Winifred Whitaker to Helen Roberts (Hooson's secretary), 9 April 1974. 'Others who have been apathetic are also in the process of coming to life . . . I will not let up until each and every one of the Welsh constituencies adopts a candidate.'
56 NLW, Lord Hooson Papers, Letter to Helen Hughes (Hooson's secretary) from Whitaker, 9 April 1974.
57 NLW, Welsh Liberal Party Papers, Resignation Letter from Winifred Whitaker to the WLP Executive, 19 June 1974.
58 Adjusted to 2023 levels, respectively, £39.38 at 5% inflation, and £145.17 at 4.6% inflation p/a.
59 NLW, Welsh Liberal Party Papers, Resignation Letter from Winifred Whitaker to the WLP Executive, 19 June 1974. Also, these roles were put forward by Whitaker as a suggestion for any future person being engaged.
60 NLW, Welsh Liberal Party Papers, Resignation Letter from Winifred Whitaker to the WLP Executive, 19 June 1974.
61 NLW, Welsh Liberal Party Papers, Memo from Hooson to the Executive, 3 April 1974.
62 NLW, Merfyn Jones Papers, File 35, Notes on the Activities of the Executive of the Welsh Liberal Party 1973/4 by John Roberts, 17 June 1974.
63 NLW, Welsh Liberal Party Papers, Memo from Hooson to the Executive, 3 April 1974. 'Lord Lloyd has now informed the Chairman that he has increased her [Whitaker's] salary and given her a bonus.'
64 NLW, Welsh Liberal Party Papers, File A4, Minutes of the Executive Committee, 25 September 1976. Ashford requested permission to leave early each day to attend a Welsh-language course. This was denied, and she was advised to attend evening courses. This was a curious decision for a party that wanted to promote its Welshness.
65 NLW, Welsh Liberal Party Papers, File A4, Minutes of the Executive Committee of WLP, 26 February 1977, p. 3.
66 NLW, Welsh Liberal Party Papers, File A4, Executive Committee Report, 19 June 1976. This is a draft by John Roberts, chairman of the executive. He has

substituted 'a great change of personnel in the Executive' for the referenced quote.
67 NLW, Merfyn Jones Papers, File 35, Minutes of the WLP Executive Committee, 22 March 1975, for example.
68 Although Martin Thomas would become the WLP president between 1977 and 1979.
69 NLW, Merfyn Jones Papers, File 35, Draft Revised Constitution, 1975. Although this is the draft, the transfer of power to the executive was approved.
70 NLW, Merfyn Jones Papers, File 35, The Constitution of the Welsh Liberal Party. This is the original constitution and sets out the council's powers. Interestingly, it points out that the duty of the council was to 'stimulate militant Liberalism', a phrase that was missing from subsequent amendments, possibly because of the rise in militant nationalism, with groups such as the Free Wales Army, MAC and, to a lesser extent, the Welsh Language Society.
71 NLW, Welsh Liberal Party Papers, File A4, Executive Committee Report, 19 June 1976.
72 Deacon, *Welsh Liberals*, p. 195.
73 NLW, Welsh Liberal Party Papers, File 18, List of Constituency Secretaries, 3 June 1976. There were thirty-three active constituencies, with thirty-one secretaries in place.
74 Deacon, *Welsh Liberals*, pp. 204–5.
75 NLW, Welsh Liberal Party Papers, File A11, Constituency Questionnaire Report, 6 October 1979.
76 Adjusted to 2023 levels, £4,712.21 at 3.6% inflation p/a.
77 NLW, Merfyn Jones, File 32, 'A Report on the 1979 General Election', unknown author, 2.
78 NLW, Merfyn Jones, File 32, 'A Report on the 1979 General Election', unknown author, 4. Adjusted to 2023 levels, £9,933.34 at 3.6% inflation p/a.
79 NLW, Lord Hooson Papers, Box 42, Memo: Accounts of the Welsh Liberal Party of Wales from 31 July 1965 to 31 August 1966, 8 September 1966. The treasurer was Major J. Parry Brown of Newport. It must be stressed that this was the income of the LPW office and not of the constituencies or the affiliated organisations. Adjusted to 2023 levels, respectively, £1,914.74 (1966) and £3,224.34 (1965), both at 4.9% inflation p/a.
80 NLW, Lord Hooson Papers, Minutes of the North Wales Liberal Federation Executive Committee Meeting, 5 November 1966. Adjusted to 2023 levels, respectively, £747.22 in the account, and £544.85 at 4.9% inflation p/a given to the honorary secretary. The final figure transferred was £8 19s. 4d (£122 at 5% inflation p/a). As per NLW, Lord Hooson Papers, Box 42, Welsh Liberal Party Accounts September 1966 to 3 March 1967, from Major Parry Brown, Treasurer.
81 NLW, Lord Hooson Papers, Letter from Mr Williams to Hooson, 16 April 1969.
82 NLW, Lord Hooson Papers, Box 42, Letter from Hooson to Mary Murphy, 08 November 1967. Adjusted to 2023 levels, £182,994.45 at 5% inflation p/a.

It was later confirmed that most of this, around £10,000 (£152,495.37), was from the sale of the Tenby Liberal Club.
83 NLW, Lord Hooson Papers, Box 42, Minutes of the Steering Committee, 2 October 1966. This was the first meeting (£467.01 and £155.67, 4.9% inflation p/a).
84 NLW, Merfyn Jones Papers, File 34, Minutes of the Council of the WLP, 23 March 1969. The idea was put to the council in October 1968 and ratified at the January 1969 meeting.
85 NLW, Merfyn Jones Papers, File 34, WLP Membership and Productivity League Table, Amounts received at Aberystwyth up to 31 July 1969. Adjusted to 2023 levels, £6,368.84 and £20.86, 5% inflation p/a.
86 NLW, Welsh Liberal Party Papers, File A18, Memo regarding 'Financial Subscription in 1970'.
87 NLW, Merfyn Jones Papers, File 34, Summary of Income and Expenditure for 31 August 1967 to 29 May 1968, Rhys Gerran Lloyd, Hon. Treasurer. Adjusted to 2023 levels, £14,636.48 at 5% inflation p/a.
88 NLW, Lord Hooson Papers, Box 42, Memo: Accounts of the Welsh Liberal Party of Wales, 31 July 1965 to 31 August 1966, 8 September 1966, Major Parry Brown, Treasurer. For this column, the average inflation is 4.9% p/a.
89 NLW, Lord Hooson Papers, Box 42, Memo: Welsh Liberal Party Accounts, September 1966 to March 3 1967, 3 March 1967, Major Parry Brown, Treasurer. For this column, inflation is 5% p/a.
90 NLW, Merfyn Jones Papers, File 34, Summary of Income and Expenditure for August 31 1967 to May 29 1968, Rhys Gerran Lloyd, Hon. Treasurer. The large jump in financial spending was due to the payment of the salary of the secretary and expenses paid for printing, travelling and speakers. This would have been for events such as the weekend schools. For this column, inflation is 5% p/a.
91 NLW, Merfyn Jones Papers, File 34, Financial Report to the Welsh Liberal Council, 2 August 1969. This is an interim report but gives a good idea of the finances of the WLP at this point. For this column, inflation is 5% p/a.
92 NLW, Merfyn Jones Papers, File 39, Financial Report to the Annual Conference, May 1970. This report was created following the departure of Emlyn Thomas. As such, not all the accounts were up to date and were still being sifted through. For this column, inflation is 5% p/a.
93 NLW, Lord Ogmore Papers, File 4, Letter from Lloyd to Lord and Lady Ogmore. Undated, but 1967. Adjusted to 2023 levels, £1,524.95 at 5% inflation p/a.
94 NLW, Lord Ogmore Papers, File 4, Letter from Lloyd to Lord Ogmore, 1 January 1968. Adjusted to 2023 levels, £175,637.75 at 5% inflation p/a.
95 NLW, Welsh Liberal Party Papers, Financial Report by the Lord Lloyd of Kilgerran for the period 1973 to February 1974 general election. Undated but 1974.
96 NLW, Welsh Liberal Party Papers, File A18, letter to HM Inspector of Taxes from Lloyd, 27 March 1972. The first depositor put in several thousand

pounds. Lloyd and his wife deposited £3,000 (£45,748.61 at 5% inflation p/a, assuming 1967 as deposit date).
97 NLW, Welsh Liberal Party Papers, File A18, Letter from H. R. Hamilton, HM Inspector of Taxes, to Lloyd, 25 February 1972.
98 NLW, Welsh Liberal Party Papers, File A18, letter to HM Inspector of Taxes from Lloyd, 27 March 1972. Adjusted to 2023 levels, £73,676.90 at 4.9% inflation p/a.
99 According to NLW, WLP Papers, File A31, Financial Report 1 April 1974, by the Chair of the Executive, John Morgan. Adjusted to 2023 levels, £7,258.74 at 4.6% inflation p/a.
100 Adjusted to 2023 levels, £4,174.22 at 5% inflation p/a.
101 NLW, Welsh Liberal Party Papers, File 18, Letter from Rhys Gerran Lloyd to Lord Ogmore, 26 March 1971. Adjusted to 2023 levels, £64,107.92 at 4.9% inflation p/a.
102 NLW, Welsh Liberal Party Papers, File A18, Letter from Rhys Gerran Lloyd to Hooson, 2 March 1971. Adjusted to 2023 levels, amounts are, respectively, £84,670.84, £967,666.77 and £96,766.68 at 4.9% inflation p/a.
103 Michael Pinto-Duschinsky, *British Political Finance 1830–1980* (London, 1981), p. 184.
104 NLW, Merfyn Jones Papers, File 34, Income–Expenditure Account: 1 January to 31 December 1972, Rhys Gerran Lloyd, June 1973. Adjusted to 2023 levels, £5,203.03 at 4.8% inflation p/a.
105 NLW, Welsh Liberal Party Papers, Financial Report by the Lord Lloyd of Kilgerran for the period 1973 to February 1974 general election. Undated but 1974.
106 NLW, Welsh Liberal Party Papers, Memo from Hooson to the Executive, 3 April 1974. Adjusted to 2023 levels, £34,932.70 at 4.6% inflation p/a. Hooson notes that £2,100 (£19,054.20) was to be used for fourteen deposits, and twenty-one constituencies benefited from financial help of between £50 and £100 (£453.67 to £907.34).
107 NLW, Welsh Liberal Party Papers, Letter from Lloyd to Hooson, 14 February 1974.
108 NLW, Welsh Liberal Party Papers, Memo from Hooson to the Executive, 3 April 1974.
109 I have been unable to locate a full income/expenditure report for 1971.
110 NLW, Welsh Liberal Party Papers, File A31, Affiliation Fees for 1971. Date unknown, but likely to be early 1972. Adjusted to 2023 levels, £3,870.67 at 4.9% inflation p/a.
111 Merfyn Jones Papers, File 34, Income-Expenditure Account: 1 January to 31 December 1972, Rhys Gerran Lloyd, June 1973. The income/expenditure report separates the income from member subscriptions, which is why the amount for 1972 in table 4 looks erroneous. These subs were kept in other accounts and appear to have just sat there accumulating interest. Adjusted to 2023 levels, £2,924.41 at 4.9% inflation p/a.

112 NLW, Lord Hooson Papers, Income–Expenditure Account: 1 January to 31 December 1973, Addendum to Letter received from Lord Lloyd of Kilgerran to Hooson, 14 February 1974. There were at least ten affiliating, but more appear to have paid since then.

113 NLW, Lord Hooson Papers, Income–Expenditure Account: 1 January to 31 December 1973, Addendum to Letter received from Lord Lloyd of Kilgerran to Hooson, 14 February 1974. Adjusted to 2023 levels, £3,486.03 at 4.8% inflation p/a.

114 NLW, Merfyn Jones Papers, File 34, Income–Expenditure Account: 1 January to 31 December 1972, Rhys Gerran Lloyd, June 1973. Adjusted to 2023 levels, £24,727.90- £32,232.34 = -£7,504.43 at 4.9% inflation p/a.

115 NLW, Lord Hooson Papers, Income–Expenditure Account: 1 January to 31 December 1973, Addendum to Letter received from Lord Lloyd of Kilgerran to Hooson, 14 February 1974. Adjusted to 2023 levels, £21,311.60-£28,939.24 = -£7,627.64 at 4.8% inflation p/a.

116 Adjusted to 2023 levels, £3,486.03 at 4.8% inflation p/a.

117 NLW, Welsh Liberal Party Papers, File A31, Financial Report 1 April 1974, by the Chair of the Executive, John Morgan. Adjusted to 2023 levels, £18,146.86 at 4.6% inflation p/a.

118 NLW, Welsh Liberal Party Papers, File A31, Financial Report 1 April 1974, by the Chair of the Executive, John Morgan. Adjusted to 2023 levels, deficit of £9,073.43 and savings of £27,220.29 at 4.6% inflation p/a.

119 NLW, Welsh Liberal Party Papers, Financial Report by the Lord Lloyd of Kilgerran for the period 1973 to February 1974 general election. Undated but 1974.

120 NLW, Merfyn Jones Papers, File 35, Notes on the Activity of the Executive of the Welsh Liberal Party 1973/74 by John Morgan, 17 June 1974, although Morgan points out, 'I am reporting this rather than complaining as these members of the Executive have done this freely and without complaint'. Morgan was unhappy, personally, with this situation.

121 NLW, Welsh Liberal Party Papers, Financial Report by the Lord Lloyd of Kilgerran for the period 1973 to February 1974 general election. Undated but 1974. '[I]nformal and generous contributions towards WLP expenses have been received from Mr Hooson MP, Mr John Morgan . . . and my family.'

122 NLW, Merfyn Jones Papers, File 36, WLP Financial Report, 31 March 1978. This lists the 'private donations' as £160 (£899.66 at 3.8% inflation p/a) for 1976/7 and £1,436 (£7,510.54 at 3.7% inflation p/a) in 1977/8.

123 Pinto-Duschinsky, *British Political Finance*, p. 187.

124 Adjusted to 2023 levels, respectively, £17,002.36 at 4.9% inflation p/a and £18,730.90 at 4.8% inflation p/a.

125 Report of the Committee on Financial Aid to Political Parties, p. 120. Available at: *https://parlipapers.proquest.com/parlipapers/docview/t70.d75.1975-066534* (accessed 5 March 2025).

126 NLW, Merfyn Jones Papers, File 35, Minutes of the WLP Executive, 18 January 1975, p. 3.

127 NLW, Welsh Liberal Party Papers, Financial Report by the Lord Lloyd of Kilgerran for the period 1973 to February 1974 general election. Undated but 1974.
128 NLW, Welsh Liberal Party Papers, File A31, Letter from Norman Lewis to Constituency Secretaries, 10 January 1978. 'As you are aware the effect of inflation is particularly hard in running the office at Cardiff.'
129 Adjusted to 2023 levels, respectively, £1,231.41 at 3.8% inflation p/a and £2,081.61 at 3.7% inflation p/a.
130 NLW, Merfyn Jones Papers, File 36, WLP Financial Report 31 March 1978. This report also covered the previous financial year.
131 NLW, Merfyn Jones Papers, File 36, WLP Financial Report 31 March 1977. This report also covered the previous financial year. Adjusted to 2023 levels, £29.284.66-£31.922.28 = -£2,637.62, at 4% inflation p/a.
132 NLW, Merfyn Jones Papers, File 36, WLP Financial Report, 31 March 1978. This report also covered the previous financial year. Adjusted to 2023 levels, £12,848.26-£22,817.61 = -£9,969.35 at 3.8% inflation p/a.
133 Adjusted to 2023 levels, £20,774.29-£32,850.78 = -£12,076.49, at 3.7% inflation p/a.
134 NLW, Merfyn Jones Papers, File 37, WLP Financial Report, 31 March 1979. This report also covered the previous financial year. Adjusted to 2023 levels, £38,828.61-£33,249.35 = £5,579.26, at 3.6% inflation p/a.
135 NLW, Merfyn Jones Papers, File 36, WLP Financial Report 31 March 1977. Adjusted to 2023 levels, £27,349.98 at 4% inflation p/a.
136 NLW, Merfyn Jones Papers, File 36, WLP Financial Report 31 March 1978. Adjusted to 2023 levels, £14,040.31 at 3.8% inflation p/a.
137 NLW, Merfyn Jones Papers, File 37, WLP Financial Report, 31 March 1979. This report also covered the previous financial year. Adjusted to 2023 levels, respectively, £3,943.56 at 3.7% inflation p/a and £5,781.88 at 3.6% inflation p/a.
138 NLW, Merfyn Jones Papers, File 35, Minutes of the WLP Executive, 22 March 1975, p. 5.
139 Adjusted to 2023 levels, £523.02 at 3.7% inflation p/a.
140 NLW, Lord Hooson Papers, Box 46, Letter from Colin A. Smith to Norman Lewis, 8 March 1978. Adjusted to 2023 levels, £130.75 at 3.7% inflation p/a.
141 NLW, Merfyn Jones Papers, File 36, WLP Financial Report, 31 March 1978.
142 NLW, Welsh Liberal Party Papers, File A31, Affiliation Fees for 1976. Adjusted to 2023 levels, £6,132.95 at 4% inflation p/a.
143 NLW, Welsh Liberal Party Papers, File A31, Affiliation Fees for 1977. Adjusted to 2023 levels, £6,055.83 at 3.8% inflation p/a.
144 NLW, Merfyn Jones Papers, File 37, WLP Financial Report, 31 March 1979. This report also covered the previous financial year.
145 NLW, Welsh Liberal Party Papers, File A31, Affiliation Fees for 1978. Adjusted to 2023 levels, £8,603.65 at 3.7% inflation p/a.

146 NLW, Welsh Liberal Party Papers, File A4, Draft Executive Committee Report by John Roberts, 19 June 1976. Adjusted to 2023 levels, respectively, £257.96 and £9,673.42 at 4% inflation p/a.
147 NLW, Merfyn Jones Papers, File 35, Minutes of WLP Executive Committee, 22 February 1975, p. 4.
148 NLW, Merfyn Jones Papers, File 35, Minutes of the WLP Executive, 2 November 1974, item 4. Adjusted to 2023 levels, £15,878.50 at 4.6% inflation p/a.
149 NLW, Welsh Liberal Party Papers, File A31, Financial Report 1 April 1974, and NLW, Lord Hooson Papers, Letter from Whitaker to the Executive of the WLP, 19 June 1974. Whitaker was given a pay rise in March 1974 by Lord Lloyd, just prior to his resignation, so she only enjoyed a couple of months of the £16 per week (£145.17 at 4.6% inflation p/a) plus expenses. Prior to that, her weekly salary was £8 per week (£72.59 at 4.6% inflation p/a).
150 The financial reports for the period state 'Wages and Salaries'. As the financial reports are for the running of the Cardiff HQ, it is safe to assume that 'Wages and Salaries' relates to Gwyneth Ashford. Even when the role of organiser was created in 1978, this was paid out of a separate fund. The amounts in parentheses have been adjusted for inflation to 2023 amounts; the inflation percentages are: 1974 4.6%, 1976 4%, 1977 3.8%, 1978 3.7%, 1979 3.6%.
151 NLW, Merfyn Jones Papers, File 36, WLP Financial Report 31 March 1977. Ashford was granted a pay rise of £250 per annum, NLW, WLP Papers, File A4, Minutes of the Executive Committee, 17 July 1976, p. 4.
152 NLW, Merfyn Jones Papers, File 36, WLP Financial Report, 31 March 1978.
153 NLW, Merfyn Jones Papers, File 37, WLP Financial Report, 31 March 1979. This report also covered the previous financial year.
154 NLW, Merfyn Jones Papers, File 36, Minutes of the WLP Executive, 4 March 1978. Item 2a.
155 NLW, Lord Hooson Papers, Letter from Lloyd to Hooson referencing a political director, 3 August 1972.
156 NLW, Welsh Liberal Party Papers, File A4, Minutes of the WLP Executive, 25 September 1976, p. 4.
157 NLW, Welsh Liberal Party Papers, File A4, Minutes of the WLP Executive, 5 February 1977, p. 4. Adjusted to 2023 levels, £28,114.35 at 3.8% inflation p/a.
158 NLW, Merfyn Jones Papers, File 59, Minutes of the WLP Executive, 3 September 1977, p. 3. Howells had been President of the WLP for the previous three years and had to step down, as per the constitution.
159 Adjusted to 2023 levels, £7,845.27 at 3.7% inflation p/a.
160 NLW, Merfyn Jones Papers, File 36, Minutes of the WLP Executive, 4 March 1978, pp. 3–4.
161 NLW, Merfyn Jones Papers, File 36, Minutes of the WLP Executive, 29 July 1978, p. 3.
162 NLW, Welsh Liberal Party Papers, File A5, Minutes of the WLP Executive, 2 September 1978, p. 1, item 4.

163 NLW, Merfyn Jones Papers, File 36, Minutes of the WLP Executive, 7 October 1978, p. 1.
164 NLW, Welsh Liberal Party Papers, File A5, Minutes of the WLP Executive, 4 November 1978, p. 1.
165 NLW, Welsh Liberal Party Papers, File A5, Minutes of the WLP Executive, 2 December 1978, p. 1.
166 NLW, Welsh Liberal Party Papers, File A5, Minutes of the WLP Executive, 2 September 1978, p. 1, item 4.
167 NLW, Merfyn Jones Papers, File 36, Minutes of the WLP Executive, 4 March 1978, item 2a.
168 NLW, Welsh Liberal Party Papers, File A5, Minutes of the WLP Executive, 3 February 1979, item 5b.
169 Deacon, *Welsh Liberals*, p. 197.
170 NLW, Welsh Liberal Party Papers, File A5, Minutes of the WLP Executive, 3 February 1979, item 4g. Upon receiving her request, the executive asked for her to take two months' unpaid leave; they would increase her pay by ten per cent to cover this.
171 NLW, Welsh Liberal Party Papers, File A5, Minutes of the WLP Executive, 9 June 1979, item 9a.
172 NLW, Merfyn Jones Papers, File 37, Minutes of the WLP Executive, 1 December 1979, p. 3.
173 NLW, Merfyn Jones Papers, File 36, Minutes of the Executive of the WLP, 7 October 1978, p. 4. Adjusted to 2023 levels, £2,647.94 at 3.5% inflation p/a.
174 NLW, Welsh Liberal Party Papers, File A5, Minutes of the WLP Executive, 6 January 1979, p. 3.
175 NLW, Merfyn Jones Papers, File 37, Minutes of the Executive of the WLP, 3 November 1979, p. 2.
176 Deacon, *Welsh Liberals*, p. 197.

3

POLICYMAKING IN THE WELSH LIBERAL PARTY

'Without any doubt, I think the greatest contribution of the Liberals in Wales in the second part of the twentieth century was to lead in the realms of ideas and policy'
(Lord Hooson, 1994).[1]

INTRODUCTION

This chapter will argue that the WLP was formed to put forward policies that affected Wales, its people and its culture. As the previous chapters have made clear, Emlyn Hooson was determined to ensure that the new party would be seen as having the best interests of Wales at its core. As such, this chapter will contend that following the creation of the independent, but federated, party in 1966, the intention was to ensure that the WLP was a Welsh party that focused on Welsh issues.

The chapter will begin with a brief overview of the Welsh policies of the Labour Party, the Conservative Party and Plaid Cymru. This overview will show that both main parties, Labour and the Conservatives, were initially reacting to the perceived and real threat posed by Plaid. It will be argued that the two main parties were hampered by the centralised nature of their organisations, whereas Plaid's sole focus was on Welsh issues that affected the Welsh people, the language and their culture.

This will be followed by a short explanation of the historical meaning of being a Welsh Liberal and the issues that the party had traditionally tackled. Having set out the background to what 'Welshness' meant to traditional Welsh Liberalism, the chapter will argue that Hooson intended to reinvigorate the WLP and offer a direct challenge to Plaid. It will be shown and argued that this sense of Welshness was threaded through the policies and pronouncements of the WLP. It will also be shown that while Plaid and the WLP were finding similar answers to the same problems, their end goals were very different. Plaid wanted dominion status for Wales, whilst the WLP wanted Wales to be part of a federal United Kingdom.

Examination of these policies will be intertwined with general discussion of the history of the policy directorate and the challenges that the WLP faced when compared with the other parties. It will be shown that the directorate was underfunded and staffed by volunteers who, although dedicated, were unable to devote the required time to policymaking. This lack of a professional policy body led to long periods of stagnation in the party's policymaking. Despite this, it will be shown that one of the initial reasons for setting up the WLP, to reinvigorate Liberalism within Wales by focusing on the party's Welsh credentials, was a success.

THE CONSERVATIVES' WELSH POLICY

> Like birds of prey, they occasionally make a foray into Welsh politics. They peck here and there, but what they are waiting for is the chance to batten onto the body-politic of Wales after it has been bruised and battered by the ravages of Labour and Nationalists . . . They have no tradition in Wales.[2]

This was part of Hooson's rallying message to the activists of the WLP just before the 1968 Caerphilly by-election. The rhetoric touched upon the popular trope of there being no Conservative tradition in Wales. Historians, primarily Edwards and Blaxland, have begun to challenge this view in recent years and have shown that the Conservative Party deserves a prominent place within the historiography and the fabric of Welsh politics. Both have highlighted this, with Edwards stating that 'Contrary to popular assumptions, Tory policies and personnel after 1945 did not always ignore or neglect Wales'.[3] Perhaps this is not the ringing endorsement that one would give to the WLP or Plaid, but during the post-war years, the Conservatives concerned themselves with improving the party's standing within Wales. For example, in 1948 Churchill promised that '[s]hould we return to power, we propose, among other steps, to make a provision for a Cabinet Minister especially responsible for Wales'.[4] As Blaxland notes, the recommendation to promise such a minister had been included in the results of a fact-finding mission by Enoch Powell, which was part of an increased focus on providing devolution to Wales. The findings were published by the Conservatives in a bilingual pamphlet[5] entitled *The Charter for Wales*.

The *Charter for Wales* (along with the 1950 and 1951 general election manifestos) called for measures to increase industry in Wales, help hill farmers and reform higher education and, perhaps most startling of all for those who presumed a Tory bias against Wales, a commitment to fostering the Welsh language and its culture.[6] Following the return of a Conservative government in 1951, Churchill's promised cabinet minister was not given a separate department. Instead, the Welsh Affairs portfolio was coupled with that of the Home Office.[7] Despite this, Edwards states that the new ministry 'not only underlined the party's determination to highlight its commitment to Wales but was part of a determined effort not to treat Wales as another English region'.[8] There is certainly agreement between Edwards and Blaxland on the reasons for implementing the role, with the latter stating that the Conservatives were jubilant that they 'had managed to wrongfoot their Labour and Liberal opponents by coming up with their own coherent message', crediting Powell as being 'a significant architect of administrative devolution in Wales', and asserting that 'In subtle but very noticeable ways, the Conservatives were helping to make specifically Welsh issues more prominent'.[9] It is of note that this position and the 1955 elevation of Cardiff to capital city status happened under a Conservative government.

Despite these seemingly warm overtures to Wales from the top of the Westminster party, it is interesting to note that the Welsh Conservatives had serious issues in obtaining concessions from the Conservative HQ for Welsh-specific policies. The rhetoric was not being met by action. As Edwards notes, despite positive policy proposals in the 1959 document *Work for Wales: Gwaith i Gymru*[10] (later to be regarded by a former Conservative Secretary of State for Wales as 'an astonishingly comprehensive analysis of the Welsh economy and social conditions'[11]), the 1959 Conservative general election manifesto did not include any meaningful reference to Wales.[12] Whilst the 1964 manifesto gave just thirty words,[13] it was the 1966 manifesto that eventually afforded ten lines to Welsh policies.[14] This represents the start of a change in focus as, following the 1964 general election, the Conservatives were out of power. Additionally, the rise of the Scottish National Party (SNP) led to fears that a similar rise in support for Plaid could occur. Couple this fear with the loss of Conway to Labour at the 1966 general election, one of the most Conservative seats in Wales, and a realisation grew that the Welsh Conservatives needed to change the direction of their organisation and policies.

The party embarked on a set of fact-finding surveys within Wales and in 1969 implemented a Welsh Policy Group within the Conservative Party.[15] This resulted in a set of policies that were eventually included in the 1970 general election manifesto, drawn from previous policy statements that included a focus on the economy, housing, health and welfare.[16] So, just at the time that Hooson was placing Wales at the heart of the WLP, the Welsh Conservatives also sought to offer a vision of their own 'Welshness'.

As Edwards and Blaxland both concede, the traditional image of the Conservatives within Wales, which harked back to the nineteenth-century image of the heartless Tory landlord, was a barrier to their advancement, despite being able to point to the economic success of the middle class in England.[17] However, the fact that the Conservatives were focusing on Welsh issues, albeit through a committee process administered by Conservative HQ in London, should have alarmed the WLP. Many of the policies, as will be shown below, touched on the same issues that the WLP were pressing for. Yet, there was one area that was distinctive to the WLP, and that was the matter of extending devolution and the creation of a federalist state. As expressed in the *Wales into the 70s* policy document, the Conservatives favoured only a limited amount of devolution. The party advocated an extension of powers to the Welsh Office to cover primary and secondary education and a reorganisation of the local authorities,[18] which was substantially less than the devolution favoured by the WLP.

Despite Hooson's rhetoric regarding the lack of a Conservative tradition in Wales, there is no doubt that the Conservatives made a real effort to redefine themselves as being relevant to the country. This was a party that was not unaware or dismissive of Wales but consciously sought to take into consideration the different nature of Welsh politics.

LABOUR'S WELSH POLICY

Despite this activity within the Conservative Party, it must not be forgotten that it was the Labour Party, which had firmly established itself as the dominant political party within Wales, which had more to lose by taking its status for granted. However, as Edwards notes, in Wales, Labour found it hard to shake off its image as the 'party of south Wales', with many in the Welsh Office believing that most of Wales's problems were in the more populous and industrial south.[19] Labour did emphasise several Welsh policies within its programme, including the founding of the Council for Wales and Monmouthshire in 1949, a nominated advisory body to the Government on Welsh issues. Admittedly, this was something of a sop to those calling for a Secretary of State for Wales, which was opposed by Clement Attlee because it could encourage Welsh nationalism.[20]

Welsh Labour was deeply divided when it came to the administration of Wales and the promotion of its culture. Members such as S. O. Davies, Jim Griffiths, Cledwyn Hughes and, later, Gwynoro Jones were sympathetic to Welsh nationalist issues, particularly concerning devolution and the language. However, on the other side of the debate were men such as George Thomas, Aneurin Bevan, Leo Abse and others, who were against devolutionary measures, albeit for differing reasons.[21] For example, Bevan believed that the centralised planning of the economy relied on the 'seizure and the extension of power at the centre', that is, in Westminster.[22] Bevan, whilst making the argument that Wales was no different from the rest of the UK, stated 'I do not know the difference between a Welsh sheep, a Westmorland sheep and a Scottish sheep'.[23] At the extreme level, George Thomas just had a base hostility towards the Welsh language and its speakers, as well as those who called for devolution. He believed they were close to the nationalist side of Welsh politics.[24]

However, in 1959, primarily through the efforts of Jim Griffiths, the Labour Party eventually agreed to establish a Secretary of State for Wales. Following the 1964 general election and spurred on by the apparent rise of Welsh nationalism, and the need to tackle it, Harold Wilson's Labour government established the post of a Secretary of State for Wales. Labour then began a set of Welsh policy initiatives that included its own mid-Wales plan, the first Welsh Language Act in 1967, and the establishment of the Royal Commission on the Constitution. The Commission was charged with looking at different governance models for the United Kingdom[25] and reported its findings in 1973. The publication of the report was followed by a five-year debate and legislation which culminated in the failure of the

1979 devolution referendum. This debate exposed the fissure within the Welsh Labour Party as to how the demands of the growing Welsh consciousness could be met.

To a certain extent, it would have been more correct to say that the problem with both the Welsh Conservatives and Welsh Labour was that they were not 'Welsh'-only parties. They relied on the centre to make the policies, albeit with input from their Welsh members. Neither party had a federalist structure or operated as a stand-alone Welsh party, like the WLP or Plaid. Arguably, to have embraced a federalist party structure would have been difficult, for both parties believed in the power of the centre to provide good governance to the United Kingdom. To devolve too much influence away from the centre, particularly in policymaking, would have been an acknowledgement that they believed in political federalism. A devolved or federalist structure was something the Liberals did believe in, purposely making it a part of its organisational structure.

PLAID CYMRU

In terms of vote share, before the 1970 general election, Plaid Cymru was the fourth political party within Wales. Yet, up until 1966, its distinction was that it was the only one of the four major parties to operate solely within Wales. Despite this placing, as pointed out above and in previous chapters, the rise of Plaid during the 1950s and 1960s meant that the other three parties began to recognise the threat it posed.

Before the 1950s, Plaid could be described as little more than a pressure group that contested elections. However, the party's involvement in two major campaigns, the Parliament for Wales and Tryweryn, brought the party some political credibility and new supporters. This was followed by the 1959 general election, when Plaid was narrowly denied a third place in the Welsh poll. Yet, as Alan Butt Philip noted, the early 1960s saw a period of 'drift and questioning inside Plaid Cymru',[26] with breakaway nationalist groups such as the Free Wales Army (FWA) and the Welsh Language Society (WLS) airing their opposition to the tactics of Plaid.

Despite this fragmentation, Phil Williams, Plaid's economics spokesperson, has argued the new supporters that had been attracted to the party made it 'more rigorously political . . . [and] more palatable in its concern for issues of interest to the ordinary voter'. Williams believed that it was this change in direction that allowed Gwynfor Evans to take the Carmarthen seat from Labour at the 1966 by-election.[27] Laura McAllister concurs with this and argues that Gwynfor Evans, as party president, oversaw a financial, organisational and policy resurgence within Plaid. For McAllister, Evans was responsible for a 'gradual widening and deepening of policy formation'.[28]

The increased focus on policies, particularly in economics, saw Plaid gradually move away from the solely cultural aspects of Wales. The main example was that the rise of the WLS had allowed Plaid to separate itself from the language issue and begin a process of trying to depoliticise it. Although it would take some time before the public stopped associating the militant actions of the WLS with Plaid, the process had begun internally. This coincided with a larger formulation of policies that had begun in the early 1960s. With a shift towards 'populist socialism', it was in 1964 that Plaid began to focus on economic planning, with policies that included a Welsh Economic Development Authority, a Welsh Transport Board, a Welsh Power Board and a Welsh Water Board. Additionally, there were policies relating to the redevelopment of towns, and to radio and television services.[29] Most striking of all was Plaid's 1970 publication *An Economic Plan for Wales*, which McAllister argues silenced critics who lambasted Plaid for not having a credible handle on the subject.[30] Many of these policies would be mirrored within the other political parties, especially within the WLP, whose own economic plans pre-dated those of Plaid.

Both parties, almost in tandem, would keep the interests of Wales at the forefront of the Westminster agenda throughout the 1960s and 1970s.

'TRADITIONAL' WELSH LIBERAL POLICIES

The founding of the WLP had more to do with reconnecting Liberalism with its historical sense of 'Welshness' and Welsh nationalism, rather than being solely a reaction to the rise of Plaid. Whilst Hooson was indeed influenced by Lloyd George and his policy book *Britain's Industrial Future*, it must be acknowledged that it had nothing practical to say about Wales. What Hooson took from Lloyd George was that, despite the odds being against the BLP in the 1920s, sound policies could reinvigorate Liberalism and show that the BLP had answers to the grave problems facing Britain. Similarly, Hooson wanted the WLP to be spearheading the policy debate and offering answers to the political issues that Wales faced in the 1960s and 1970s.

For Hooson, positioning the WLP as a political party that emphasised its 'Welshness' was an opportunity to harness the historical tradition of the party. To put this tradition to use in a contemporary manner was key to facilitating the Welsh Liberal revival that he believed was on its way.[31] Lloyd George, at the start of his parliamentary career, championed Welsh radical issues such as home rule, temperance and the disestablishment of the Church in Wales. Lloyd George and his Welsh contemporaries, such as Tom Ellis, had pushed Wales to the top of the political agenda within the BLP and government. There was also another facet to Lloyd George's career that Hooson wanted to emulate, the so-called 'New Liberalism' which emphasised social issues and laid the foundations for the creation of the Welfare State.

Although there is a debate as to whether the New Liberalism became a part of Welsh Liberalism in the late nineteenth and early twentieth centuries,[32] there is no doubt that the Welsh

Liberals advocated policies that promoted social, economic, political and administrative reforms within Wales. Many of the policies were linked to the party's nonconformist roots and emphasised its Welsh nationalist credentials, resulting in legislation that disestablished the Church in Wales in 1920 (the law was passed in 1914, but was delayed by the First World War) and the Sunday Closing Act of 1881. The latter was the first Act of Parliament that treated Wales as a separate entity, as opposed to the usual legal jurisdiction of 'England and Wales'.[33] Additionally, the support and establishment of institutions, such as the National Library of Wales and the universities, can be viewed as attempts to strengthen the growing sense of nationhood within Wales.

Added to this were campaigns against Tory landlordism and land reform in general. As Morgan has argued, the economic aspect of Welsh Liberal policy in the late nineteenth century centred around the rural areas of Wales and tenant farmers. The Welsh Land League was set up in 1886, demanding fair rents, a land court to adjudicate on rents and security of tenure for tenants.[34] Land reform and procuring rights for tenant farmers was an enduring policy of the Welsh Liberals, and Lloyd George was an avid supporter throughout his life. This interest and support informed one of his famous coloured policy books, *The Land and the Nation*, otherwise known as the 'Green Book'. Although the 'Green Book' did not solely relate to Wales, it was an extension of the Liberal campaign against the feudal system of land control that existed within Britain. The book's proposals on 'cultivating tenure', whereby the state would appropriate cultivatable land and distribute it to tenants, were seen as semi-nationalisation of the land by some Liberals and were opposed by many.[35]

However, the BLP's most distinct policies relating to Wales were those of education and Home Rule/devolution, followed by the party's support for the Welsh language and culture. As these policies were discussed in chapter one, we will not re-examine them here. It is worth remembering that these policies would remain as part of the LPWs official programme, but due to disinterest from most of the Welsh Liberal MPs, the party did not campaign seriously on these issues between 1930 and 1949. Even on devolution, we see that members of the WLP, such as Clement Davies and Roderick Bowen, were indifferent to the campaign and did not lend their full support to the activities. However, what can be stated about the nineteenth-century and the early twentieth-century LPW was that its members had a long tradition of adopting Welsh issues and fighting for a cause. Deacon's comment, quoted in chapter one, about causes being the *'raison d'être'* of nineteenth-century Liberals[36] was just as true in the mid-twentieth century. From David Lloyd George's social reforms to Megan Lloyd George's leadership of the Campaign for a Welsh Parliament and Hooson's quest to revive Liberalism within Wales, each had a cause that they were to champion. Each was radical in their own way, looking back to the past to inform the present, and with a belief that those traditions could remain relevant. It would take members such as Glyn Tegai Hughes and Emlyn Hooson, both rising stars in the party during the 1950s, to lay claim to these policies once again. Hooson pointed to this 'new generation' as taking over the policy direction of the LPW by the end of the 1950s, but commented that the party was 'still encumbered with an antediluvian organisation safeguarded with grim determination by highly conservative Liberal inheritors'.[37]

Having tackled the reorganisation of the LPW and founding a new party, attention had to be paid to re-establishing policies that demonstrated the WLP's 'Welshness'.

'WELSHNESS' RECLAIMED

One of the most startling facets of Welsh Liberalism is how individual members were able to articulate the history and tenets of the party. To be a Welsh Liberal in the 1890s, the 1960s or 2024 included the ability to articulate what it meant or means to be a Welsh Liberal. This is not as easy as it may sound, as there is a common misconception that to be a Liberal voter is and was to occupy the middle ground, to be all things to all people. Although this line is usually peddled at general elections, it was rarely true for the BLP and even less so for the WLP.

As the first chapter argued, Hooson understood that the LPW had been neglected and this extended to the policies of the party. Due to the serious divisions between the NWLF and SWLF, coupled with the lack of attention from the leadership of the BLP, the LPW suffered from a serious policy deficit in the years after Lloyd George left the Liberal leadership. As such, Hooson's belief in a Liberal revival rested upon organisational change and a sound set of policies that focused on Wales. The formation of the WLP was a chance to reset and re-examine what the Liberals in Wales stood for. The WLP had to show that Liberalism was still a relevant force within Wales and not just a mouthpiece for the English party or a middle way between the Conservatives and Labour. The WLP had to regain its sense of Welshness if it were to survive and remain relevant in the coming decades.

The policies of the new party were to reflect the Welsh Liberal tradition, whilst building an alternative vision for Wales that was not espoused by any of the other political parties. 'Welshness', which can be defined as Welsh people, Welsh culture and the Welsh language, would be at the heart of the policy process. In effect, the WLP existed to promote Welsh issues and to consider UK-wide policies through the prism of Wales. This meant that issues such as the mid-Wales depopulation crisis could be considered alongside a UK-wide policy on trade unions.

Before the decision to dissolve the LPW, Hooson had already set in motion something of a policy revival within Welsh Liberalism. Hooson convened the Welsh Radical Group to investigate and provide a report on the issues of depopulation and industry within mid-Wales. The proposals were wide-ranging and provided an impetus to other policy initiatives that were taken before the 1970 general election, such as the WLP's economic policy.

THE HEARTLAND

The Heartland report began by identifying that rural depopulation in Wales had become a significant problem by the 1950s. It was primarily caused by the young moving away from the rural areas and seeking employment opportunities elsewhere, usually in England. Likewise, there was an understanding that inward migration to Wales, particularly in the rural areas, was the result of retirees looking to spend their remaining days in the idyllic countryside. The youth were not being replaced and those that stayed were unable to find suitable work in traditional industries, such as agriculture, following mechanisation and the amalgamation of small holdings into larger units. Added to this were unsuitable housing, a disabled transport infrastructure, the closing of schools and a lack of further education options.[38] As an illustration of how grave the depopulation issue was in mid-Wales, table 15 shows the estimated population change in five mid-Wales counties between 1903 and 1965.[39] Table 16 shows a starker picture of the decrease in population in these counties due to migration trends.

Table 15: Population change (+/-)in mid-Wales, 1903–65[40]

County	1903 Mid-year population (estimated)	1965 Mid-year population (estimated)	Difference (+/-)
Breconshire	54,023	54,460	+437
Cardiganshire	82,021	53,330	-28,691
Merionethshire	64,278	38,270	-26,008
Montgomeryshire	63,332	43,690	-19,642
Radnorshire	20,979	18,240	-2,739
Total population	284,633	207,990	-76,643 (-26.93%)

Table 16: Migratory changes to mid-Wales, 1951–61[41]

County	Total change (amount)	Total change (%)	Natural increase (amount)	Natural increase (%)	Net migration (amount)	Net migration (%)
Breconshire	-1,323	-2.34%	+1,340	+2.37%	-2,663	-4.71%
Cardiganshire	+370	+0.69%	-1,020	-1.91%	+1,390	+2.61%
Merionethshire	-3,155	-7.61%	-199	-0.48%	-2,956	-7.13%
Montgomeryshire	-1,825	-3.97%	+1,481	+3.22%	-3,306	-7.19%
Radnorshire	-1,522	-7.61%	+260	+1.30%	-1,782	-8.91%

As these two tables ably demonstrate, there was a serious problem with depopulation within mid-Wales. These were the problems that Hooson and Geraint Jenkins (along with other members of the Welsh Radical Group) wanted to provide answers to. As noted in an earlier chapter, Hooson was an admirer of both Lloyd George's policy documents, particularly *Britain's Industrial Future*, and Lyndon Johnson's Appalachian Regional Development Act (1965). The latter was an attempt to tackle depopulation in the Appalachian area, caused by high unemployment and severe poverty, which the Act looked to deal with through the Appalachian Regional Commission and extensive infrastructure projects.[42] This appealed to Hooson; he wanted to emulate the Act and provide an answer to the problems of Wales. However, it would be wrong to give the impression that Hooson had suddenly decided to tackle this topic because of the Appalachian Act. *The Heartland* was not Hooson's first foray into the issues facing rural Wales. He had begun to assess the topic in 1956, hoping to publish a plan in the aforementioned 'Welsh Yellow Book', but it was never published.[43]

In preparation for his 'Welsh Yellow Book', Hooson co-authored the LPW manifesto for the 1959 General Election. The plans for the manifesto were summarised in an article for the *Wales Magazine*, where it was somewhat confusingly titled 'Charter for Wales', the same title as the earlier document issued by the Conservatives. The LPW's plans were concerned with the whole of Wales, rather than just mid-Wales, and provided the following recommendations:

1. Four new towns, each consisting of 30,000 people, in Gwynedd, mid-Wales, south Cardiganshire and north-east Cardiganshire.
2. A Welsh Rural Development Corporation, with a budget of £120,000,000,[44] which would be spent on reorganising rural areas and building factories over twelve years. This would be a nationalised body for six years, at which point it 'would issue stock so that Welsh people could invest their savings in the development of their own country'.
3. Direct farm grants until 1965, after which they would be replaced by a Land Bank capital development scheme. This was so Welsh farmers could be equipped to survive without tariff protection in a European Free Trade Area.
4. A Welsh Water Board and nationalisation of local water undertakings.
5. A new north–south trunk road.[45]

Hooson's plan, as noted in the article, was an early attempt at tackling a crisis that affected many rural areas in Wales. Interestingly, the extension of nationalisation, in this case of 'local water undertakings', was something that Hooson generally had no time for. Hooson was always a pragmatist and would support nationalisation if it had a goal. So, the Water Board would come under the remit of the Welsh Rural Development Corporation and would be privatised within six years.[46]

Before the publication of Hooson's recommendations, there had been other plans to tackle the depopulation crisis in mid-Wales. The most famous of these was authored by the Mid-Wales Industrial Development Association (MWIDA) and had recommended the building of a new town near Caersws (between Llanidloes and Newtown), close to the Welsh/English border.[47]

This was followed, in 1964, by the Beacham Committee's report on depopulation, which recommended attracting further manufacturing industries to secure employment and the establishment of a new town or the development of some existing towns. The report highlighted twelve towns that could be attractive to industrialists and could be expanded; however, the Labour government chose to accept the single town option and put this forward to a group of consultants.[48]

THE INQUIRY AND RECOMMENDATIONS

The Welsh Radical Group (WRG) was set up, under the chairmanship of Hooson, in four regional sub-committees, with the London section issuing the initial report. It was hoped that *The Heartland* would become part of the Liberal development plans for the whole of the UK. However, this is the only report that was published. The WRG aimed to 'investigate the problems of Mid-Wales',[49] requesting expert advice from people in academia, local government and further afield. One of the experts asked to contribute was Professor Edward Nevin,[50] to whom Hooson would turn on occasion to produce economic papers for the WLP, although it needs to be pointed out that he did not sit on the panel for this report.[51] Hooson had informed him of his initial thoughts regarding a development authority, which Nevin supported. However, Nevin was sceptical as to whether another report on the decline in rural Wales was needed, stating that 'There is, surely, general agreement about this. Nor is there any real dispute about the broad nature of the way a solution should be attempted'.

Nevin went further, producing a scathing opinion of the MWDIA, and he believed that Hooson had aligned his

> proposals pretty firmly to Mid-Wales Industrial Development Association, both in terms of membership of your study group

and in terms of the 'nucleus' (your word) of the proposed Development Corporation. I believe this to be a fundamental mistake. In my view the M.W.I.D.A. has failed . . . in the more fundamental sense of having compromised itself beyond redemption. It is essentially a pressure group body which . . . has relied on the Highest Common Denominator in order to remain intact . . . the present Chairman's emphasis on Mid-Wales' potential as a 'Playground' of the Midlands is symptomatic-and a new start in Mid-Wales is essential.[52]

The reason this has been highlighted is because Hooson took notice of this suggestion. Hooson had written to Nevin outlining elements from the *Charter* as a starting point for the group (particularly in terms of the Rural Development Corporation), with a note about a new town in Caersws.[53] The MWIDA had specifically included the proposal to site a new town close to Caersws, whilst also seeking to attract industry into the area. This had caused consternation in many quarters. Many local people had said that they did not want people from Birmingham moving to the area. Plaid voiced its opposition because it would further erode the language and culture of Wales.[54]

The *Times* initially called the MWIDA plan 'ambitious', where 'local people and skilled men from the Midlands would work side by side', and suggested a prosperous mid-Wales could 'fill a regretted vacuum and so unite the north and south of the country'.[55] However, just shy of a year later the MWIDA's attempts to attract industry to the area, no doubt by highlighting the beautiful landscape, was treated with derision by the newspaper, which called Wales a 'holiday country' and said that businessmen had enough trouble persuading their workers to work. In addition, 'any misgivings will be increased rather than stilled by the presence . . . of an assortment of girl factory workers'.[56]

However, by the time that *The Heartland* was published, the idea of a new town being the 'Playground of the Midlands' had been thoroughly considered and rejected. The solution found by the WRG was to distance its recommendations from advocating a 'Playground of the Midlands' and to focus on improving Aberystwyth. The final report[57] recommended a three-phased approach.

In phase one, the panel recommended:

1. A National College of Agriculture be established at Aberystwyth.
2. The establishment of a Rural Development Corporation.
3. The encouragement of industry.
4. A first-class north–south Wales trunk road to be built.
5. An east–west motorway, from Shrewsbury to Aberystwyth.
6. Maintaining the current railway line from Shrewsbury to Aberystwyth.

Phase two recommendations were:

1. A New Town Corporation to be set up.
2. Expanding Aberystwyth into 'virtually a complete regional centre'.
3. The expansion of towns as satellites to Aberystwyth.
4. Building an airport near Aberystwyth and another close to Shrewsbury.
5. A coastal toll road to be built down the west coast of Wales.
6. Building dams to regulate the supply of water and to stop the frequent flooding in mid-Wales.

Phase three recommendations were still being thought out at the time, with a plan to publish them in 1966. However, the WRG felt that the Rural Development Corporation (RDC) would become an investment board, which would transfer its assets into stock to attract public investment. In addition, the report made it clear that local government reform would be needed in the future, which would be facilitated by the establishment of a parliament for Wales.[58]

The policy proposals were far-reaching and, as one would expect, Welsh in their outlook. The report pointed out that 'Agriculture is the basic industry of mid-Wales' and identified that its success depended on a national policy. It further notes that agriculture is threatened by a lack of marketing knowledge and advocates a grading system for Welsh meat, as well as establishing a better processing chain. This would involve an area that had an abattoir also having factories to process the 'valuable by-products'.[59] By starting the report off with a section on agriculture, the WRG can be seen to be playing to its strengths. The LPW was dependent on its rural votes, especially as both of its MPs (Hooson and Roderic Bowen) represented rural constituencies. The Liberals had a long tradition of supporting farmers and tenant farms, something that would carry on throughout Hooson's tenure. It was important to have an agricultural policy that looked to modernise the sector in mid-Wales.

The report does tread some other safe ground, particularly in its recommendations for attracting new industries into the region. The report suggested continuing to attract 'light engineering industries', but stopped there. Yet, there is a recommendation to 'foster' the woollen and leather manufacturing industry, 'on which much of the nineteenth century economy of the area was based'.[60] This seems a tad out of place in a section that sought to suggest new ways of revitalising the Welsh economy, and should probably have been under the agricultural proposals. The true recommendations lay in the loans and grants enticements that were designed to keep industry in the area for some time, which included grants to construction workers and towards building costs and plant and machinery expenditure.[61]

Aberystwyth was chosen because it had 'amenities far greater than any other town in the region'. The town was felt to be far enough away from the border to deter people from the Midlands or the creation of 'a dormitory of commuters from the Black Country'. The report argued that 'it is more likely that any town farther east would be subject to such pressures'.[62] Transport was another major proposal, and the report linked the building of roads and airports with the expansion of Aberystwyth and its satellite towns. The major infrastructure building scheme was one of the more radical proposals and it was something that would be looked at in future reports by the government and Plaid Cymru.

CRITICISM

This was quite an extensive report and the proposals were certainly ambitious, yet the fact that the report was initially issued due to 'intense public interest', and was still being finalised,[63] has left it open to criticism. Nevin called the plan 'a valuable piece of work' but then criticised the group for

> publishing ambitious proposals without indicating the manner in which they are to be implemented . . . your group has laid itself wide open to criticism of being mere pipe-dreamers who pull targets out of thin air and expect achievements to arrive from a similar direction.[64]

Whilst it is true that *The Heartland* did not provide clear mechanisms on how it expected the plan to be implemented and was not costed, it should be seen as a set of proposals and was presented in that way. However, the lack of costings was indicative of a plan that had been hurriedly released. A possible reason why the plan was rushed out was that the MWIDA's plans had progressed, and the group were in discussions with the government about the expansion of five existing towns in Wales.[65]

Another criticism that Nevin levelled towards the plan was that the figures, that is, the statistics, were laid out with no explanation as to how they were reached.[66] This criticism is very relevant, particularly in the case of the Aberystwyth proposals. The report states that 'It is envisaged that the population (of Aberystwyth) should be trebled within the next 20 years and achieve a population of about 60,000 by the end of the century'.[67] It is not clear how the authors arrived at that figure, but they do state that most of the new population would come from Wales, as Aberystwyth became more accessible from the north and the south. It mentions that Cardiff would have an overspill population, by 1980, of approximately 200,000.[68] There were a lot of assumptions made, and the potential population growth was a damaging one. In the ten years between the 1961 and 1971 census, the population of Aberystwyth increased by only 241 people, rising from 10,427 to 10,688.[69] By 2001, the population of Aberystwyth town had only risen to 11,607 people, with the surrounding areas adding another 5,321 persons.[70] For an 'accessible' town, with the amenities of a university, the Forestry Commission and the National Library of Wales already in place, the figures quoted seemingly had no evidential basis. If these amenities had not already attracted a sufficient baseline population from the rest of Wales, then it was not feasible to believe that tens of thousands of people would arrive within twenty years.

There were other criticisms, such as the claim that the proposed National College of Agriculture should be 'established forthwith at Aberystwyth . . . No such educational establishment exists in Wales'.[71] Except that there already was an agricultural college in existence, the Farmers' Education Centre in Felin Fach, which opened in 1952. Internally, the South Wales Liberal Federation and the Gibbses (Jennie and John) were very vocal opponents. In a foretaste of the opposition that Hooson would face when he and others pushed for the formation of the WLP, Geraint Jenkins complained that:

> I have just emerged from a battle royal [*sic*] with members of the South Wales Liberal Federation. The Gibbs' have heard of our proposed plans and I do not think that they entirely approve of our getting on with the work without having John Gibbs in on everything . . . Jennie argues that they produced a Liberal Manifesto for Wales a few years ago and she's not at all convinced that we need something else.[72]

Despite the criticisms, the plan was met with enthusiasm in some areas. For example, the Aberystwyth town clerk, W. Philip Davies, wrote to Hooson stating that the recommendations had been discussed and the following noted:

> The basic principles thereof be approved subject to the reservation that certain aspects thereof might, from time to time, require further detailed consideration as appeared to be necessary and advisable. Having regard to the provisions of the Highland Development (Scotland) Bill, it was hoped a Bill appropriate to Mid-Wales be prepared at an early date.[73]

The *Birmingham Daily Post* credited the clerk as saying that 'the problems of mid-Wales would have to be solved without much further delay', whilst Aberystwyth's Mayor, Alderman Cecil Owen, commended many of the recommendations. The Mayor of Welshpool was not quite so pleased with the plan for village clusters, stating that:

> The drift to the towns continues and it is the towns like Welshpool that I would like to see developed. Welshpool could become a buffer against depopulation. At the same time, I do not want to see the surrounding countryside plundered by a vast overspill population.[74]

INFLUENCE

Despite the Aberystwyth town clerk's urging, no such Bill was prepared, but many of the recommendations found their way into the WLP's 1970 manifesto. Agriculture was a large part of the manifesto, but so were other aspects of *The Heartland*, in particular, the Rural Development Corporation and increasing the communication network in Wales by building roads and airports, whilst maintaining the existing railway network.[75] Hooson believed that the legacy of the plan, especially the proposal for a mid-Wales Rural Development Corporation, 'were seized upon by, for example, the Labour Government but interpreted in a vastly different way'.[76]

The belief that the Labour government adopted aspects of *The Heartland* has never been seriously explored. It is interesting to note that Bryan Keith-Lucas, who was a member of the Liberal Party and had just been appointed to the Local Government Commission, sent the following note to Hooson: 'By the way, I have made sure that Jim Griffiths read our Plan for Wales before formulation of the Government's proposals.'[77] Of course, this does not in itself provide concrete evidence that Griffiths paid any heed to the recommendations. However, the proposals that Keith-Lucas referred to were included in the White Paper on the Development of Agriculture, issued in August 1965, which made provision for a rural development board. Following publication, the Agriculture Minister, Fred Peart, described the intended role of the development board:

> Their responsibility will be to promote in their areas the co-ordinated development of agriculture and forestry, together with such complementary uses as tourism . . . A board must coordinate its development programme with the Forestry Commission. It must also be able to make sure that private afforestation schemes do not cut across its programme.[78]

This aligns, somewhat, with the proposals in *The Heartland* that stated:

> We see no reason why the Rural Development Corporation should not itself . . . equip a certain number of larger farms for letting on marginal and hill land. It seems to us wrong that whereas much hill and marginal land is taken over by the Forestry Commission no comparable Commission exists . . . for agriculture purposes. Controlled afforestation must be married more closely to agriculture.[79]

However, whereas Hooson's proposals spoke about large farms 'letting' out marginal and hill land, the Labour government felt their boards[80] should be able 'to control the sale of agricultural land in their areas so as to ensure that such land is not sold for purposes contrary to the rural development programmes'.[81] Following the enactment of the Agriculture Act (1967), the Rural Development Board (RDB) was indeed able to limit the sale of land, with any sale requiring the 'Board's written consent'.[82] Later, in 1969, both the Farmers' Union of Wales (FUW) and Hooson presented a petition signed by ninety per cent of the farmers in his constituency against the proposed RDB being set up in Montgomery. The petition argued that the RDB would 'inhibit the freedom to purchase and/or sell land within the area of the Board'.[83] Butt Philip points out that the FUW were able to claim credit for the delaying of the board, which was dissolved in 1970 when Labour lost power.[84]

As with Aberystwyth, the Labour government initially wanted to put a new town in Caersws,[85] which would expand the population to 70,000. These proposals were later scrapped in the face of fierce local opposition,[86] which resulted in the 'growth town' proposal (the aforementioned twelve towns now being whittled down to seven – Aberystwyth, Bala, Brecon, Llandrindod Wells, Newtown, Rhayader and Welshpool[87]) being adopted. Although Aberystwyth was to be part of a seven-town scheme, there were some similarities between the criteria chosen by the government and those used by the WRG. For example, both mentioned[88]

1. The climate – the need to have an 'attractive climate' (in the Labour government's criteria), and the WRG observation that 'Aberystwyth has an extremely good climate'.
2. Communications – Labour: 'It should not be too remote from the large centres of population with which the communications system should be adequate'; WRG: 'Once the programme outlined in phase 1 is complete, there would be no difficulty of access to Aberystwyth.'
3. Employment – Labour: 'It should . . . act as an employment centre for a substantial area of the surrounding countryside'; WRG: 'It is . . . accessible to North and South Wales to establish itself as a regional centre in its own right . . . We envisage that the town would develop along the coast and inland. Industrial belts could be developed up the valleys.'

There were other criteria, such as the local authorities being 'willing to assist incoming labour', but the point to make is that the interconnecting nature of the plans by the Labour government, the MWIDA and *The Heartland* lend credence to Nevin's observation about there being general agreement on the causes and remedy for the depopulation issue. It also provides circumstantial evidence that *The Heartland* had some influence over government policy.[89]

PLAID CYMRU'S *ECONOMIC PLAN*

Although it appeared a full five years after the publication of *The Heartland* and a year after *Life to a Nation*, Plaid's *Economic*

Plan has been credited with 'maturing'[90] Plaid Cymru. Butt Philip notes that the idea of an economic policy had occurred to the leaders of Plaid, whilst engaged in the 1967 Rhondda by-election, which had been fought on the 'issue of pit closures and local unemployment'.[91] His point that Plaid realised they could 'exploit the grievances of the Welsh valleys with political profit'[92] should probably be taken as hyperbole, especially considering Butt Philip's association with Hooson and the WLP.[93] Edwards points to the formation of Plaid's Research Group as the impetus for the development of the plan.[94]

Interestingly, the *Economic Plan* was influenced by the writings of economists such as Professor Nevin,[95] who would also aid Hooson. Plaid's plan was published in 1970 and, at 286 pages, it was a significant policy document. Despite the difference in length, there were some similarities with *The Heartland*. The main one is that both plans were formulated with the depopulation crisis as the starting point. However, the two plans take quite divergent routes in tackling the economic needs of Wales, for example where the WRG envisioned that after thirty years there would be a 'great development in the holiday industry', and that 'the basic industry of agriculture, and its sister industry of forestry would have been greatly developed',[96] neither was considered by Plaid as viable industries to substantially increase employment within Wales.[97] Instead, the *Economic Plan* argued that manufacturing (such as in the engineering and electrical field) was the growth industry to transform the Welsh economy, as Plaid's analysis had shown that these were likely to be 'attractive and successful'.[98]

The proposals that bore some resemblance to those in *The Heartland* were the town plans. The WRG identified in the first phase eight towns as 'potential growth points': Welshpool, Newtown, Corwen, Blaenau Ffestiniog, Lampeter, Rhaeadr, Brecon and Cardigan.[99] The 'growth points' were towns that could feasibly achieve a measure of growth and would attract industry. There would also be satellite towns around these larger towns, which would be developed and feed workers into these 'growth points'. As has already been noted above, the planned growth of Aberystwyth was also designed to attract industry and workers into the area. The *Economic Plan* had similar intentions of building upon existing towns, as they had the infrastructure and amenities already available.[100] However, the main difference between the two proposals was that *The Heartland* could envisage the satellite towns/villages feeding workers into the larger towns, which would also be 'cultural and shopping centres'. However, the smaller towns and villages would have their infrastructures, such as village schools and a community centre.[101] The *Economic Plan* argued that the towns chosen should be 'freestanding communities', defined as their not being a 'parasite' on 'a nearby, larger community . . . i.e. it does not depend on any other community for secondary schooling or hospital services'.[102]

Despite some similarities, the *Economic Plan* was larger in scope than *The Heartland*, as it was considering the whole of Wales rather than just mid-Wales. In addition, the *Economic Plan* laid out its reasons for the choices it made and backed those up with statistics, displaying a better grasp of the economics. This is not to say that these statistics were entirely correct, as both Butt Philip[103] and Edwards[104] have identified the flaws, yet it was a leap forward when compared with the proposals in *The Heartland*. Despite this, both plans had one crucial thing in common: both were plans that placed the onus on Wales and a Welsh parliament to sort out the problems. The difference was whether that would be as an independent state or within a federal UK.

THE POLICY DIRECTORATE 1966–79

The constitution and policymaking

Following the formation of the WLP, under the original constitution, the general council was the ultimate authority within the party, delegating some of its powers to the executive and keeping other powers in reserve. The original constitution only allowed for the general council to 'pass in its own name resolutions on current political issues as they arise',[105] whereas the executive was only allowed to appoint a sub-committee 'for . . . the policy formation of the Party'.[106] These policy proposals would then be fed to the Annual Conference, along with those of affiliated organisations and Local Associations. Figure 2 shows the process of enacting policies up until 1975.

Figure 2: 1967–75 Policy-enacting process of the WLP

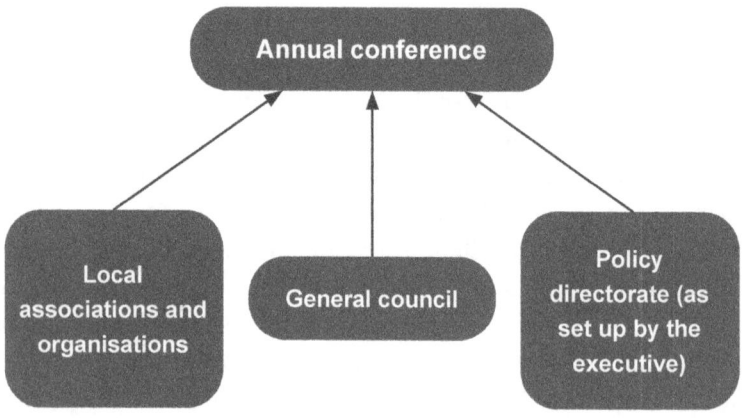

By 1975 the status of the general council had declined, later described as 'an informal talking shop',[107] and a revised constitution transferred most of the organisational and policy powers to the executive. This allowed the executive to 'be responsible for the formulation and drafting of Party policy'.[108] The reasoning was that the executive met monthly and could respond to issues in a timelier manner. Effectively, this meant that the executive was able to pass its own policy measures, whilst bypassing the annual conference, but was also able to submit policies to that body. In practice, the executive reconstituted the policy directorate to formulate policies for its consideration, with these being submitted to the annual conference. In addition, affiliated local associations could submit public policy resolutions to the annual conference too. The reasons for this change will be explored later. As figure 3 shows, this was how the revised policy-enacting process was to work.

Figure 3: 1975–9 Policy-enacting process of the WLP

Budgeting for the policy directorate

There was not a great deal of money available for the formation of WLP policies. As detailed in the previous chapter, the finances of the WLP's central organisation were for the administration of the party and very little was left for policymaking. Added to this was that the organisation was staffed by volunteers, and those that were directly employed were often guaranteed their first-year salary but were then expected to fund themselves through their activities. This lack of financial stability was also a factor when it came to providing a budget for its committees – they were generally not provided with one. This was most certainly the case with the policy directorate, which was completely volunteer-based and often staffed by members of the executive committee.

The 1975 reinvigoration of the policy directorate, after years of lying dormant, would have been an ideal opportunity to address the funding issue. The newly convened members of the directorate felt that:

> Consideration ought to be given at some time as to whether it is possible for the PD to raise some money itself. It may well be that some companies may be prepared to donate money for policy development, which they are unwilling to do for general political purposes.[109]

As happened with the general secretary and constituency organisers, the directorate was to seek external funding to finance its activities. In effect, this meant approaching industrialists and other persons with the idea that if they liked the policy, they could fund it. It soon became clear that this was not a practical solution, and some members of the executive argued, in vain, for the directorate to be given a budget.[110] The party even considered appointing a Director of Policy, who would have had oversight of the process.[111] The idea was initially accepted and it was decided that someone should be 'appointed soon . . . Finance would be provided by a decision of the Executive Committee'.[112] As usual, due to a lack of funds the idea of a paid position had to be rejected, but the originator of the proposal, Terry Thomas, was asked to undertake the role voluntarily 'should his health permit'.[113]

The only accounted for expenditure to the policy directorate from central WLP funds was in 1967, when the group was given £72 1s. 11d.[114] Other than this, there was no direct reference to any funding of the policy directorate or policymaking in the accounts between 1966 and 1979. The only accounted money which could feasibly have been used for policy was that used for printing. Over the years, some policy documents were published, for example, in 1977 the party published 'Social Security Benefits: A Discussion Document'. The same financial year (1977/8) saw quite a heavy expenditure on printing costs, £633, and in the period up to 31 March 1979, the printing costs were £368,[115] yet had been only £76 in the 1976/7 period.[116] These extra costs would have included amounts associated with the devolution campaign, the 1979 general election and the annual conference. The accounts are not clear on where the money was spent.

The Weekend Schools (also known as the Pantyfedwen Schools) were a strange financial beast, as no income or expenditure was recorded centrally by the WLP. Although these had been started in the early 1950s by Hooson, Glyn Tegai Hughes, Maldwyn Thomas and his sister, Mair,[117] any financial benefit or deficit to the LPW or the WLP was not recorded. It is only in 1978 that these begin to be shown in the accounts, bringing an income of £200[118] and, in 1979, £210.[119] These amounts are listed as income for the party and no expenditure was listed for hosting these schools. It is unlikely that these amounts would have been directly used to fund the policy directorate, especially when we consider that the WLP was facing a very precarious financial position during this period.

This analysis, particularly in the post-1970 period, is the accepted truth and was certainly the situation when the party provided its accounts to the 1976 publication of the *Report of the Committee on Financial Aid*, led by Lord Houghton. The report gave a stark indication of the financial disparity between the political parties operating in Wales and the UK. Table 17 shows the income and policy budgets for the four main parties operating in Wales, whilst table 18 shows the income and policy budget for the constituent parts of the federated Liberal Party. Both demonstrate how disadvantaged the WLP was in terms of money and policy budgets, even within its own party.

Table 17: Total income and policy expenditure by the four main parties in Wales, 1970–6[120]

Political party	Income	Policy expenditure
Conservative Party[121]	£7,401,000	£1,104,000
Labour Party[122]	£5,367,000	£329,000
Plaid Cymru[123]	£262,000	£8,000
Welsh Liberal Party[124]	£8,900	£0

Table 18: Total income and policy expenditure for the Federated Liberal Party, 1970–6[125]

Party	Income	Policy expenditure
British Liberal Party[126]	£668,000	£71,000
Scottish Liberal Party[127]	£66,000	£5,000
Welsh Liberal Party	£8,900	£0

The figures show that between 1970 and 1976, Plaid had an income that was almost thirty times that of the WLP. This gap was further reflected in the amount that Plaid spent on policy formation: although not a great deal over six years, it reflected how Plaid had attracted finance, due to its greater electoral appeal, and was willing to put more of that money into its policymaking. As established in the previous chapter, this was not an option for the WLP, as it relied too heavily on internal financing.

When it was a regional section of the BLP, the WLP could expect to have its policy expenditure included in that organisation's budget, although inevitably that would have meant less of a focus on Welsh policies. However, by extricating itself from the BLP, the WLP was unable to properly afford a policymaking platform. As table 18 shows, the total policy expenditure of the BLP was nine times the total income of the

WLP. However, as with the discussion on finances in chapter two, it is advisable to treat these figures with a little scepticism. There can be little doubt that personal funds from members of the executive and the policy directorate, for example, were used for policy purposes. These payments, as detailed in the previous chapter, were always discretionary and were never detailed.

Yet, this was not the full picture. Before 1970, despite there being no set budget, the WLP published some major policies, including *The Heartland* and *Life to a Nation*, and it would be incorrect to say that there were no funding streams open to the party. For example, Hooson approached the future president of the WLP,[128] the Hon. Edward Davies, for funding whilst engaged in the *Heartland* project.[129] However, following the disastrous results of the 1970 general election, obtaining outside funding for the party and policymaking became more difficult. In 1971, Lloyd wrote to Lord Ogmore asking if he 'might be able to arouse adequate interest amongst . . . South Wales industrialists to make a contribution to our fund'.[130] Unfortunately, no one wanted to invest in the party because the 'industrialists felt that the Welsh Liberal industrial policy was non-existent or non-credible',[131] which is understandable, as the seats contested in 1970 by the WLP and the wider BLP had not shown that the Liberals were serious about power. This situation would continue, and any outside funding would usually be given with the express purpose of funding elections.

What is clear is that it is difficult to rely on the published figures for the WLP when trying to explain how the party funded the policy directorate. Depending on the period, it appears to have been through a mixture of wealthy benefactors, internal donations or members of the directorate footing the costs of research themselves. This was in keeping with the loose financial arrangements of the WLP itself. Most of its income came from affiliation fees, but these would then be supported by the informal payments made by the officers of the party and wealthy donors.

SPOKESPERSONS

The executive of the WLP established its first policy directorate in January 1967. It consisted of nine members, with their portfolios running the gamut of the Welsh economy and culture.[132] Hooson, who wanted to provide the WLP with a 'political direction',[133] became the chairman of the directorate. The spokespersons were chosen for their experience or standing within the party. For example, the future first chair of the Welsh Council of the National Farmers' Union, Meuric Rees, was given Agriculture and Rural Economy.[134] Wilfred McBriar, the adviser on trade unions, was the branch chair of the Caernarfon and vice chair of the Wrexham TGWU.[135] Other members of the directorate held other titles within the party, such as Martin Thomas, who became vice president in 1967. Some members stood for parliament, sat on the executive or were local councillors.[136] Each incarnation of the policy directorate would ensure that roles were matched to experience. For example, David Hando, a teacher in Newport, would later take on the Education role and Dr Jennifer Lloyd, a renowned psychiatrist, took on the Health portfolio.

The years 1965 to 1970 were a period of intense policymaking within the party, and included specialist groups being set up or brought in. These groups worked specifically on items such as the *Heartland* report into the depopulation issue in mid-Wales and *Life to a Nation*, the WLP's economic proposals that became the bulk of the 1970 manifesto. However, these groups proved to be short-lived, and following the disappointing results of the 1970 general election, where Plaid gained more votes than the WLP for the first time, the policy process of the WLP became more disorganised and the directorate was convened less and less.

This meant that more of an emphasis was to be placed on the spokespersons of the party, yet this was a very grey area from the start. The issuing of policy statements or, more to the point, properly defining the role of the spokespersons was something that the WLP never seemed to master. Right from the beginning, there were indications that the spokespersons for the party had little oversight from either the directorate or the executive committee, especially concerning the issuing of press statements. In 1967, Leslie Jones, a member of the annual conference committee, complained that:

> The Western Mail rang me a few days ago for a statement . . . I gave them a statement and they mentioned that they were also going to contact Elfyn [Morris]. His statement was eventually quoted . . . A typical example of 'crossing the wires' once again. The officers of this party have not sufficient definitely defined duties so that a person who thinks that they should be doing something, in fact, finds someone else doing it.[137]

The role of the spokespersons was further hampered in the post-1970 period by the apparent lack of interest in convening the policy directorate. There is no record of any meetings, planned or otherwise, of this body in the years between 1970 and 1974.[138] This lack of attention to convening the policy directorate was due to the circumstances that the BLP found itself in and Hooson's increasing role in the parliamentary party. The absence of Liberal MPs following the 1970 general election meant that Hooson's parliamentary workload had increased, and by 1973 the Liberal leader, Jeremy Thorpe, had given him several substantial spokesperson portfolios. These included the Law, Agriculture and Wales, which, along with his busy law practice, offers a clue as to why the policy process began to break down. The person who had spearheaded the policy directorate in the WLP's first three years was no longer able to devote the time to policy formation.

However, there is obvious evidence that policies were being issued between 1970 and 1974 (see below), although this is not detailed, often consisting of a paragraph issued to the press or even a page or two that would be passed to the executive committee and debated at the annual conference. Deacon points out that Martin Thomas had become more involved with encouraging policy formation,[139] yet it was often left to the individual spokespersons to formulate ad hoc policies and issue press statements.

By 1973, the policy directorate was non-existent. There was an acceptance within the executive and council that the WLP spokespersons were not being proactive enough and the WLP's messaging was not being relayed to the press. Hooson provided a hint of how redundant the spokespersons and policy process had become when he tried to set out the role of the former and how advanced Plaid were in comparison:

> Research was vital for any spokesman – he must be very knowledgeable about his subject. Any reliable source of information must be tapped and that information stored. *Spokesmen should not be afraid of making statements on reports issued by the government, or on burning issues . . . Some spokesmen were to be congratulated on this . . . Yet, Plaid Cymru had a better overall record when making statements . . . and this counted very much in their favour.*[140]

It was this over-reliance on a team of volunteers, many of whom had other roles within the executive, which exposed the WLP's lack of press management skills, something that had hampered the party since the beginning. Willingness to be engaged as spokespersons was severely lacking, and this was further highlighted by Hooson's request for the executive to submit 'names of those with suitable knowledge and expertise who might be designated as Spokesmen of the Party', saying that there needed to be 'better liaison between policymakers and candidates in relation to public announcement of policy'.[141]

The volunteer aspect of the role, whether that of spokesperson or policy directorate member, could be a serious disadvantage to the party. Furthermore, the difficulty in finding spokespersons meant that some of the more proactive members were given quite diverse remits. For example, David Hando[142] held the Education portfolio but was then asked to be the spokesperson for Commonwealth Affairs, the United Nations, the NHS and Social Services.[143] Yet, he would also issue statements supporting the Conservative government's 'belated' efforts to curb soaring inflation and urging gas workers not to strike.[144] This was too much work to be placed on individual volunteers, and many of the more proactive members, such as Hando, would take a step back from the directorate.

A CHANGE OF THE GUARD

By any estimation, the results of both 1974 general elections were a success for the WLP, with the election of two MPs and every Welsh constituency being fought. It also showed that there was still an interest in the WLP and its policies within Wales. Coupled with the 1975 referendum on continuing EEC membership and the constitutional status of Wales, the WLP could have the potential to shape or contribute to these debates. This interest did not go unnoticed within the WLP and it coincided with a gradual personnel change within the executive. Some of those who had helped start the WLP, such as Lord Lloyd of Kilgerran, had resigned and taken up positions elsewhere. Mary Murphy had fought her last parliamentary battle in October and concentrated more on her position as a local councillor.[145] It was left to those new members of the executive to try to bring a renewed sense of purpose to the policy directorate. The former PPC for Barry, Dr Jennifer Lloyd and Gareth Morgan were tasked with reviving the group in 1975.

Lloyd and Morgan decided that the group had to be 'responsible over-all for the development and publication of the policies of the Welsh Liberal Party' and had to be incorporated more thoroughly within the structure of the WLP. They set out a proto constitution, which included the objects of the directorate and how they saw the group developing in the long term. Initially, the directorate was to keep the role of spokesperson, who would have their brief and specialist subject, but this requirement would be gradually replaced once the directorate issued more policy documents. The intention was that each spokesperson would become a polymath of WLP policy and speak accordingly. Further, they wanted to collate existing WLP policies and develop these with the aid of geographical sub-committees and grass-root involvement. There would be regular meetings, and a further aim would be to professionalise the candidates of the party. In achieving these goals, the document proposed that the chair of the executive would also sit as the chair of the directorate, with the leader of the party (Hooson) being an *ex officio* member. The directorate would be overseen by a steering committee, with the power to co-opt members and set up sub-committees from the executive. The directorate was to be small, and they noted that there were steps taken to prepare six policy papers.[146]

The areas that would prove most contentious were to do with finance and the continued voluntary nature of the directorate. As indicated above, the idea of the directorate approaching businesses was a non-starter. It was also a contentious asking because similar requirements had been made for the appointment of Emlyn Thomas in 1968 and John Spiller in 1979, both of whom were either unable or unwilling to finance their roles. By 1977, it was obvious that this proposal was harming the policy directorate, as some believed it to not be feasible to expect companies to finance the policies of the WLP and called on the executive to furnish the policy directorate with a budget.[147] These calls would be echoed in 1979, with the executive being urged to 'make clear what it wants done, and what it is prepared to pay for'. The policy directorate survived in this condition between 1975 and 1979, but it would be incorrect to suggest that policies were not formulated in this period. As with the previous incarnations of the directorate, even in its dormant period, the policies that were formulated were Wales-orientated and were often quite detailed. Yet, between 1978 and 1979, the publication of policies had ground to a near halt, with just one leaflet having been produced on the Welsh language.[148]

The lack of finances meant that the old problems still existed, namely that each member had to act as their own researcher and spokesperson, which could be time-consuming. There was also no leadership; the role of spokesperson had not evolved as planned, and the party was still relying on the conscientious few:

> We need to bring our list of spokesman [sic] up to date. I was looking at the list the other day and, although there was no one on the list who was actually dead, there was certainly quite a few names of people who give precious little indication of continued life on this earth.[149]

This was despite the increasing size of the directorate, which numbered around a dozen members when it was reformed in 1979. Gwyn Griffiths, who would reform the policy directorate following the 1979 general election, commented that the size of the directorate was hampered by being unable to convene regularly, by a lack of leadership within the group or by the executive and the lack of a budget. The lack of policy publications meant there had been very little publicity for the party, something that would have been needed in the run-up to the crucial devolution referendum and the general election.

Following the results of the disastrous 1979 general election and referendum, Gwyn Griffiths recognised that the party needed either a full-time research officer or a director of policy, but could afford neither. His solution was a reform of the structure of the directorate, which would allow it to use the present resources of the party. This would mean that:

1. The executive would decide which issues the directorate should concentrate on.
2. The chairman would also be a member of the executive and would have a leadership role that included managing those doing research or who were spokespersons for the party, making use of the secretarial skills, liaising with the weekend schools and taking minutes.
3. A publications officer would properly prepare the leaflets and their distribution.
4. A conference officer would prepare the motions to be passed to the conference.
5. There would be close liaison with the weekend school committee, so any proposals could be discussed by the directorate.[150]

These proposals are outside of the current remit of the book, as they occur in the post-1979 period, but it should be noted that, from 1975, a greater emphasis was being placed on the policy directorate. The party recognised that reform was needed and that all organs of the WLP needed to better communicate with each other. The points relating to the weekend schools are pertinent because, despite the number of experts that attended the gatherings, there had been a recognition that no one had recorded or kept notations of the lectures and their contributions 'were lost to the party immediately after the weekend'.[151] Better communication between the different organs of the WLP could have provided the party with a ready supply of expert testimony and informed the policymaking process.

1966–70: THE POLICIES AND MANIFESTO

Before the formation of the WLP, Martin Thomas set out a vision for the WLP:

> To take full advantage of the situation, the (Welsh) Liberal Party must proclaim not a political but an economic nationalism . . . Given a solid Welsh image, Labour seats are there to be won . . . To revive the Welsh Candidates Association, merging with the Welsh Radical Group to initiate a Welsh policy of economic and social development.[152]

The September 1966 meeting that formed the WLP sought to make good on Thomas's words by immediately endorsing a draft bill for a Welsh parliament and the less Wales-centric policies of compulsory comprehensive education and the abolition of the 'selective employment tax and the introduction of a payroll tax'.[153] The Government of Wales Bill was a firm statement of intent from Hooson.

THE GOVERNMENT OF WALES BILL

Following the September 1966 meeting that set up the WLP, where Martin Thomas had written a draft devolution Bill, Hooson and Thomas began the process of refining that document. The Government of Wales Bill was presented by Hooson, with cross-party backing from Gwynfor Evans and S. O. Davies, the Labour MP for Merthyr Tydfil, to Parliament on St David's Day, 1967.

The Bill set out the WLP's position on what a domestic parliament, in a federal United Kingdom, would look like for Wales. The main points of the Bill were:[154]

1. The UK Parliament would retain certain powers including those relating to defence, international trade, currency, the Crown, and criminal law.
2. The Welsh Parliament would be single-chambered and titled The Senate/Y Senedd.
   It would be able to pass and enact laws, enforceable by penal sanctions. Also, any law enacted in Wales would have primacy over those of the UK Parliament, as long as they are not reserved powers, in which case, the UK Parliament would have primacy.
3. There would be seventy-two members of the Senedd, two from each constituency in Wales, elected via the alternative vote. Thirty-six MPs would still be sent to Westminster but would not vote on matters relating exclusively to England, Scotland and Northern Ireland.
4. Executive power would remain vested in the monarch and would be exercised by a Governor of Wales.
5. The Welsh language would have equal validity with the English language in the Parliament/Senedd.
6. The Parliament/Senedd could make laws to raise taxes including the rates, purchase taxes, sale taxes and land taxes. All other taxes would be reserved for the UK Parliament.
7. There were clauses for setting up a Welsh Exchequer and a Joint Exchequer Board.
8. Any conflict in law would be subject to the interpretation by the Appellate Committee of the House of Lords.

Although the Bill did not make it past the first reading, it was a radical addition to the debate and would be the preferred model of the WLP. Its radicalism was in how it set out a coherent plan for the devolution of powers to a federal Welsh parliament. Although federalism had been the primary goal of the BLP, the manifestos were not always consistent and often only urged the devolution of powers to a Welsh parliament. By presenting the Bill, Hooson was indirectly stating that the new WLP, the third party in Wales, was a nationalist party that believed in Wales as a nation and backed a degree of separateness. Interestingly, unlike the economic direction the WLP was taking at this point, during the presentation of the Bill, Hooson stated that:

> As all hon. Members know, I am not an economic nationalist and I never shall be, but I believe that Wales, like Scotland and Northern Ireland, has the right to organise its own domestic affairs . . . I see the Parliament at Westminster as a federal Parliament concerned with foreign affairs, overseas trade, defence and the overall direction of the economy.[155]

Hooson's denial that he was an economic nationalist was not strictly true, as the Bill made provision for the collection of certain taxes and for Wales to be provided with the Welsh share of reserved taxes. Additionally, other policy documents that were released at this time point to the WLP pursuing an economic nationalism (see below). These policies would have had a bearing on the Welsh economy, and were designed to do so. However, this economic nationalism was tempered by cultural nationalism, which Hooson pointed to in his speech:

> We inherit a small but distinct culture whose origins are lost in antiquity. Our language is an expressive language of lyrical and emotive beauty. But we are bound by something beyond language, beyond culture only, by that curious blend of romanticism and radicalism which in one way or another finds expression in every son of Wales.[156]

It would not have escaped the notice of the Labour government that one of the backers of the Bill was the Plaid Cymru president, Gwynfor Evans. Evans is likely to have backed the Bill as part of a long-term goal toward dominion status, and the idea of a Governor would have appealed to him. For the Labour government, the potential for both nationalist parties to work together, albeit with different goals, would have been taken as a warning. If the WLP were to achieve its goal of federalism, then a demonstration of a competent federal parliament could have serious implications for the unity of the UK.

As an indication of how seriously the WLP took the issue of federalism, in January 1968 Lord Ogmore, President of the WLP, presented another Government of Wales Bill in the House of Lords. It was a very similar Bill to Hooson's, in that it contained the core provisions listed above (except for having just eighteen MPs sent to Westminster), yet it did not proceed any further than Hooson's Bill and was defeated on the first reading.[157] As noted by Lord Ogmore, when giving evidence to the Royal Commission on the Constitution, his Bill and, by extension Hooson's, were the basis of 'our economic policy and our social policy'.[158]

THE POLICIES

From 1967, Hooson and the policy directorate began to set the policy tone for the next three years. As chapter one noted, Hooson had already begun that process with the 1959 manifesto, and many of these policies would be refined for the *Heartland* (1965) and *Life to a Nation* (1969) policy documents and the 1970 general election manifesto. Additionally, the policy directorate and spokespersons issued statements reacting to government policies which may not have always been straightforwardly Wales-centric. As ever, and like all good Liberals, the WLP would emphasise international affairs.

Concerning Wales, Martin Thomas's words were certainly the blueprint for how the WLP wanted to differentiate themselves from Plaid. At this juncture, Plaid was still seen as a party that cared more about the cultural side of Wales and sought independence, but had less to say about the economics of Wales. This image of Plaid would change once its *Economic Plan* was published in 1970, but before this, it was clear that if the WLP were to mount a nationalist challenge then it had to be on an economic basis.

The first major policy document was *Life to a Nation*; this collated and revised the WLP's economic policy. This document was produced by the policy committee, which established several sub-committees, each headed by a designated expert.[159] At just ten pages long, this was half the size of *The Heartland*, but it was designed to be an abridged version of the WLP's economic policies, rather than a comprehensive look into each area.[160]

The proposed policies within *Life to a Nation* assessed the need to attract new industry into Wales. This would be a notable departure from the Labour government's 'Welsh Development Area' grants to businesses, as these were based on unemployment levels, rather than the potential for future development: that is, training the workforce and providing adequate accommodation. The policy contained proposals to improve the transport and port infrastructure within Wales, including a 'free port area', with proposals on education, the retention of wealth in Wales, a Land Bank and agriculture.[161] It is worth noting that since the 1965 *Heartland* policy and in light of Hooson's 1967 Government of Wales Bill, all of the major policy proposals of the party would hinge on the 'existence of a Welsh Domestic Parliament . . . A Parliament is a vital necessity for our programme to become reality'.[162] This was placing the WLP's federal and domestic parliament policy at the heart of its existence as a party. Unsurprisingly, the proposals were the basis of the 1970 general election manifesto.

In the wake of the Tryweryn campaign, one of the most contentious policies, particularly in Welsh nationalism, related to water and the flooding of the valleys. The manifesto did not go much further than demanding the establishment of a Welsh Water Board and seeking assurances from the government 'that no more Welsh valleys will be drowned until such a board is created'.[163] However, following the general election, it was Hooson who developed the policy further by suggesting that a levy could be placed on the resources, which could be split evenly between the Exchequer and the proposed Welsh Development Fund. Hooson, knowing how emotive the issue was in Wales, stated:

> I see this proposal as one which could unify the people of Wales. It does not matter how views differ upon how Wales should be governed . . . It could be administered under dominion status, under a domestic parliament, under an elected council, under a development commission or even under the Welsh office.[164]

This was quite a step forward, as the WLP looked to offer a definitive proposal on a topic that had become the preserve of the nationalists. Plaid was advocating the creation of a National Water Board and that English local authorities

> should pay a fair price for all water they take from Wales . . . that in future only small, isolated and unpopulated sites should be considered for drowning and even these should not be permitted unless some direct economic benefit accrues to the areas where the reservoirs are situated.[165]

This call for a Welsh Water Board and compensation for the people in Wales affected by the drowning of valleys was not exclusive to the WLP or Plaid, as the Conservatives and Labour had similar policies or recommendations. For example, although not a policy and ignored by Conservative HQ, there was certainly support expressed within the Welsh Conservatives for 'the payment of royalties to Welsh areas providing water for England'.[166] Within Labour, there was support for a Welsh Water Board, notably from Cledwyn Hughes, the Secretary of

State for Wales.[167] In the end, the 1973 Water Act established the Welsh National Water Development Authority.

Despite the WLP's initial focus on setting out an economic nationalism, the party had developed several of its cultural policies, the most obvious being related to the Welsh language. The 1962 formation of the WLS had allowed Plaid to attempt to jettison the issue and no longer make it a party-political point. This had not been successful, and the WLS's disruptive actions were causing problems for Plaid. Hooson and the WLP had been critical of the WLS's actions, with Hooson prosecuting members of the WLS who had been convicted of damaging English-language road signs.[168] Hooson and the WLP were sympathetic to the cause, but not to the group's disruptive actions.

The 1970 trial and imprisonment of the Welsh folk singer Dafydd Iwan, for refusing to pay a fine for defacing road signs, was a case in point. Around twenty Justices of the Peace (JPs) contributed to his fine and Iwan was released after three weeks of a three-month sentence. Whilst some within Wales called for the removal of the JPs, including the Monmouth Labour MP Donald Anderson,[169] the WLP took a different approach and issued a statement that said the JPs' actions were 'ill-advised'. The statement went further:

> I deplore the daubing of road signs as childish, annoying and potentially dangerous, but I would have thought that Welsh MPs would do better to urge the introduction of bilingual signs rather than to demand the dismissal of sympathetic JPs or congratulate bad-tempered judges on the severity of their sentences.[170]

Statements such as this were designed to show that the WLP believed in the language and had a mature outlook on its survival. Additionally, the WLP understood that the actions of the WLS could alienate the English monoglot majority of Wales. Party policy was directed towards detoxifying and depoliticising the language issue. The 1970 manifesto stated that:

> The Welsh language will live if the people of Wales will it to live . . . What worries Liberals is the unpleasant climate being created in Wales. The principle of equal validity points to the Welsh language having its rightful place in the land, but no one should try to ram the language down the throats of others.[171]

Not only was it a pointed challenge to Plaid, but the manifesto also displayed Hooson's influence on the policy. Hooson, a Welsh-language speaker, had a keen interest in its survival and was the director of the Welsh-language publisher Gwasg Gee. The WLP policy was one of encouraging bilingualism and for people to cherish and learn the language. Whereas Plaid edged towards bilingualism, the party could not completely divorce itself from its previous position. As Butt Philip notes:

> It is not exactly clear when Plaid Cymru changed its view on the language from demanding the return to an all Welsh-speaking Wales . . . to the demand for a bilingual Wales . . . (because) The Blaid avoided conflict on this issue by refusing to state its complete position.[172]

However, the WLP's policy on the language having 'equal validity' with English, which was also written into Hooson's Government of Wales Bill, was contentious. Many thought the goal should be 'equal status and dignity'[173] with English. The equal validity argument was a compromise to those who felt the language was being 'rammed down people's throats' and decried the cost of official bilingual literature.[174]

Despite this emphasis on equal validity, the WLP recognised that if the language was to survive, people had to be encouraged to learn and speak it. In recognition of this, the 1970 manifesto also stated that they wanted separate channels for Welsh and

English television programmes, as the former had only a limited amount of time (around six hours a week in 1964[175]) and were being transmitted to 'large numbers of people who are unable to understand them'.[176] In a later policy document, Hooson argued that the WLP should be advocating more money should be allocated towards Welsh-language TV programmes and, in particular, children's programmes.[177] In the 1974 general election manifestos, the WLP joined calls being made for a Welsh-only television channel.[178]

POLICY BREAKDOWN, 1971–9

The 1970s were, to say the least, an economically tumultuous decade, punctuated with strikes,[179] the three-day week, high unemployment, fuel shortages and soaring inflation. As table 19 shows, unemployment in Wales rose dramatically after 1974. The fact that the WLP were unable to formulate a set of economic policy proposals, as they had done before the 1970 general election, spoke volumes about the breakdown within the WLP policy process. This is not to say that there was no policy to tackle the rising inflation or the high unemployment levels, it is just that these were left as part of a UK-wide set of BLP policies.

Table 19: Total unemployed in Wales, 1971–6[180]

Year	Male unemployed	Female unemployed	Total unemployed
1971	34,567	7,520	42,087
1972	45,728	9,977	55,705
1973	39,019	9,161	48,180
1974	29,877	6,511	36,388
1975	49,831	15,091	64,922
1976[181]	59,148	22,340	81,488

Yet, the WLP were not devoid of policies in this period. The 1974 February and October general election manifestos demonstrated that there were some noteworthy policies, which included a levy on water resources pumped to England, a Welsh-language television channel and a Celtic Sea oil levy.[182] The last of these was a reaction to the oil found in the North Sea which had begun to benefit Scotland's economy, albeit with the revenues going to the British Exchequer. Hooson had earlier suggested that should oil be found off the coast of Wales, then the planned Welsh Development Board and the Exchequer could split any revenues evenly.[183] However, despite the 'creative'[184] nature of the policies, they were not significantly 'new' and were either rehashed from the 1970 manifesto or had been modified. Yet, they showed that the WLP policies were consistent with its intent to focus on economic and social issues. The election of Geraint Howells as MP for Ceredigion, followed by his re-election in October, ensured that Welsh policy issues, particularly relating to the language and agriculture, would remain at the heart of the WLP.

The October 1973 publication of the report by the Royal Commission on the Constitution, with its recommendations for a Welsh legislative parliament, was coupled with the relative success of the 1974 general elections. Although funding remained an issue, these events sparked a renewed interest in policy formation within the WLP. The reconstituted policy directorate began to meet regularly and there were some interesting policy papers on agriculture, health and transport which were devised and presented to the executive. Experts were approached and asked to write papers as well.[185] Apart from the policy papers, the group produced rather lengthy (for the WLP, at least), documents on a wide range of topics. These included social security,[186] transport policy[187] and evidence to the Royal Commission on the NHS,[188] to name just a few. Many of these documents were produced with the belief that a Welsh parliament was on the horizon, and the party was contributing to the overall debate about powers that could be devolved to Wales. For a brief couple of years, the WLP began to have confidence in its policymaking.

However, closer inspection shows that some of these policies were not always Wales-specific and that BLP policies had been issued under the WLP banner for sale to the public. One such was the social security policy document, which did not mention Wales at all, yet the fact that the WLP had issued it shows that the party still believed that it was important for any Welsh parliament to eventually have this power. There were some remarkable policy achievements, such as Gwyn Griffiths's transport policy document. The impetus for the new transport policy had been the Labour government's 1976 White Paper on Transport, with the Transport Act being passed in 1978. Griffiths had begun taking evidence in 1976, and based his proposals on responses and reports from around thirty organisations and business leaders. The policy document ran to ten pages and was adopted as policy at the WLP's annual conference that year.[189] The difference between this major policy piece and those adopted before 1970 is that this was the work of one person. It was to the detriment of the WLP that they did not have other members of the policy directorate who were willing or able to invest the time and research in producing a comprehensive policy platform.

Whether it was the financial issues that the party faced between 1977 and 1979, or that the proposed Welsh Assembly, rather than the hoped-for parliament, had sapped the enthusiasm for policymaking, as it would be an executive rather than a legislative body, the policy process became more of an afterthought. Griffiths pointed out that the only policy that was published in 1978 was his updated Welsh-language policy. This lack of policymaking, coupled with the failure of the March 1979 devolution referendum and the loss of Hooson's Montgomery seat, prompted the WLP to reassess the policy directorate.

AGRICULTURAL POLICY

It would be remiss not to remark on one of the key successes of this period, which was in the party's agricultural policy. Defining an agricultural policy was of interest to Hooson, as he had grown up on and owned a working farm. Additionally, he represented a rural and hill farming constituency and was very much involved in that way of life. This was also true of Geraint Howells, who was a well-known sheep farmer in Cardiganshire, the county that he would represent from 1974 to 1992. Howells would become the WLP spokesperson on agricultural affairs and Hooson would have the same role in the Parliamentary Liberal Party (PLP). Unfortunately, space in the present volume does not allow for a detailed analysis of the WLP's agricultural policy, but what can be noted is the effect it had on BLP policy and British government policy.

As one would expect, the BLP manifestos issued during the 1966 and 1970 general elections included some shared agricultural policies with the WLP. For example, in both elections, the BLP called for the establishment of a land bank,[190] and in 1970 there was an emphasis that the 'Small farmers and growers, who are efficient and whose holdings are viable deserve to survive'.[191] Although the influence of the WLP could be detected, the latter policy was somewhat different from that of the Welsh Liberals, in that they emphasised that every assistance should be given to ensure economic viability,[192] whereas the BLP supported those small farms that were already 'viable'. It is a subtle difference in language, but it showed that the BLP was prepared to allow the market to decide the future of the smallholder.

However, the WLP's influence on BLP policy would change when Jeremy Thorpe appointed Hooson as PLP spokesperson for Agriculture, Wales and the Law, in November 1973. There is evidence that Hooson was able to align the policies of both the BLP and the WLP: for example, the policy documents *The*

Heartland and *Life to a Nation*, and the 1970 WLP general election manifesto, gave a lot of attention to the issue of young farmers. In June 1974, BLP agricultural policy was to be amended in this direction and called for:

1. Security for tenants and their sons – support for the alignment of English and Welsh law with Scottish law. This meant that 'sons, engaged full time in agriculture, can automatically succeed their fathers as tenants'.
2. Provision of farm holdings for young farmers – by amending the Smallholdings Act of 1908, the Liberals would set up an Agricultural Holding Act, designed to 'transform the Smallholdings Committees of the County Councils into Agricultural Holdings Committees' allowing them to purchase land and set up agricultural holdings to be let, thus 'providing the first rung in the farming ladder for many people'.
3. The postponement of death duties – death duties would be postponed 'until whenever the farm or farm stock is eventually sold'.[193]

The above policies had not been included in the BLP's 1970 general election manifesto,[194] but had been included in the WLP's manifesto that year.[195] These policies highlighted the influence of the WLP, through Hooson, on the BLP. This transfer of policies, to affect a national policy, had not occurred since the time of Lloyd George. There was also a shared policy on income and price guarantees which had been included in both the WLP and BLP manifestos. The WLP had proposed in 1970 the 'Wages and conditions of employment for farmworkers to be brought into line with those in other industries'.[196] The BLP pointed to real incomes increasing by forty-six per cent in the preceding ten years, while in the same period farmers had an increase of only seven per cent. The BLP manifesto stated that 'Liberals support the farmers' claim for more generous treatment'.[197] These were policies that remained within both the WLP and BLP general election manifestos.

THE FARMERS' UNION OF WALES

As a final note on the agricultural influence of the WLP, it must be noted that it made an impact on government policy during the Lib-Lab Pact. In April 1978, the FUW, which had hitherto been seen as a poor relation to the National Farmers' Union (NFU), was given equal validity as an official negotiating partner with the Ministry of Agriculture, Fisheries and Food and the Welsh Office.[198] This was at the instigation of Geraint Howells, one of the founder members of the FUW and a keen supporter. Howells, by then the PLP agricultural spokesperson, had approached his opposite number in the pact, John Silkin, and asked him outright for full recognition of the FUW. 'That is what you are going to get', replied Silkin.[199] This was a major step for the FUW and was another example of the WLP influencing the policy of other parties. In a pact that held very little for the Liberals, this showed that the WLP was able to gain something tangible from the association.

CONCLUSION

The policy goal of the WLP was to promote Wales and its interests. The WLP wanted to wear its Welshness as a badge of honour, reclaiming its rightful place as the Welsh party. The party emphasised its economic nationalism from the start, which differentiated it from Plaid. However, this did not preclude the WLP from developing a coherent social and cultural policy, as evidenced by its Welsh-language proposals. These policies were intertwined with an overarching economic policy, as evidenced by their inclusion in the television channel debate and education.

However, the chapter has shown that the WLP had secured funding for its major policies *The Heartland* and *Life to a Nation* but found it difficult to secure funding after the 1970 general election. Additionally, the financial organisation of the WLP meant that there was very little money within the party and the policymaking process ground almost to a halt. It was only following the success of the 1974 general elections and the renewed hope in a Welsh parliament, following the 1973 Royal Commission report, that the policy directorate was reformed.

The reformed policy directorate started with an ambitious and workable remit. However, the requirement to seek out external funding and a lack of direction from the executive meant that it became rudderless. It did not help that at the point of formation the WLP was close to bankruptcy. Policymaking began to suffer and, by 1979, it became harder to arrange meetings. With 1979 being a crucial year, one wonders whether the watered-down devolution proposals had sapped the enthusiasm from the policy directorate.

It is difficult to assert that the WLP always led from the front on its general policies, particularly after 1970. What can be asserted is that throughout Hooson's tenure as the leader of the WLP, the emphasis was placed on Wales. The policy directorate may have suffered from a lack of funds and a lack of direction but the policies were distinctly Welsh. However, there were notable successes, none more obvious than the WLP's agricultural policy. Additionally, Hooson's Government of Wales Bill was a defining moment in the early life of the WLP, setting out its Welsh nationalist credentials and intertwining them with its policies on the establishment of a legislative Welsh parliament.

The next chapter will assess the electoral record of the WLP under Hooson and will argue that the party has been unfairly overlooked, due to its lack of MPs. The chapter will argue that the WLP's popularity, especially when compared with Plaid, should have afforded it a higher status than the current historiography gives the party.

Notes

1. Lord Emlyn Hooson, *Rebirth or Death?* (Aberystwyth, 1994), p. 5.
2. NLW, Merfyn Jones Papers, Box 34, 'Our Task in Wales – We Start at Caerphilly', address by Hooson prior to the 1968 Caerphilly by-election.
3. Andrew Edwards, *Labour's Crisis: Plaid Cymru, The Conservatives and the Decline of the Labour Party in North-West Wales, 1960–74* (Cardiff, 2011), p. 155.
4. J. Graham Jones, 'The Parliament for Wales Campaign, 1950–1956', *Welsh History Review*, 16/2 (1992), 209.
5. In fact, bilingualism.
6. Sam Blaxland, *The Conservative Party in Wales, 1945–1997* (Cardiff, 2024), p. 67.
7. Initially, the post was coupled with that of the Home Secretary, but from 1957 to 1964, it became part of the Minister of Housing and Local Government's remit.
8. Edwards, *Labour's Crisis*, p. 158.
9. Blaxland, *The Conservative Party*, pp. 68–70.
10. Edwards, *Labour's Crisis*, p. 162. This was a 35,000-word policy document published in 1959.
11. Lord Crickhowell, *The Conservative Party and Wales* (National Library of Wales, 2006), p. 14. This is the revised and expanded text of the twentieth Welsh Political Archive annual lecture delivered to the National Library of Wales on 3 November 2006. Lord Crickhowell was formerly known as Nicholas Edwards, the Secretary of State for Wales between 1979 and 1987.
12. 1959 Conservative Party General Election Manifesto. Available at: http://www.conservativemanifesto.com/1959/1959-conservative-manifesto.shtml (accessed 5 March 2025).
13. 1964 Conservative Party General Election Manifesto. Available at: http://www.conservativemanifesto.com/1964/1964-conservative-manifesto.shtml (accessed 5 March 2025).
14. Edwards, *Labour's Crisis*, p. 164, and 1966 Conservative Party General Election Manifesto. Available at: http://www.conservativemanifesto.com/1966/1966-conservative-manifesto.shtml (accessed 5 March 2025).
15. Blaxland, *The Conservative Party*, pp. 192–5.
16. 1970 Conservative Party General Election Manifesto. Available at: http://www.conservativemanifesto.com/1970/1970-conservative-manifesto.shtml (accessed 5 March 2025). The Conservatives also published separate manifestos for Wales and Scotland.
17. Edwards, *Labour's Crisis*, p. 188, and Blaxland, *The Conservative Party*, p. 122, for example.
18. Edwards, *Labour's Crisis*, pp. 183–4.
19. Edwards, *Labour's Crisis*, p. 87.
20. Peter Stead, 'The Labour Party and the Claims of Wales', in John Osmond, *The National Question Again: Welsh Political Identity in the 1980s* (Llandysul, 1985), p. 105. 'By its very nature the Council of Wales was a concession and a compromise.'

21 J. Graham Jones, 'The Union Jack, The Red Flag and the Welsh Dragon: The Dilemmas of Goronwy Roberts and James Griffiths', *Llafur: Journal of Welsh People's History*, 12/1 (2016), 46. Although I have lumped them together in two opposing camps, a better description is by Jones of Welsh Labour as being split into three camps: a group avidly supportive of devolution (including S. O. Davies and Cledwyn Hughes), those diametrically opposed to devolution (including Ness Edwards and George Thomas) and, finally, those in the middle, such as Jim Griffiths, who were greatly sympathetic but hamstrung by their official positions within the Labour Party and government.
22 R. Merfyn Jones and Ioan Rhys Jones, 'Labour and the Nation', in Duncan Tanner, Chris Williams and Deian Hopkin (eds), *The Labour Party in Wales, 1900–2000* (Cardiff, 2000), pp. 258–9. It must be said that Bevan's attitude was echoed by others within the wider Labour Party and movement. The socialist strategy was to unite the workers, not impede or separate them with artificial barriers. The state was the organ of nationalisation and for improving people's lives.
23 Nye Davis, 'The difference between sheep: Bevan and the "Welsh Day" debate'. Available at: *https://blogs.cardiff.ac.uk/thinking-wales/the-difference-between-sheep-bevan-and-the-welsh-day-debate/#_ftnref2* (accessed 5 March 2025).
24 Martin Shipton, *Political Chameleon: In Search of George Thomas* (Cardiff, 2017), pp. 63 and 109. Shipton states that Thomas considered Welsh speakers as anti-English and a troublesome group.
25 *Royal Commission on the Constitution, 1969–1973* (1973), vol. 1, p. 5. 'We have no doubt that the main intention . . . was that we should investigate the case for transferring or devolving responsibility . . . from Parliament . . . to new institutions.'
26 Alan Butt Philip, *The Welsh Question: Nationalism in Welsh Politics 1945–1970* (Cardiff, 1975), p. 85.
27 John Davies, 'Plaid Cymru in Transition', in John Osmond (ed.), *The National Question Again: Welsh Political Identity in the 1980s* (Llandysul, 1985), p. 137.
28 Laura McAllister, *Plaid Cymru: The Emergence of a Political Party* (Bridgend, 2001), pp. 70–2.
29 Edwards, *Labour's Crisis*, pp. 132–3.
30 McAllister, *Plaid Cymru*, p. 71.
31 Russell Deacon, *The Welsh Liberals: The History of the Liberal and Liberal Democratic Parties in Wales* (Cardiff, 2014), p. 171. 'The Welsh Liberal Party had been established with the idea of achieving nothing short of a Welsh Liberal revival.'
32 Kenneth O. Morgan, *Modern Wales: Politics, Places and People* (Cardiff, 1995), p. 65. Morgan argues that it barely existed, whereas Peter Clarke argues that Morgan's argument closed 'too many doors' and that the survival of Welsh Liberalism up to 1914 can be explained once it is seen in the 'framework of progressivism'. P. F. Clarke, *Lancashire and the New Liberalism* (Cambridge, 1971), p. 401.

33 Kenneth O. Morgan, *Rebirth of a Nation: Wales 1880–1980* (Oxford, 1990), p. 36.
34 Morgan, *Rebirth*, pp. 38–9.
35 Kenneth O. Morgan, *The Age of Lloyd George: The Liberal Party and British Politics, 1890–1929* (London, 1978), p. 102.
36 Deacon, *Welsh Liberals*, p. 40.
37 Hooson, *Rebirth or Death?*, p. 5.
38 NLW, Lord Hooson Papers, File 116/1, Emlyn Hooson and Geraint Jenkins, *The Heartland: A Plan for Mid-Wales* (London, 1965), pp. 5–6.
39 These five counties were also the basis for the Mid-Wales Industrial Development Association reports.
40 John Williams, *Digest of Welsh Historical Statistics, Vol. 1* (Pontypool, 1985), pp. 50 and 52. It must be noted that Hooson's report assessed 'a greater part of Brecon', so the figure here is just illustrative.
41 Williams, *Digest*, pp. 69–74. These figures have been used as they were the ones used by Hooson and were the latest census calculations available at the time. The 'Total change' column is the difference between the previous census and this one. 'Natural increase' was calculated by subtracting the total deaths from the total births. The 'Net migration' amounts are the difference between the 'Total change' and 'Natural increase'. The rise in Cardiganshire is probably due to the intake at UCW Aberystwyth (see Williams, *Digest*, p. 62, for the population increase in Aberystwyth).
42 Appalachian Regional Commission, 'ARC History'. Available at: *https://web.archive.org/web/20160407014958/http://www.arc.gov/about/archistory.asp* (accessed 5 March 2025).
43 Minutes of the Liberal Party Organisation's Executive Committee, 14 December 1956, p. 9: 'it was <u>agreed</u> to ask Mr. Emlyn Hooson if the draft of the Welsh Yellow Book, which was in the course of preparation, could be made available to the Executive before publication'. Available at: *https://microform.digital/boa/collections/81/volumes/585/grimond-and-thorpes-liberal-revival-1954–1976* (accessed 5 March 2025).
44 Adjusted to 2023 levels, £232,323,858.58 at 4.7% inflation p/a.
45 'Charter for Wales', *Wales Magazine*, 41 (1959), 11–13. No author given. Available at: *https://journals.library.wales/view/1214989/1218069/#?xywh=-2068%2C-201%2C6483%2C4005* (accessed 5 March 2025).
46 'Charter for Wales', 12–13. Available at: *https://journals.library.wales/view/1214989/1218069/#?xywh=-2068%2C-201%2C6483%2C4005* (accessed 5 March 2025).
47 Ian C. Thomas, 'The Beginnings of an Economic Development Policy in Mid-Wales: The Mid-Wales Industrial Development Association, 1957–1974', *Welsh History Review*, 17/3 (1995), 433.
48 Thomas, 'The Beginnings', 434. These were Bala, Tywyn, Aberystwyth, Lampeter, Cardigan, Welshpool, Newtown, Llanidloes, Brecon, Llandrindod Wells, Rhayader and Builth Wells.

49 NLW, Lord Hooson Papers, Box 50, Statement issued by the Liberal Party, 18 March 1965.
50 Nevin was a noted economist from University College Wales, Aberystwyth. *Independent*, George Clayton, 'Obituary, Professor E. T. Nevin CORRECTED', 20 and 23 September 1992. Available at: *https://www.independent.co.uk/news/people/obituary-professor-e-t-nevin-corrected-1552650.html* (accessed 1 August 2024).
51 NLW, WLP File C11, Minutes of the Policy Directorate, 4 September 1976, p. 1. 'Mr. Emlyn Hooson was to contact Professors Nevin and Sadler with regard to them writing an economic paper for the Directorate.'
52 NLW, Lord Hooson Papers, Box 42, Letter from Professor E. T. Nevin to Hooson, 22 January 1965.
53 As the original letter is not available, this has been gleaned from Nevin's reply on 22 January 1965.
54 *The Times*, 15 June 1965.
55 *The Times*, 27 June 1960.
56 *The Times*, 24 May 1961.
57 There is some discrepancy as to what the final report was. *The Heartland* was published in March 1965 and there is a further document, *The Forgotten Land*, which was drawn up in July 1965. J. Graham Jones, 'Emlyn Hooson and Montgomeryshire Politics 1962–79', *The Montgomeryshire Collections*, 97 (2009), 180, states that *The Forgotten Land* was published in July, and included the information from *The Heartland*, namely 'the party's strategy for Mid Wales while retaining agriculture as its main industry'. I have a copy of both documents (the latter in draft form) and Jones's report is the only one I have seen that mentions it was published. I have seen no other evidence that it was published, although there is evidence that the Welsh Radical Group continued to work on the project. From the copy that I have, there is nothing substantially different.
58 NLW, Lord Hooson Papers, File 116/1, Emlyn Hooson and Geraint Jenkins, *The Heartland: A Plan for Mid-Wales* (London, 1965), pp. 9–18.
59 Hooson and Jenkins, *The Heartland*, pp. 9–10.
60 Hooson and Jenkins, *The Heartland*, p. 13.
61 Hooson and Jenkins, *The Heartland*, p. 11.
62 *The Times*, 29 March 1965, 11. Letter from Hooson to the Editor.
63 NLW, Lord Hooson Papers, Box 50, Statement issued by the Liberal Party, 18 March 1965.
64 NLW, Lord Hooson Papers, Box 50, Letter from Professor E. T. Nevin to Hooson, 25 March 1965.
65 *The Times*, 13. The report suggests these will be in 'Aberystwyth, Builth Wells, Llanidloes, Dolgelley and Llandrindod Wells'.
66 NLW, Lord Hooson Papers, Box 50, Letter from Professor E. T. Nevin to Hooson, 25 March 1965.
67 Hooson and Jenkins, *The Heartland*, pp. 15–16.
68 Hooson and Jenkins, *The Heartland*, p. 16.
69 Williams, *Digest*, p. 62.

70 This is based on the 2001 census figures. See Aberystwyth population statistics, 2001, available at: *https://www.citypopulation.de/en/uk/wales/admin/ceredigion/ W04000359__aberystwyth/* (accessed 5 March 2025).
71 Hooson and Jenkins, *The Heartland*, pp. 9–10.
72 NLW, Lord Hooson Papers, Box 50, Letter from Geraint Jenkins to Hooson, 17 May 1965.
73 NLW, Lord Hooson Papers, Box 50, Letter from W. Philip Davies, the Aberystwyth Town Clerk, 9 April 1965.
74 *Birmingham Daily Post*, 30 July 1965, 5.
75 NLW, Cardiganshire Liberal Association, File 120, *Welsh Liberal Party Manifesto: The Liberal Case for Wales*, pp. 3 and 4.
76 Hooson, *Rebirth or Death?*, p. 9.
77 NLW, Lord Hooson Papers, Box 50, Letter from Bryan Keith-Lucas, 15 June 1965.
78 HC Deb 30 November 1965, col. 1248 Available at: *https://api.parliament.uk/ historic-hansard/commons/1965/nov/30/agriculture-bill#column_1267* Hansard: *Hansard's Parliamentary Debates*, vol. 721, cols 1236–352 (1 August 2024).
79 Hooson and Jenkins, *The Heartland*, p. 10.
80 HC Deb 30 November 1965, col. 1248. Available at: *https://api.parliament. uk/historic-hansard/commons/1965/nov/30/agriculture-bill#column_1267* Hansard: *Hansard's Parliamentary Debates*, vol. 721, cols 1236–352 (accessed 1 August 2024). At this stage, Fred Peart was considering two areas in mid-Wales, each to have their own board.
81 HC Deb 30 November 1965, col. 1248. Available at: *https://api.parliament. uk/historic-hansard/commons/1965/nov/30/agriculture-bill#column_1267* Hansard: *Hansard's Parliamentary Debates*, vol. 721, cols 1236–352 (accessed 1 August 2024).
82 The Agriculture Act 1967, Part III, Section 49. Available at: *https://www. legislation.gov.uk/ukpga/1967/22/part/III/crossheading/special-measures-for-certain-areas/enacted* (accessed 1 August 2024).
83 NLW, Lord Hooson Papers, Box 50, Petition – Farmers and landowners in Montgomeryshire opposing the establishment of the Wales Rural Development Board in any part of the county – presented by Emlyn Hooson, QC, MP, on Monday 13 October 1969.
84 Butt Philip, *The Welsh Question*, p. 270.
85 See HMSO, *A New Town in Mid-Wales: Consultants' Proposals* (HMSO 1966), p. 32.
86 *The Times*, 15 June 1965, 13. When speculation was rife about which towns would be selected, some of the criticism concerned who would be in the overspill: 'There is also a trace of feeling against siphoning off some of the Dark Million, which it is thought the town might do. In Llangurig, Mr G. E. St. Johnston told me: "The population would be mainly coloured. This would not be a good thing for mid-Wales."' This attitude was prevalent and Thomas, 'The Beginnings', p. 436, highlights the attitudes of the MP for

Wrexham, Idwal Jones, who believed it would result in mid-Wales becoming 'Pakistanized'.
87 Thomas, 'The Beginnings', p. 441.
88 Thomas, 'The Beginnings', pp. 441–2, and Hooson and Jenkins, *The Heartland*, p. 16.
89 It must be admitted that this is circumstantial evidence, as I did not find any reference to *The Heartland* in the James Griffith archive at the NLW.
90 Edwards, *Labour's Crisis*, p. 135.
91 Butt Philip, *The Welsh Question*, p. 180.
92 Butt Philip, *The Welsh Question*, p. 181.
93 NLW, Lord Hooson Papers, Letter from Hooson to David Hando, 30 August 1972, recommending Butt Philip's application to stand in Monmouthshire and enclosing his curriculum vitae.
94 Edwards, *Labour's Crisis*, p. 133.
95 Butt Philip, *The Welsh Question*, p. 180.
96 Hooson and Jenkins, *The Heartland*, p. 19.
97 Plaid Cymru Research Group, *An Economic Plan for Wales* (Cardiff, 1970), p. 285.
98 Plaid Cymru Research Group, *An Economic Plan*, p. 147.
99 Hooson and Jenkins, *The Heartland*, p. 13. The proposals also chose Llandrindod, Borth, Bala and Machynlleth as holiday centres.
100 Plaid Cymru Research Group, *An Economic Plan*, p. 82.
101 Hooson and Jenkins, *The Heartland*, pp. 13–14.
102 Plaid Cymru Research Group, *An Economic Plan*, p. 82.
103 Butt Philip, *The Welsh Question*, pp. 181–2: 'inadequate figures and projections because of the dearth of available statistical information'.
104 Edwards, *Labour's Crisis*, p. 136: 'the party admitted that its solutions were, in some areas, partial and patchy'.
105 NLW, Merfyn Jones Papers, File 35, Constitution of the WLP, undated but the 1975 update shows this to be the original constitution. Item 9 (e).
106 NLW, Merfyn Jones Papers, File 35, Constitution of the WLP, undated but the 1975 update shows this to be the original constitution. Item 13.
107 NLW, Welsh Liberal Party File A4, John Roberts's Executive Committee Report, 19 June 1976.
108 NLW, Merfyn Jones Papers, File 35, Draft Revised Constitution of the WLP, undated but the draft fits with the ongoing discussions by the executive.
109 NLW, Welsh Liberal Party File A40, Policy Directorate – General Guidance, 25 June 1975.
110 NLW, Merfyn Jones Papers, File 49, Discussion Paper on the Proposal to Set Up the Post of Directorate of Policy, by Terry Thomas. Document undated but there is reference to it in the Minutes of the Policy Directorate, 1 May 1976.
111 NLW, Merfyn Jones Papers, File 49, Discussion Paper on the Proposal to Set Up the Post of Directorate of Policy, by Terry Thomas. Document undated

but there is reference to it in the Minutes of the Policy Directorate, 1 May 1976.
112 NLW, Welsh Liberal Party File C11, Minutes of the Policy Directorate Committee, 1 May 1976.
113 NLW, Welsh Liberal Party File C11, Minutes of the Policy Directorate Committee, 4 September 1976, p. 1.
114 NLW, Merfyn Jones Papers, File 34, WLP Summary of Income and Expenditure 31 Aug 1967 to 29 May 1968. Adjusted to 2023 levels, £1,097.97 at 5% inflationp/a.
115 NLW, Merfyn Jones Papers, File 37, Balance Sheet as at 31 March 1979. Adjusted to 2023 levels, respectively, £1,7364.09 at 3.6% inflation p/a and £1,463.23 at 3.3% inflation p/a.
116 NLW, Merfyn Jones Papers, File 36, Welsh Liberal Party Financial Report 1977/78, 31 March 1978. Adjusted to 2023 levels, £427.34, at 3.8% inflation p/a.
117 Deacon, *Welsh Liberals*, p. 140. They were founded in Pantyfedwen, Borth, hence the alternate name.
118 NLW, Merfyn Jones Papers, File 36, Welsh Liberal Party Financial Report 1977/78, 31 March 1978. Adjusted to 2023 levels, £1,046.04, at 3.7% inflation p/a.
119 NLW, Merfyn Jones Papers, File 37, Welsh Liberal Party Balance Sheet 1978/79, 31 March 1979. Adjusted to 2023 levels, £989.56 at 3.6% inflation p/a.
120 *Report of the Committee on Financial Aid to Political Parties*, British Parliamentary Papers (1976). Available at: *https://parlipapers.proquest.com/parlipapers/docview/ t70.d75.1975–066534* (accessed 1 August 2024). These are the central accounts in both tables and do not include constituency funds. For each party, I have combined all the years together, as it gives a good overview of income and budget, especially as the report sets the 'Income At Constant (1970) Prices'. On the face of it, the figures quoted do not reflect the actual amounts each party received, as the parties were submitting figures at 1970 prices. This allowed for a more accurate picture of the finances, as inflation averaged 12.6% between 1970 and 1976 (Bank of England inflation calculator). The WLP and Plaid Cymru did not provide any figures prior to 1970, despite the report accepting figures from 1967 onwards. No reason appears to have been given. Also, the amounts in the tables have not been adjusted to 2023 prices.
121 *Report of the Committee on Financial Aid to Political Parties*, pp. 96 and 98. Available at: *https://parlipapers.proquest.com/parlipapers/docview/t70.d75.1975–066534* (accessed 1 August 2024). Note that, as the Conservatives are not a federated party, this is the total declared to the committee for the whole party. The portion afforded to the Welsh section of the party is not given. Also, I have not included the amounts provided to consultants and companies for public research, as these were lumped together with other budgets and had not been broken down. Adjusting 1970 amounts for 2023 inflation (at 5% p/a) – income: £97,149,105.32; policy expenditure: £14,491,637.92.

122 *Report of the Committee on Financial Aid to Political Parties*, pp. 102 and 104. Available at: *https://parlipapers.proquest.com/parlipapers/docview/t70.d75.1975-066534* (accessed 1 August 2024). The explanation for the Conservatives is relevant to the Labour Party too, including why the budget to consultants and companies has been left out. I have included the amounts allocated to the general election funds too, just for completeness, as the party paid for policy programmes out of this. The 1975/6 figures were provisional, as the report was completed prior to those figures being known. 1970, adjusted for 2023 at 5% p/a – income: £70,449,837.62; policy expenditure: £4,318,613.11.
123 *Report of the Committee on Financial Aid to Political Parties*, pp. 132 and 134. Available at: *https://parlipapers.proquest.com/parlipapers/docview/t70.d75.1975-066534* (accessed 1 August 2024). Plaid only gave details for policy expenditure between 1974 and 1976. In 1970, adjusted for 2023 at 5% p/a – income: £3,439,138.71; policy expenditure: £105,011.87.
124 *Report of the Committee on Financial Aid to Political Parties*, pp. 120 and 122. Available at: *https://parlipapers.proquest.com/parlipapers/docview/t70.d75.1975-066534* (accessed 1 August 2024). In 1970, adjusted for 2023 at 5% p/a – income: £116,825.70.
125 *Report of the Committee on Financial Aid to Political Parties*. Available at: *https://parlipapers.proquest.com/parlipapers/docview/t70.d75.1975-066534* (accessed 1 August 2024).
126 *Report of the Committee on Financial Aid to Political Parties*, pp. 108 and 110. Available at: *https://parlipapers.proquest.com/parlipapers/docview/t70.d75.1975-066534* (accessed 1 August 2024). The 1975/6 figures were provisional, as the report was completed then. In addition, in 1974 the BLP paid out £30,000 (£272,202.85 at 4.6% p/a) towards consultants and agencies for public opinion research, public relations and advertising. In 1970, adjusted for 2023 at 5% p/a – income: £8,768,491.06; policy expenditure: £931,980.34.
127 *Report of the Committee on Financial Aid to Political Parties*, pp. 114 and 116. Available at: *https://parlipapers.proquest.com/parlipapers/docview/t70.d75.1975-066534* (accessed 1 August 2024). The Scottish Liberals declared policy expenditure in 1970 and 1972–4. In 1970, adjusted for 2023 at 5% p/a – income: £866,347.92; policy expenditure: £65,632.42.
128 Davies was the first president of the WLP before Lord Ogmore took over in 1967.
129 NLW, Lord Hooson Papers, Box 50, Letter from The Hon. Edward Davies, 13 May 1965. Davies was the son of David Davies and the great-grandson of the industrialist David Davies. This was a powerful family that had made a fortune during the nineteenth century. Both of Edwards's forefathers were influential Welsh Liberal MPs. Edward would be the very first president of the newly formed WLP.
130 NLW, WLP File A18, Letter from Rhys Gerran Lloyd to Lord Ogmore, 26 March 1971.
131 Deacon, *Welsh Liberals*, p. 178. From the minutes of the Welsh Liberal Council Meeting, 19 November 1972.

132 NLW, Lord Hooson Papers, Box 42, Members of the Policy Directorate, 9 January 1967.
133 NLW, Lord Hooson Papers, Box 42, Letter to Elfyn Morris from Hooson, 1 July 1966. However, Hooson wanted to be president of the WLP.
134 'Proud record of knighted Meuric', *Daily Post*, 21 June 2007. Available at: *https://www.dailypost.co.uk/news/local-news/proud-record-of-knighted-meuric-2872280* (accessed 1 August 2024).
135 Rees, *Welsh Hustings*, p. 199. TGWU – Transport and General Workers' Union.
136 NLW, Lord Hooson Papers, Box 42, Members of the Policy Directorate, 9 January 1967. Excluding Hooson, six members had fought in general elections, and one member was a current councillor on Swansea Council.
137 NLW, Lord Hooson Papers, Box 42, Letter from Leslie Jones to Hooson, 2 July 1967.
138 This, of course, could mean that these were among the records that did not survive being stored in a damp garage.
139 Russell Deacon, 'The Steady Tapping Breaks the Rock', *Journal of Liberal History*, 22 (Spring 1999), 15.
140 NLW, Minutes of the WLP Council Meeting, 29 September 1973, p. 3. My emphasis.
141 NLW, Merfyn Jones Papers, File 35, Minutes of the WLP Executive Committee, 20 July 1974.
142 Hando, a former teacher, is currently Newport County AFC's honorary president and former chairman.
143 NLW, Letter from Lord Hooson to David Hando, 28 February 1973. Hooson decided to take the NHS from Hando and give it to Dr David Williams.
144 NLW, WLP Press Release by David Hando, 19 February 1973.
145 Steve Belzak, 'Swinging in the '60s to the Liberals: Mary Murphy and Pontypridd Urban District Council', *Journal of Liberal History*, 68 (Autumn 2010), 33.
146 NLW, WLP Papers, file A40, Policy Directorate – General Guidance, 25 June 1975. NLW, WLP Papers, File C11, Meeting of the Policy Directorate, 1 May 1976. Apart from Hooson, the members included Gareth Morgan, Dr Jennifer Lloyd, Dr David Williams, Geoffrey Heys, Gwyn Griffiths and Richard Livsey. The directorate would have different members passing through it, but these were the initial members.
147 NLW, Merfyn Jones Papers, File 40, Discussion Paper on the Proposal to Set Up the Post of Directorate of Policy by Terry Thomas, 1977.
148 NLW, WLP File C11, Letter from Gwyn Griffiths to the Members of the Executive and Policy Directorate, 16 March 1979.
149 NLW, WLP Papers, File A4, Executive Committee Report (Draft) by John Roberts, 19 June 1976, p. 3.
150 NLW, WLP File C11, Letter from Gwyn Griffiths to the Members of the Executive and Policy Directorate, 16 March 1979.
151 NLW, WLP Archive, File C11, Memo to the Policy Directorate from the Chairman of the WLP Weekend Schools Committee, 10 November 1976.

152 NLW, Lord Hooson Papers, Box 42, Memorandum to the Executive of the LPW from Martin Thomas, 28 July 1966. Items 5 and 8(e).
153 *North Wales Weekly News*, 15 September 1966, 15.
154 Government of Wales Bill 1967. Available at: *https://parlipapers.proquest.com/parlipapers/* (accessed 1 August 2024).
155 HC Debate, 1 March 1967, vol. 742, col. 418. Available at: *https://hansard.parliament.uk/commons/1967-03-01/debates/73586515-ebae-47fe-8160-d1de6a0837a0/GovernmentOfWales* (accessed 1 August 2024).
156 HC Debate, 1 March 1967, vol. 742, col. 418.
157 HL Debate, 30 January 1968, Fifth Series, vol. 288, col. 762. Available at: *https://hansard.parliament.uk/Lords/1968-01-30/debates/f6458a99-f92c-4cce-97e4-2ed65bd47394/GovernmentOfWalesBillHl* (accessed 1 August 2024).
158 *Royal Commission on the Constitution, Minutes of Evidence I*, 19 November 1969, p. 17. Available at: *https://archive.org/details/op. 1267081-1001/page/n15/mode/2up?q=The+Structure+of+the+Welsh+Economy* (accessed 1 August 2024).
159 Deacon, *Welsh Liberals*, pp. 179–80. Deacon states, on p. 180, that *Life to a Nation* was the WLP's 1970 general election manifesto. Whilst the manifesto drew on the policy document, the WLP manifesto was unimaginatively titled *Welsh Liberal Party Manifesto: The Liberal Case for Wales*.
160 NLW, Lord Hooson Papers, File 116/1, *Life to a Nation: An Economic Policy for Wales*, p. 10.
161 NLW, Lord Hooson Papers, File 116/1, *Life to a Nation: An Economic Policy for Wales*, pp. 1–7.
162 NLW, Lord Hooson Papers, File 116/1, *Life to a Nation: An Economic Policy for Wales*, p. 10.
163 NLW, Cardiganshire Liberal Association, File 120, *Welsh Liberal Party Manifesto: The Liberal Case for Wales*, p. 6.
164 NLW, WLP File A29, 'The Liberal Proposal for a Welsh Development Fund', a message from Hooson to the Council of the WLP, undated but around 1971.
165 Cwmdeithas Hanes Plaid Cymru History Society, 'Leaflets before 1970', Image 6, 'water water everywhere: alwen efyrnwy tryweryn elan claerwen clywedog – dulas?' No date, but after 1967. Available at: *www.hanesplaidcymru.org/taflenni-cyn-1970/nggallery/thumbnails?lang=en* (accessed 1 August 2024).
166 Edwards, *Labour's Crisis*, p. 165, n.54.
167 Edwards, *Labour's Crisis*, p. 102.
168 *Daily Mirror*, 14 May 1971, 2.
169 *Birmingham Daily Post*, 6 February 1970.
170 NLW, Lord Hooson Files, Box 54, Welsh Language File, Press Release from David Hando/Monmouth Liberal Association to Donald Anderson, 5 February 1970.
171 NLW, Cardiganshire Liberal Association, File 120, *Welsh Liberal Party Manifesto: The Liberal Case for Wales*, p. 5.
172 Butt Philip, *The Welsh Question*, pp. 117–18. 'Blaid' can be used as well as Plaid to denote Plaid Cymru. In Welsh, the initial consonant 'p' undergoes a soft

mutation to 'b'. See Charlotte Aull Davies, *Welsh Nationalism in the Twentieth Century: The Ethnic Option and the Modern State* (New York, 1989), p. 20, n.3.
173 NLW, Lord Hooson Papers, Box 12, Government of UK (No.1) Bill, Archbishop of Cardiff's correspondence. The document is an amalgamation of correspondence relating to the drafting of Lord Ogmore's Bill. Undated but prior to the 30 January 1968 debate in the House of Lords.
174 HL Debate, 30 January 1968, Fifth Series, vol. 288, col. 737. Available at: *https://hansard.parliament.uk/Lords/1968-01-30/debates/f6458a99-f92c-4cce-97e4-2ed65bd47394/GovernmentOfWalesBillHl* (accessed 1 August 2024).
175 Butt Philip, *The Welsh Question*, p. 69.
176 NLW, Cardiganshire Liberal Association, File 120, *Welsh Liberal Party Manifesto: The Liberal Case for Wales*, p. 6.
177 NLW, WLP File A29, Emlyn Hooson, 'The Future of the Welsh Language', draft policy for consideration by the WLP Council, 5 December 1971.
178 Deacon, *Welsh Liberals*, p. 185. S4C (Sianel Pedwar Cymru) would begin on 1 November 1982.
179 *Digest of Welsh Historical Statistics, 1974–96*, p. 149. Available at: *https://gov.wales/digest-welsh-historical-statistics-0* (accessed 1 August 2024). For example, in 1974 there were 1,325,000 working days lost to industrial stoppages in Wales, compared with 255,000 in 1975.
180 Williams, *Digest*, ch. 2, table 2.7. These figures show the total number of people unemployed for eight weeks or less to those with over twenty-six weeks of unemployment. The figures between 1971 and 1973 start at the age of 14 and end at 65. From 1974 onwards, the figures for age are classed as 'under 20' to '40 and over'. All unemployment figures are from January of each year except for 1974 and 1975, which are mid-year, due to an energy crisis and industrial action, respectively.
181 *Digest of Welsh Historical Statistics, 1974–96*, p. 145. Available at: *https://gov.wales/digest-welsh-historical-statistics-0* (accessed 1 August 2024).
182 Deacon, *Welsh Liberals*, p. 185.
183 NLW, WLP File A29, *The Liberal Proposal for a Welsh Development Fund*, a message from Hooson to the Council of the WLP, undated.
184 Deacon, *Welsh Liberals*, p. 185.
185 NLW, WLP File C11, Minutes of the Policy Directorate Committee, 4 September 1976, as an example of all this activity.
186 NLW, Merfyn Jones Papers, File 47, *Social Security Benefits: A Discussion Document*, March 1977.
187 NLW, WLP Archive, File H5, Transport Policy, Gwyn Griffiths, 31 July 1977.
188 NLW, Merfyn Jones Papers, File 35, Written Evidence to the Royal Commission on the NHS, December 1976.
189 NLW, WLP File H5, Resolution to Conference – Addition to Resolution No. 3 – Transport.
190 Iain Dale (ed.), *Liberal Party General Election Manifestos, 1900–1997* (London, 2000), pp. 124 and 140.
191 Dale, *Liberal Party*, p. 140.

192 NLW, Lord Hooson Papers, File 116/1, Hooson and Jenkins, *The Heartland*, p. 10.
193 NLW, Merfyn Jones Papers, File 35, Memo Regarding Proposed Changes to the Agricultural Policy of the United Kingdom, 20 July 1974.
194 Dale, *Liberal Party*, p. 140.
195 NLW, Cardiganshire Liberal Association, File 120, *Welsh Liberal Party Manifesto: The Liberal Case for Wales*, pp. 4–5.
196 NLW, Merfyn Jones Papers, File 47, A Summary of the Agricultural Policy Recommendations made by the Policy Directorate, 16 May 1970.
197 Dale, *Liberal Party*, p. 140.
198 Deacon, *Welsh Liberals*, p. 204.
199 'From humble beginnings... A history of the FUW', *Daily Post*, 17 November 2005. Available at *https://www.dailypost.co.uk/business/business-news/humble-beginnings-history-fuw-2902984* (accessed 1 August 2024).

4

THE ELECTORAL LEGACY UNDER EMLYN HOOSON

INTRODUCTION

The accepted history of the Welsh Liberals in twentieth-century Wales is one of eclipse. The party was gradually eclipsed by Labour during the 1920s, reducing the Liberals from the first party of Wales to the second. In the 1930s, they were eclipsed by the Conservatives and were pushed into third place. The LPW/WLP maintained this position until the 1970 general election, when the party was briefly relegated to the fourth position, behind Plaid Cymru.[1] In his study of Plaid Cymru, Labour and the Conservatives in north-west Wales, Edwards states that: 'Because the Liberals did not pose a realistic threat to Labour after 1959, [this book] pays less attention to the party's activities than its closest rivals'. Edwards's explanation for leaving out the WLP has also been the often-unacknowledged reason the party has been ignored by many Welsh historians, namely that they did not have the MPs and, by extension, no longer had any real influence in Wales. At best, they are viewed as a party that held no relevance to the Wales of the 1960s and 1970s.

Yet, these assumptions and analyses have rarely been challenged. This chapter will argue that the WLP was still an electoral force that enjoyed a great deal of support. It will be divided into two sections. The first will examine the electoral record of the WLP between 1967 and 1979, the year that Hooson lost his seat. This section will demonstrate that the WLP progressed during this period, and that it was the vagaries of the British electoral system that denied the standing that the party's share of the vote demanded. It will argue that historians have placed too much importance on the contest between Labour and Plaid, spending too little time examining the electoral support of the WLP. As such, this chapter will be framed by the electoral battle between the WLP and Plaid, as they were competing against each other. Labour and the Conservatives will be considered, where necessary, but this is an examination of the two smaller parties in Wales. The chapter will also give an insight into how the candidates were chosen and the financial burden placed on the local associations during elections.

The second section will examine why Hooson lost his Montgomery seat at the 1979 general election. There have been many explanations as to why, ranging from an influx of English migrants, to his support for the Lib-Lab Pact and the devolution referendum, to the demands of Hooson's legal career. This section will examine those arguments and will show that Hooson understood that his seat was in peril but still stood by his political principles. It will be argued that there was no one cause for the loss of Hooson's seat but that it was due to a combination of factors, primarily his support for the Lib-Lab Pact and devolution, the state of his local constituency and the historical 'small c' conservative nature of the constituency.

This chapter will be an unashamed revisionist history of the WLP's electoral fortunes during this period. It will show that the WLP has been incorrectly ignored by historians that have been more focused on the issues between Plaid and the Labour Party. This chapter aims to show that the WLP are deserving of a place within the historiography of the 1970s, rather than being dismissed from it.

ELECTORAL RECORD

No history of a political party is complete without an analysis of its electoral record. Remarkably, there has been very little analysis of the electoral fortunes of the WLP (as opposed to the LPW) in the political historiography of Wales or the Liberal Party. There have been fleeting references to Hooson's by-election win in 1962[2] and the WLP election results in the 1974 general election,[3] and a few more to Hooson losing his seat at the 1979 general election.[4] However, the two main historians of this period in Welsh Liberal history, Russell Deacon and J. Graham Jones, have followed the accepted wisdom that the WLP was eclipsed by Plaid and remained as 'also-rans'.

Between 1967 and 1979, there were only three by-elections held within Wales: Rhondda West in 1967, Caerphilly in 1968 and Merthyr Tydfil in 1972. The WLP fought the latter two seats but also considered fighting the first. Two of the three by-elections occurred before the 1970 general election and it is quite clear that there were reservations about standing a candidate in these seats.

Following the death of the Rhondda Labour MP, Iorwerth Thomas, a by-election was held on 9 March 1967, which would have been an early test for the newly founded WLP. However, the lack of organisation in the constituency was particularly evident and the WLP steering committee decided not to contest the seat unless a well-known candidate could be secured.[5] The seat was held by Labour, with Plaid coming second and reducing the larger party's lead from 16,888 votes to just 2,306.[6] Hooson was particularly scornful of the steering committee's decision not to field a Liberal candidate, stating 'I think their decision was wrong and all I hope is that we have learnt our lesson'. Hooson further explained, 'my own view is that they will now accept my proposal that every single by-election in Wales must be fought as well as the 36 Welsh seats at the next General Election'.[7]

However, the standing committee's decision may have been quite prescient, under the circumstances. On 18 July 1968, the Caerphilly by-election was held following the death of Ness Williams, the Labour MP, and the WLP entered its first election for a parliamentary seat. The constituency had last been contested by the Liberals in 1929 and this was reflected in the results, with the candidate, Peter Sadler, finishing last, with 3.6% of the vote. The real significance of the by-election, though, was that the second-placed Plaid candidate, Dr Phil Williams, reduced Labour's lead from 21,148 votes in 1966 to 1,874 in 1968.[8] Including Carmarthen in 1966, this was the third Welsh by-election in a row in which Plaid was able to challenge the Labour Party. However, it was clear that the WLP were in no position to mount an electoral attack on a staunchly Labour seat, especially with a resurgent Plaid Cymru contesting the seat as well.

The candidate, Peter Sadler, on the eve of the poll, stated, somewhat naively, that 'I think we can be a good third',[9] but, in the event, came a distant fourth behind the Communist candidate. An internal WLP report noted, 'This was frankly a shambles . . . nearly every basic mistake that could be made was made'.[10] However, the mistake was putting up a candidate at all. In an eve of election address to the party activists, Hooson lays bare that, due to its last having been fought by a Liberal in 1929, the by-election was 'Not a very propitious constituency . . . to begin our campaign, but nevertheless, this is where we are going to begin it'. Hooson also mentioned that 'we have spent two years setting up our party, finding our candidates . . . *creating a basic skeletal organisation*'.[11] To have pitted themselves against two powerful adversaries that were adept at fighting by-elections, before the basic local and central Liberal organisation was properly in place, was foolhardy. As noted in a previous chapter, Plaid had significant experience in mounting successful by-election campaigns throughout the 1950s and 1960s. They would target their resources (finances and people) specifically to maximise the potential vote of the party, whereas the Liberals preferred to fight general elections, had little experience of fighting by-elections and were unable to match Plaid in campaign style or finances. Despite this, the WLP had to begin somewhere, and the decision to not contest the Rhondda West by-election had been criticised internally and externally.[12] It also gave the WLP a chance to understand what the party was up against, especially in a seat that had not seen a Liberal candidate in forty years.

This lack of by-election experience would have continued to hamper the WLP, especially in seats that had not been fought since the 1929 general election. Luckily for the WLP, there was just one by-election in the 1970s, Merthyr Tydfil. As if in acknowledgement of the mountain that they would have to climb, Hooson wrote in October 1967, 'I live in dread of a by-election in the completely barren constituencies. One such is Merthyr Tydfil where S. O. Davies is the Member; he is over 80.'[13] The LPW/WLP had refrained from putting up a general election candidate against Davies, and it is not difficult to ascertain why. Finances and organisation had been an issue, but Davies was also a very popular politician. This was evidenced by his decision to stand as an independent Labour candidate in 1970 after the Labour Party tried to force him to retire. He retained his seat against the official Labour candidate and with a sizeable majority, albeit reduced when compared with 1966.[14] He was something of a maverick, unafraid to express his Welsh nationalism, and worked cross-party on the Parliament for Wales campaign and sponsored Hooson's 1967 Government of Wales Bill. Angus Donaldson, standing for the WLP and famous for wearing a deerstalker hat, lost his deposit and, to add insult to injury, was presented with a bill for £25.57[15] for the rates of premises hired during the by-election. The WLP stance was that Donaldson and his agent, Kenner Jones, were 'responsible in law for the running of the campaign and declaring and meeting your expenses'.[16]

This was a bill that Donaldson felt the WLP should pay, 'this for the general sake of the good name of the Party', further noting that 'We all made mistakes at Merthyr'.[17] The campaign was further brought into disrepute by another unpaid bill, this time for election leaflets totalling £54.75,[18] a bill that could not be met by the Merthyr Tydfil Liberal Association 'as they do not appear to have any funds'.[19] Although there is little doubt that these bills were paid by the head office in Cardiff, it shows a naivety on the part of the WLP that they expected the candidate to cover his expenses and a derelict association to do likewise. This was an issue that had shown its head before, most notably with the financial issue surrounding the Gibbs (see chapter one).

Again, it was the WLP's lack of by-election experience, coupled with an equal lack of finances, which saw the party come last. It was at this, albeit belated, point that Hooson put forward several proposals for fighting a by-election that included not entering 'any by-election unless we are prepared to spend £1,000[20] on the campaign'. Hooson also suggested that the WLP 'should prepare a blueprint . . . for fighting a by-election in various categories of seat'.[21] It is unclear as to whether such plans were implemented, as there was not another by-election in Wales until 1982.[22] However, what is clear is that the WLP were not adept at fighting by-elections, especially on the same level as Plaid, who 'build up an atmosphere (through heavy cost) and this is very important with regard to wavering voters'.[23] By-elections were not indicative of the electoral performance of the WLP, but it was undoubtedly correct to contest them, even if they were sure to lose. This is because they provided an electoral experience to the party activists and the WLP, particularly as targeting a specific seat is different from a general election, where every seat is in play. However, as by-elections were too few and far between to be of any use as a barometer of the electoral state of the party, the first true electoral test of the WLP would be the 1970 general election.

CANDIDATE SELECTION

In terms of candidate selection, a lot of the work had been undertaken by both general secretaries, Mary Murphy and Emlyn Thomas (see chapter two). However, thirteen of the nineteen candidates were members of the executive or were known, through professional friendships, to members of the executive and Hooson. It would not be unfair to point out that they were selected based on their ability to pay for or contribute to the election costs. Table 20 shows the breakdown of professions.

Table 20: Professions of 1970 general election candidates[24]

Profession	Law	Medicine	Business	Education	Agriculture
Number of candidates	7	1	5	5	1

This situation is hardly surprising, especially when one considers the financial state of the WLP. However, it did not do much for the egalitarian image that the party wanted to portray. After all, the preamble to the 1970 manifesto read: 'The Welsh Liberal Party is a Welsh Party. And it is a party not only for the people of Wales, but of the people of Wales.'[25] Yet, this need to attract wealthy candidates points to how unlikely it would have been for a person from a less affluent or professional background to contest a seat. This type of selection, based on who could pay, was a feature of the election process throughout the 1970s and beyond.

As an example of the lengths the WLP would go to entice a prospective candidate, one needs to look no further than the case of W. Armon Ellis. Ellis was a solicitor, a Liberal county councillor and a former prospective parliamentary candidate (PPC) in 1950 and 1951. Hooson felt that Ellis was 'the only one who could win Denbigh for us, but, at the moment, he's very much a man of the periphery of Liberalism', but 'as quite a power in North Wales', it was decided to try and entice Ellis with the offer of lunch with Lord Ogmore in the House of Lords.[26] Although his candidacy did not come to fruition, as Idris Hughes-Evans stood in the seat, it is indicative of the lengths that the party would go to for the 'right candidate', and especially one that could pay their way.

Nominally, the local associations were free to choose who would be their candidate but, as the above shows, these decisions were open to influence from the centre of the party. As another example of the influence of the centre, Hooson wrote to Tom Crowther, one of the three potential candidates for Newport, to ask him to 'persuade the association to adopt someone as soon as possible, if only to release the interest and attention of the remaining two to pass to "pastures elsewhere"'. Hooson even suggested that, due to one of the candidates being Welsh speaking, he 'would do very well in one of the west Wales constituencies. Do have a word with him'.[27] Clearly, Hooson was trying to influence the outcome of the proceedings, one way or another. In the end, only one of the candidates would stand for the WLP, David Hando in Monmouth. There would be no candidate in Newport until 1974.

INFLUENCING CONSTITUENCY CHOICE

Before the October 1974 general election, discussions began on forming a candidate committee, which would have 'no power to impose a choice on any constituency, it was recommended that the committee should vet potential candidates and advise constituencies not to adopt until the committee had had an opportunity to express its views'.[28] It was initially hoped that the recently departed Lord Lloyd of Kilgerran would be able to chair the committee, but he declined to do so.[29] Following the October 1974 general election, it was decided that the candidate committee would be 'reconstituted on a permanent basis' and that the 'powers of the Candidates' Committee would be to make a recommendation, or to withhold official WLP support, rather than to force any choice on a constituency'.[30] It is difficult to believe that the intention was not to force the will of the WLP's executive committee, with regard to a candidate, on that of the constituency. This committee was a coercive tactic by the WLP to vet and, essentially, approve a candidate.

Yet, the WLP also had other methods at its disposal for dealing with recalcitrant constituencies when it came to candidate selection. In September 1978, the Brecon and Radnor Liberal Association (BRLA), informed the WLP executive that they had voted by nineteen votes to sixteen not to contest the next general election. Those sixteen who had decided to contest the election formed a breakaway group called the 'Brecon and Radnor General Election Committee' (BRGEC), and adopted Norman Lewis as their candidate. The WLP immediately disaffiliated the BRLA and recognised the BRGEC. Although the executive committee's authorisation for disaffiliating the BRLA was a tad spurious, in that they cited clauses 16 and 19a of the WLP constitution,[31] with clause 16 referring to a constituency being able to affiliate if they have 'at least 20 paid up members'. In this instance, the WLP appear to be stating that they only have nineteen members (ignoring that the breakaway group had sixteen). Clause 19a stated that: 'The Executive Committee may refuse or revoke the affiliation of any Constituency Association which in its opinion does not support the aims and objects of the Party'.[32] By disaffiliating the BRLA, they were going against the results of the democratic vote of the local party. Of course, by recognising the breakaway BRGEC, they were securing a candidate for the next general election.

WELSHNESS

It has already been established that Hooson wanted to promote the WLP's Welsh cultural credentials. Between 1945 and 1983, every Liberal MP in Wales could speak Welsh,[33] and it was an important consideration when it came to choosing the candidates. In an obvious piece of targeting, Welsh-speaking candidates were deployed to areas that were traditional bastions of the language. It is no accident that of the seventy-four candidates chosen as prospective parliamentary candidates (PPCs) between 1970 and 1979, thirty-three of them were Welsh speaking.[34] Nearly all of them, with some exceptions,[35] fought in Welsh-speaking constituencies.

Although it was important for the WLP to field Welsh speakers, the results were a mixed bag. In counties where more than twenty per cent of people could speak Welsh[36] and an identifiable Welsh-speaking WLP candidate stood, a Plaid candidate would often be behind the Liberal. It must be pointed out that the WLP was relatively weak in the areas that Plaid captured or came second in.[37] The opposite is true for areas that the WLP captured or came second in.[38] Table 21 demonstrates this by showing the number of times that each party finished ahead of the other, whilst table 22 shows the relative weakness of either the WLP or Plaid in seats that either party won or came second in. Both tables relate only to an identified Welsh-speaking WLP candidate standing against Plaid.

Table 21: Results of identifiable Welsh-language candidates in direct competition with Plaid Cymru, 1970–9

Party	1970 General election[39]	Lost deposits[40]	Feb. 1974 General election[41]	Lost deposits	Oct. 1974 General election[42]	Lost deposits	1979 General election[43]	Lost deposits
WLP	5	4	4	1	4	2	6	5
Plaid Cymru	5	5	3	3	3	3	3	5
Total	10	9	7	4	7	5	9	10

Although table 21 does not provide the full picture of those contests, it demonstrates that the WLP's strategy would often pay off. Table 21 shows that the WLP was able to do well in constituencies that had a high number of Welsh speakers and would lose fewer of their deposits too, albeit marginally. Table 22 is interesting, as it provides some good examples of how far the WLP had come, whilst showing the mountain they had to climb to reclaim constituencies that were once LPW strongholds.

Table 22: Weakness of WLP or PC in seats where either took first or second placing[44]

	1970 WLP% of vote, placing	1970 PC % of vote, placing	Feb.1974 WLP % of vote, placing	Feb.1974 PC % of vote, placing	Oct.1974 WLP % of vote, placing	Oct.1974 PC % of vote, placing	1979 WLP% of vote, placing	1979 PC % of vote, placing
Cardigan/ Ceredigion	29.6% 2/4	19.6% 3/4	40.2% 1/4	13.3% 4/4	42.1% 1/4	13.2% 3/4	35.6% 1/4	14.5% 4/4
Carmarthen	21.8% 3/4	30.1% 2/4	19.4% 3/4	34.3% 2/4	10.4% 3/5	45.1% 1/5	8% 4/6	32% 2/6
Denbigh	18.1% 3/4	11% 4/4	30% 2/4	8.1% 4/4	29.3% 2/4	11.9% 4/4	28.2% 2/4	9.3% 4/4
Merioneth	22.6% 3/4	24.3% 2/4	18.4% 3/4	34.6% 1/4	15.4% 3/4	42.5% 1/4	12.1% 4/4	40.8% 1/4
Montgomery	38.4% 1/4	6.7% 4/4	45.4% 1/4	8.3% 4/4	43.1% 1/4	9.3% 4/4	34.9% 2/4	8.5% 4/4

Ceredigion had fallen out of Liberal hands at the 1966 general election and had become a Labour seat. It became a Labour/Liberal marginal seat in 1974, when Geraint Howells became MP. However, Plaid were in a minor position up until 1992, when they unexpectedly took the seat. The reason for Plaid's lack of success here was due to a strong Liberal presence. In other seats, the strategy had been to target Labour, but in the marginal seats, where both main parties were strong, it would have been difficult for Plaid to offer a credible alternative. Denbigh was slightly different, in that a Conservative held the seat, but the Liberals had held the second position at every general election since 1955, with Labour only taking that position in 1970. Denbigh, like Montgomery, was a rural, 'small c' conservative seat that had elected a National Liberal or a Conservative since 1931, with the LPW/WLP running a close second. Again, Plaid could not offer something different in a seat that was conservative and where the Liberals and/or Labour were strong.

In the seats that Plaid won, there was a different reason as to why the Liberals posed no threat to them. Both Merioneth and Carmarthen had been Liberal seats until 1951 and 1957, respectively. In Merioneth, from 1931, the Labour Party had been able to appeal to Liberal voters and turn it into a marginal constituency, but a heavy Liberal presence remained. The rural nature of the constituency, the language and the sense of Welshness had kept the Liberals as the main challenger to Labour. Yet, like so many former Liberal seats that fell to Labour between the 1920s and 1950s, once Labour was able to demonstrate that they could appeal to the traditional Liberal base, whilst offering something new or ingratiating themselves with links to the trade unions, then the Liberal support fell. In such circumstances, Plaid were able to appeal to the Liberal base but also beyond. Plaid's candidate, Dafydd Elis Thomas, was young, he had an active organisation and, coupled with being able to speak Welsh, he understood the rural issues and interests in trade unionism, he was able to demonstrate a natural appeal to the electorate.[45] He took the seat in February 1974 during Plaid's onslaught in north-west Wales.

Similarly, in Carmarthen, the seat had fallen to Labour; however, as previously noted, it was to the former deputy leader of the Liberal Party, Megan Lloyd George. When Gwynfor Evans took the seat in 1966, it was lost to the WLP. Labour was in second place at the 1966 by-election but had retaken it by the slimmest of margins in 1970, retaining it in February 1974 but losing it to Plaid in October 1974, with Labour regaining it in

1979. Following that, it remained a Labour seat, with Plaid and the Conservatives vying for second place during the 1980s and 1990s.

The pattern established in table 22 is different from that established by most of the seats that make up the results in table 21. If we were to look at the pattern for areas such as Llanelli and Anglesey, a more mixed set of results appears, once we factor in a WLP candidate that was not identified as Welsh speaking. Other than a steady increase in the party's share of the vote, the WLP were never able to escape from fourth place behind Plaid on Anglesey. A Welsh-speaking candidate would have provided the WLP with a level of respectability, but Plaid had established itself more fully since 1966. The LPW did not contest the seat in 1966 and the party's share of the vote had fallen from 20.4% in 1964 to 6.2% in 1970, whilst Plaid had increased its vote from 6.5% in 1964 to 22.1% in 1970.[46]

Conversely, Llanelli was a real battleground for the Liberals and Plaid during the 1970s. In 1964, the LPW had taken 12.2% and Plaid were on 7%, taking third and fourth place, respectively.[47] The LPW did not contest the seat in 1966, the WLP stood in 1970 but had dropped to fourth place with just 7.7% of the vote to Plaid's second-placed 16.8%.[48] Yet by October 1974, the WLP would switch this result and take second place to Plaid's third. However, Llanelli had a strong Labour majority throughout the 1960s and 1970s, so we find the Conservatives, Plaid and WLP within a few percentage points of each other. Again, in such a constituency that was both rural and industrial, any advantage in appealing to these areas would be taken, and the Welsh language was a prime example of this.

What we need to take away from this is that the WLP understood that it had to promote its Welshness if it was to progress and tackle the threat from Plaid. It is difficult to say whether it was a successful policy but, undoubtedly, if they had not placed a Welsh-speaking candidate, they were in danger of alienating a significant part of the electorate in some seats.

GENERAL ELECTIONS 1970-9

Harold Wilson's Labour government had been expected to win the 1970 general election but had become a victim of circumstances. Between the 1966 and 1970 general elections, the government faced several headwinds that included a devaluation of sterling in 1967, large trade deficits necessitating budget cuts and tax increases, and, finally, abandoned trade union legislation in 1969. These issues were perceived to be mute when the trade figures started to improve in 1969, and the polls were running in Labour's favour. Yet, as Clarke notes, when polling day approached the tide began to turn in the Conservatives' favour, with disappointing trade figures, a random poll that gave a Tory lead and a five per cent drop in voter turnout, meaning that many people who might have voted Labour stayed at home.[49] The result was that a Conservative government, under Edward Heath, came to power.

The 1970 general election was a difficult election for the Liberals, whether Welsh, Scottish or English. The Liberal Party was faced with its own issues, which included the Young Liberals, who were generally seen as being to the left of the mainstream party. Commonly referred to as the 'Red Guards', the Young Liberals advocated worker control of nationalised industries and would be militant in their campaigning. A case in point was the 'Stop the Tour' protests, which were against South African sporting teams playing in the UK, which saw cricket grounds vandalised. Added to this was a sense that the UK Liberal revival of the early 1960s had run its course, and the by-election wins had petered out. Wallace points to the 'apparent irrelevance of the Liberals to the central issues of the campaign' meaning that the Liberals did not have anything to say on economics or industry.[50] The manifesto has been described as lacking a 'coherent overall theme, merely listing a set of grievances afflicting the British people'.[51] All of this was compounded by the party only contesting 332 of the 630 seats available. Essentially, the Liberal Party did not even pretend that it was a serious contender to form a government, and was in danger of losing its identity.

There is no doubt that the WLP had a manifesto that was better thought through than the national manifesto. The WLP manifesto was Wales-centric and based on its two economic policy documents *Life to a Nation* and *The Heartland*. The WLP had something to say and offer on issues that mattered to Wales, from a domestic parliament to local government reform, rural development agencies and agriculture to Welsh-language television programmes. As the manifesto was examined in the previous chapter, there is no need to comment further on this, which will be the same for the 1974 and 1979 manifestos.

Although the general elections have been touched upon in previous chapters, there has not been any analysis of the results and what they meant to the progress of the WLP. The aim here is to show that the WLP made significant progress under Hooson and that it was the correct decision to form the new party. We cannot divorce the LPW and the WLP from the wider issues affecting the Liberal Party in the UK, as these did have a bearing on the WLP, particularly in 1970 and 1979. However, the WLP under Hooson made great strides electorally, even if it was not always reflected in the number of MPs elected.

For several reasons, it is logical to take the 1966 general election as our starting point. Firstly, it was the final general election before the formation of the WLP; secondly, apart from 1959, it was the LPW's lowest percentage share of the vote; and lastly, the number of candidates was the least it had fielded since 1959 (there had been twelve candidates in 1964). As such, it provides a perfect base to measure the WLP's advance. It will be shown that at every subsequent general election, the WLP made a noticeable advancement in both candidates and positioning. Throughout, there will be a comparison made with Plaid, as it will be the contention that the LPW/WLP were generally a more popular party.

Table 23: LPW and PC positions in every constituency with a candidate, 1966[52]

Party	Vote share	Number of candidates	Direct contests (LPW/PC)	First position	Second position	Third position	Fourth position
LPW	6.3%	11	9	1	4	6	0
Plaid Cymru	4.3%	20		0	1	12	7

As table 23 demonstrates, it was not all bad news for the LPW in 1966, as the party had finished ahead of Plaid in terms of its share of the vote, despite fielding nine fewer candidates than its opponent. Also, in the nine contests where both parties faced each other, the LPW was ahead of Plaid in every seat. However, this was small comfort to the LPW and it was these election results, coupled with the Carmarthen by-election, that sealed the LPW's fate and ushered in the formation of the WLP.

As the previous chapters have shown, the WLP pushed for a greater cohort of candidates for the 1970 general election. Other than the by-elections which, as we have established, were not the best way to examine the WLP's electoral chances, the 1970 general election would be the party's first real electoral test. Yet, the WLP faced several challenges for this general election. The first was that the number of seats fought was well below the standard Hooson had set for the WLP. In 1967, Hooson stated that the aim was to contest all '36 seats at the next general Election',[53] and by 1969 had boasted that 'we have adopted Candidates in 22 of the 36 constituencies. We are anxious to fight all the constituencies, if this is humanly possible within our resources.'[54] However, when it came to the actual general election, the WLP would field only nineteen candidates. It is not clear what happened to the three extra candidates, but two examples could shed light on the internal rifts within the party.

The first example is that of Peter Jacobs, the WLP spokesperson on foreign affairs and PPC for Barry. Jacobs resigned his position in a letter to Hooson, which he also made public via the *Western Mail*. Jacobs's reason for resigning was what he perceived to be the rightward shift that had taken place since the formation of the WLP. He stated that the party had 'shown itself to be more conservative on such issues as the South African political situation, Rhodesian sanctions, the European Common Market and Industrial Democracy'. He took further issue with his fellow candidates:

> Mr Huw Thomas came to Barry and took a Powellite line on immigration . . . Cllr. Angus Donaldson has advocated the death penalty for those who cause death by blowing up pipelines. He has conducted a witch hunt against a fellow councillor who opposed the Springbok tour. I was dismayed at Cllr. Mary Murphy's opposition to the 'Killing of Sister George', a film of some merit being shown in Pontypridd . . . I find it ironic that I feel compelled to resign because my policies have remained orthodox Liberal Policies.[55]

In many ways, this was just as much an attack on Hooson and the direction of the WLP, as it was on the individuals mentioned. This is even acknowledged as such by Hooson in his reply, where he makes it clear that he did not support the boycotting of the Springbok rugby tour. Hooson's views on continuing trade with South Africa, as well as other dubious regimes, were quite well known. Explaining his opposition to a conference amendment by the National League of Young Liberals (NLYL), which urged sanctions against South Africa, Hooson argued that:

> I hate many aspects of the Chinese Government particularly the way it deals with minorities, but I think we should trade with China. All of us, as Liberals, hate many aspects of the

South African Government, but I think we should trade with South Africa.[56]

These remarks could cast Hooson as an apologist for such regimes, but they were entirely consistent with his internationalist outlook and Liberal principles on free trade.

Further, Hooson initially chastises Jacobs on the EEC issue by arguing that 'I think you will find I was advocating entry into the Common Market long before you were against other people in our party'. However, Hooson then concedes that he now has 'increasing reservations' on joining, 'largely on political grounds', which included EEC members wanting to get hold of 'British atomic know-how for a European nuclear deterrent'.[57] Hooson's opposition to joining the EEC was just as well-known as his opinions on the South African issue. Hooson was by no means the only Liberal MP with misgivings about joining the Common Market[58] but, following the 1970 general election, the others had lost their seats and he remained a lone voice against entry.

The other example is the famous case, within Liberal circles at least, of Winston Roddick, PPC for Anglesey. In March 1970, the Anglesey Liberal Association sent a letter to Roddick, requesting his resignation, as the

> Association had not made the anticipated headway over the past twelve months, and consequently . . . the Executive agreed that the distance between your home and the constituency made it impracticable that you should continue . . . I therefore, very regretfully have to . . . request that you . . . consider resignation of your candidature .[59]

Roddick forwarded the letter to Hooson, stating that 'I was given no hint at all of this "coup". I think I'm being blamed for their faults . . . I can only presume that they are telling the truth when they say that the reason for all this is that I don't live in the constituency'.⁶⁰ Hooson wrote to the constituency treasurer, Mrs Edwards, reminding her that he had 'the highest regard for Mr Roddick', and chastised the constituency officers for the lack of progress, stating that 'what happens in Anglesey has its effect on other constituencies'. Hooson then asked for her confidential views on the real reason and whether it was financial.⁶¹ The response received amounted to an accusation that Roddick was not prepared to fulfil any of the engagements that he had promised to attend, had his travel expenses paid and requested that his wife's expenses be paid, too. The constituency felt this was unfair. Roddick, who lived outside the constituency, was their first choice over a more local person, on the basis that he promised to visit once per month.⁶²

It is unclear as to whether Roddick was informed of the contents of this follow-up letter, as the myth appears to be that the constituency were acting to oust him either in favour of another candidate or because he lived elsewhere and they did not want to pay his expenses. Regardless, Roddick remained the PPC for Anglesey, and Hooson's intervention probably secured his position. Yet, Mrs Edwards also referred to 'a lack of leadership since we went over to the Welsh Liberal Party. We have lost many faithful and valued members of the Executive Committee as a result of the changeover'.⁶³ This sense of alienation within the constituency parties, coupled with a loss of senior members, would rear its head in subsequent general elections. It might not be too much of a stretch to state that the problems of Anglesey were felt in the other seventeen constituencies that were not fought in 1970. Equally, there were also issues at the candidate level, whether one that was seemingly uninterested in nurturing a constituency like Anglesey or one that felt they were too liberal for the WLP.

Other issues that affected the WLP included the already mentioned 'Stop the Tour' protests, which saw the NLYL targeting both the 1970 Springboks rugby tour and the South African cricket tour. The vandalising of cricket grounds had become a major topic, nowhere more so than within the WLP. Angus Donaldson wrote to Hooson lambasting the NLYL as 'tools of a Communist type organisation . . . These people must, in my opinion, be asked to leave the Liberal Party, and join their "extreme left" friends of the Socialist Party'.[64] Robert Ingham has cited Jeremy Thorpe's battles with the NLYL, along with the quality of the members of the Parliamentary Liberal Party, as being the main reasons why the BLP did so poorly at the 1970 general election.[65] Roy Douglas concurs that the NLYL did the BLP no favours, but he also cited the BLP's support for entry into the Common Market, a policy that was unpopular and may have had a bearing.[66] Tudor Jones takes a different route and quotes Hooson, who laid the blame squarely at the feet of Jo Grimond and his policy of a 'Realignment of the Left'. This policy had been heavily criticised by Hooson when it was first mooted by Grimond and, following the 1970 general election, he let it be known that the policy had led to an impression 'that the Liberals regarded themselves as some form of superior, enlightened coterie in a tacit informal coalition of the Left – remembering that Left to most people now connotes Socialist rather than Radical'.[67] It would be hard to argue with any of these historians' analyses of what affected the BLP in the 1970 general election, as each of these issues were widely reported and had inflicted varying amounts of damage on the BLP. Regardless, twelve Liberal MPs were elected in 1966 (thirteen entered the 1970 election), but just six MPs were returned in 1970, with Hooson being one of them.

As one might expect, despite the new federal structure, the WLP was not immune to the national picture and the issues with the BLP affected the fortunes of the WLP. However, the WLP had to contend with Welsh domestic politics. As has been pointed out before, the years since 1966 had seen a significant surge in the fortunes of Plaid. The party's by-election record was one that the WLP could be envious of, and they had published their Economic Plan just in time for the 1970 general election.

This meant a perfect storm for the WLP, as for the first and only time during the twentieth century, Plaid had taken third place in terms of the popular vote. Yet, the fact that the WLP was able to field nineteen PPCs in 1970 was a significant step forward when compared with 1966. It had been the party's highest number of candidates since the February 1951 general election and its highest number of votes since 1964. Additionally, in the nineteen seats that the WLP and Plaid contested against each other, the WLP was ahead of its rival in eleven of those seats.[68] Table 24 demonstrates that the 1970 general election held several positives for the WLP. The WLP finished above Plaid in eleven of their contests, demonstrating that the WLP was stronger in the mid and south of Wales.

Table 24: The relative strength of the WLP in nineteen direct contests with Plaid Cymru, 1970[69]

Party	Seats in which each party finished above the other	Seats where the share of the vote was above 10%	Number of lost deposits
Welsh Liberal	11	10	10
Plaid Cymru	8	11	13

However, while it was not the Liberal breakthrough that the WLP and Hooson had hoped for, it was also not the disaster that befell the wider BLP. The best that could be said for the 1970 general election is that it showed that the WLP were in a holding pattern and were able to show the party could finish ahead of Plaid.

The 1974 general elections would be the breakthrough that the WLP had longed for, but one that would be ignored by the media and many historians. Referencing the February and, by extension, the October 1974 general election, K. O. Morgan acknowledged 'A partial recovery for the Liberals in mid-Wales', but was rather scathing of the WLP's performance, stating 'although overall the Liberals, with just two seats and only 16 per cent of the vote, were still in feeble condition in Wales'.[70] Whilst acknowledging that Plaid's performance was not that impressive, Morgan then proceeds to focus on the seats that Plaid had won because 'it was seats that mattered'.[71] On the other hand, John Davies barely mentioned the WLP's performance at either general election but, to be fair, he gave only a one-page synopsis of the results before discussing devolution.[72] Edwards also acknowledged a 'Liberal mini-revival that had more in common with the pattern of political change that was evident across Britain', but cautioned against overstating the extent of this revival in north-west Wales.[73] Johnes also gave the WLP short shrift, mentioning them only in passing and giving no real analysis, preferring to focus on the decline in Labour and the rise of Plaid Cymru.[74]

Since the WLP's electoral record being overlooked by those historians more interested in the fate of Labour and Plaid Cymru, it has been left to the few historians of Welsh Liberalism to give any kind of commentary on the general election results of 1974 and 1979. Both J. Graham Jones and Russell Deacon write in spirited terms about both 1974 general elections. Jones comments that 'there was indeed . . . some substance in the claims of a Liberal political revival' and goes on to briefly demonstrate that, except in north-west Wales, the WLP had exceeded expectations.[75] Likewise, Deacon points to UK opinion polls showing the BLP reaching highs of 28% in August 1973 and points to February 1974 being a good election for the WLP, with the party now having two seats in Wales, Montgomery and Cardigan. He does point out that, despite this, the Welsh newspapers 'did not lead with the story of a Liberal revival in mid Wales but with the nationalist surge North Wales instead'.[76] Deacon was less upbeat about the October 1974 general election, pointing out that whilst retaining the two seats in Wales, the WLP had been pushed into the fourth position by Plaid's three seats. He does note that despite this position, the WLP stated they were 'pleased that they held the two seats and came third (in terms of votes won) over Plaid'. Deacon then gives an analysis of some of the contests, pointing out that 'the Welsh party's possible seats were beginning to look less possible'.[77] It would be fair to say that neither Deacon nor Jones, let alone the other historians, emphasise the relative strength of the WLP in this period, preferring to focus on Plaid. Yet, this chapter contends that the 1974 general elections were the beginning of the revival of the WLP in Wales and it was these elections that demonstrated that the party was a popular force in Welsh politics.

The February 1974 general election was a sudden leap forward for the WLP, with the party gaining 255,423 votes, a 16% share of all those cast in Wales.[78] As already noted above, the 1970 general election saw the WLP pushed into fourth place with a 6.8% share and 103,747 votes, there is no doubt that the WLP was experiencing the beginning of an upturn in its fortunes. To put this further into perspective, the last time that the Liberals had bettered this percentage was in 1935, when the LPW gained an 18.3% share with just 159,887 votes.[79] Since 1951, the party had not risen above a 7.7% share of the vote.[80] Added to this, the thirty-one WLP candidates were its largest number of candidates since 1929, when Lloyd George was the leader. The campaign was properly funded by the central BLP and this also allowed for a full contingent of thirty-six candidates at the October general election.[81]

If we compare this overall progress in the share of the vote with that of Plaid, we can see that the WLP were able to keep Plaid's popularity to a bare minimum. As already established, this 16% share of the vote was a hefty progression for the WLP; however, Plaid's share of the vote had declined from 11.5% (175,016), in 1970 to 10.8% at both of the 1974 general elections, taking 171,364 votes in February and 166,321 votes in October.[82] Although the WLP's share of the vote fell slightly to 15.5% (238,997)[83] in October 1974, on numbers alone this demonstrates that at these two crucial general elections, fought against the backdrop of a declining Labour Party,[84] the WLP's achievements have been written out of the historiography in favour of Plaid. In terms of votes cast, the WLP was the third most popular party within Wales. To further labour this point, for the rest of the twentieth century Plaid's share of the vote would not rise above 9.9%,[85] whilst the WLP (and its later incarnations) would not see its share fall below 10.6%,[86] reaching a high of 23.2% in 1983,[87] during the alliance with the Social Democratic Party, before settling around the 12% mark in 1992 and 1997.[88]

Although the WLP's true electoral strength during this period in Welsh history has been ignored, the same cannot be said for Plaid. The February 1974 general election had seen the party capture Caernarvonshire and Merioneth from Labour, just missing Carmarthen by three votes. Carmarthen would be added to Plaid's tally at the October general election. The WLP, as we know, beat Labour in February 1974 to win back the Cardigan seat after Labour had taken it eight years previously, and, along with Montgomery, retained it at the October general election. There are some parallels between these wins that are not usually pointed out. As noted above, Edwards points to the calibre of the candidates in Caernarvonshire and Merioneth as being key to Plaid's success, along with their youth, local appeal and a good local organisation.[89] Although true, Caernarvonshire and Carmarthen had both become Labour/Plaid Cymru marginal seats, the former in 1970 and the latter in 1966. In 1970, Caernarvonshire had been contested by Robyn Lewis and he took Plaid within 6.6% of victory.[90] When Lewis was swapped for Dafydd Wigley, Plaid were able to turn that into a slight majority of 4.9%,[91] which increased to 8.5% in October 1974.[92] The same was true for the Cardigan seat: Roderic Bowen had narrowly lost the seat in 1966 to Labour, who won it by 523 votes (1.7%).[93] In 1970, Labour had only increased its majority to 3.3% (1,263 votes).[94] When Geraint Howells took the seat, he achieved a 7%, 2,476 vote majority,[95] which was duplicated in October 1974.[96] Not only was Labour facing a Plaid Cymru nationalist challenge in north-west Wales, but they also faced a similar WLP nationalist challenge in mid-Wales. Both parties were demonstrating the ability to take a Labour seat with a popular candidate and a local organisation focused on winning.

As a further example of how crucial the 1974 general elections were to the continued electoral progress of the WLP and its attempts to keep Plaid at bay, we need to examine the individual contests in a bit more detail. Tables 25 and 26 demonstrate that the WLP were in a much stronger electoral position than Plaid during both general elections in 1974.

Table 25: The relative strength of the WLP in thirty-one direct contests with Plaid Cymru, February 1974[97]

Party	Seats in which each party finished above the other	Seats where the share of the vote was above 10%	Number of lost deposits
Welsh Liberal	24	26	6
Plaid Cymru	7	10	24

Table 26: The relative strength of the WLP in thirty-six direct contests with Plaid Cymru, October 1974[98]

Party	Seats in which each party finished above the other	Seats where the share of the vote was above 10%	Number of lost deposits
Welsh Liberal	26	29	12
Plaid Cymru	10	13	26

Both tables show that the WLP, throughout Wales, was the more dominant nationalist party. Of course, as already remarked upon, Plaid were dominant in the north-west seats, particularly Anglesey, Caernarvon and Merioneth, but what these results show was the WLP dominating Plaid elsewhere in Wales. Even when we consider the effect of the 'Liberal revival' in the rest of Britain, this was a remarkable feat for the WLP and followed a pattern that had been established in 1970.

To further demonstrate that the WLP were not the 'also-rans' in 1974, but a Welsh nationalist party that had sought a different constitutional settlement for the UK, we need to remember that these general elections were held a few months after the release of the report by the Royal Commission on the Constitution, the Kilbrandon Report. As Jones and Gibbard state, it should be acknowledged that Hooson was a 'vociferous champion' and an 'active contributor to the devolution debate in Westminster'.[99] Further, in their talks with the Labour government, David Steel acknowledges that 'our talks on devolution were virtually the forerunner of the "Lib-Lab Pact" itself'.[100] Although the first Scotland-Wales Bill had been drafted with no consultation with the Liberals, Plaid Cymru or the SNP, and predictably failed, it must be assumed that, by engaging with the Liberals from all three nations, the Labour government were of the opinion that they were the acceptable face of Welsh and Scottish nationalism. The Lib-Lab Pact began in March 1977, and it is through the combined work of these two parties that the original Scotland-Wales Bill was pulled apart and that separate Scottish and Welsh Bills were reintroduced into Parliament. Although the Labour government were not as open to amending the Welsh legislation as they were to changing the Scottish legislation, members of the WLP (particularly Geraint Howells, as spokesperson on Welsh devolution), attended the talks.[101] The rise of the SNP in the 1960s, coupled with the perceived threat from Plaid, may have triggered the constitutional question, but there is no doubt that by polling so well in 1974, the WLP and the Scottish Liberal Party were seen as contributing to the nationalist threat. It is just that the Liberals were easier to bring into the conversation with Labour, as they were not advocating the separation of the nations.

Despite this cooperation with the Labour government, the 1979 general election was held after the failure of the referendums on Scottish and Welsh devolution. Both Hooson and Howells had played an important part in the referendum campaigns, unpopular roles, given the outcome. It was a dejected WLP that entered the general election, one that had been in financial straits and organisational chaos. Not only was the WLP dejected, but the wider BLP was facing something of a perfect storm. Jeremy Thorpe, the BLP's former leader, was about to be tried at the Old Bailey on charges of conspiracy to murder his former lover, Norman Scott. The trial was set for 8 May 1979, which allowed Thorpe to stand in the general election on 3 May. The newspaper coverage had been relentless and salacious, and did nothing but harm to the party. Added to this was the unpopularity of the Labour government, which had just come through the 'Winter of Discontent' and, following the failure of the referendums, had lost a vote of no confidence in the Commons. The Lib-Lab Pact, which had come to an end in September 1978, associated the Liberals with keeping an unpopular government in office. The Conservative Party, under Margaret Thatcher, was on the ascendancy and would gain a forty-three-seat majority, including eleven seats in Wales, at the general election. This was the Conservatives' largest share of seats in Wales since 1874.[102]

In Wales, the 1979 general election confirmed a downward trend in Labour's hegemony within Wales. Despite being the dominant party within Wales, Labour had begun to lose ground from its highest tally of thirty-two of the thirty-six seats in 1966, falling to twenty-seven in 1970, twenty-three in October 1974 and twenty-two in 1979.[103] This lessening of Labour's power was to the benefit of the smaller parties in Wales, particularly the WLP and Plaid. However, on the back of a national upswing in support, it was now the Conservatives who were benefiting, and it was possible to travel from Holyhead in the north to Newport in the south without leaving a Conservative constituency.

The WLP had twenty-eight candidates, eight fewer than the thirty-six candidates at the October 1974 general election. This was still a decent number and showed the WLP continued to be able to attract candidates, despite the issues raised above. Plaid had thirty-six candidates and, as table 27 shows, the WLP was still able to hold off its main competitor in most seats that they jointly contested.

Table 27: The relative strength of the WLP in twenty-eight direct contests with Plaid Cymru, 1979[104]

Party	Seats in which each party finished above the other	Seats where the share of the vote was above 10%	Number of lost deposits
Welsh Liberal	22	19	18
Plaid Cymru	6	6	22

Despite the WLP's more dominant electoral position, Plaid still retained two MPs, having lost Carmarthen again. However, the WLP had lost Emlyn Hooson in Montgomery and was back in the position of having just one MP, Geraint Howells in Cardigan, whose own share of the vote declined by some seven per cent.

This was also the general election when serious issues within the WLP's constituencies became more evident. The most significant, after the Brecon and Radnor case, was in Cardiff South East, the Prime Minister's constituency. With minutes to spare before nominations had to be handed in, Christopher Bailey decided, along with the reported assistance of his local association, not to submit his nomination papers. Instead, he urged the electorate to support the Conservative candidate. He further pledged the constituency's support for any other pacts in Labour areas, and stated that 'This Liberal-Conservative pact makes Cardiff South East a marginal seat. A five pc swing will result in the Prime Minister losing his seat'.[105] This unauthorised pact resulted in the WLP being unable to contest the constituency and it was obviously not prudent to invite any more adverse publicity by disciplining the constituency during the general election. Due to the illness of the constituency chairman, which appeared to be a delaying tactic, Cardiff South East was disaffiliated from the WLP 'and their members cease to be members of the Liberal Party'.[106]

In a scathing internal report that followed the 1979 general election, it was pointed out that in ten constituencies, there was a 'serious division in principle over whether we should fight'. Also, in ten constituencies, the decision whether to fight or not was left until after Easter 1979, which fell on 15 April that year. The report stated: 'As a whole . . . the campaign revealed to the world what we have all known privately and done nothing about. Our local organizations, with a few notable exceptions, are in an appalling condition'.[107]

Despite the state of the local constituencies in 1974, which had worsened by 1979, it can be said that the WLP's performance at each general election of the 1970s was one of steady progression. Whether it was in the number of candidates put forward at each election, the increase in the share of the vote in 1974 or being able to keep Plaid from deposing them as the true third party of Wales, the WLP had succeeded, despite the odds being stacked against them. The WLP had become an electoral force and it survived. Whether that was due to its brand of Welsh nationalism, a mini-Liberal revival that began in England and swept the shores of Wales, the stance that its leader took on entry into the EEC or devolution, the WLP was electorally strong enough to enter the 1980s and the challenges that were to follow.

THE FALL OF EMLYN HOOSON

There have been competing theories as to why Hooson lost his seat to the Conservatives in the 1979 general election. K. O. Morgan points to the increase of light industries around

Newtown, which by 1974 had brought inward migration, increasing the electorate by 2,000, and by another 2,200 between October 1974 and 1979.[108] Further, Morgan notes that 'Of the 888 new families living in housing estates built by the Newtown corporation, 435 had come from England'.[109] Jones agrees with this analysis and with Morgan's assertion that the county had become more anglicised. Both argue that this new influx of migrants was less inclined to accept their MP's support for the Lib-Lab Pact or devolution.[110] This analysis does have its merits. Official figures show that between 1974 and 1979, the estimated mid-year population of Montgomery (which included Newtown within its boundaries) rose from 45,000 to 47,800, a rise of approximately 2,800 persons.[111] When compared with the data for the period between 1970 and 1974, which showed an estimated rise of just 630 persons (43,270 to 43,900[112]), the population of Montgomery had seen a dramatic rise in the latter part of the 1970s. Although the electorate rose by 2,200 (from 33,575 to 35,786[113]), we know not all the electorate turned out to vote, but the percentage of those voting did rise by 11.3% when compared with October 1974, equating to an extra 2,962 voters.[114] This supports both Morgan's and Jones's analyses that the influx had benefited the Conservative candidate. However, this argument seems a bit of a stretch, as it assumes that migrants from England were instinctively Conservative voters.

Moreover, this analysis does not consider the issues surrounding the Montgomeryshire County Liberal Association (MCLA) at the time. Neither does it consider the traditional nature of the constituency, which was 'small c' conservative. It is also telling that Deacon did not include the migratory influx as a factor when considering why Hooson lost his seat.[115] As such, we should initially consider the state of the MCLA, something that Deacon points out (although without going into any further detail) was an issue in 1974, but had been masked by the 'national tide that was carrying the Liberals forward. It could not rely on this in 1979 when the opposite was the case.'[116] The main issue was one of finances: in 1973/4 the MCLA had an income of £2,771.04, which had risen to £3604.92[117] in the 1974/5 period, the year of the general elections. Expenses were £3,284.04 and £3,636.51, respectively.[118] The MCLA was existing above its means during this crucial period. Part of the issue is that the constituency was a target seat for the Conservatives and Plaid in October 1974, both of which had hoped to unseat Hooson. Both parties spent a substantial sum of money on contesting the seat, sums that the MCLA matched. Table 28 demonstrates how much was paid by each party to fight the October 1974 general election.

Table 28: Montgomeryshire electoral expenses by party, October 1974[119]

WLP	Conservative	Plaid Cymru	Labour
£1,259 (89% of the maximum allowed)	£1,277 (90% of the maximum allowed)	£1,233 (87% of the maximum allowed)	£850 (60% of the maximum allowed)

As the 1979 general election approached, the MCLA began to find itself in dire financial straits. Aside from the complaint referenced in chapter three, pertaining to the party sending a part payment for the affiliation fees, the association also referenced a 'full-time professional employee'.[120] This employee was the organiser and, just like the WLP, there appears to have been little financial oversight of his activities. In July 1978, the treasurer reported that he had arranged to pay the organiser's salary during a period of sickness, but it appears that the organiser had also claimed sickness benefits. Although he had agreed to pay it back, there was no 'written agreement between the MCLA and its employee'.[121] Although the organiser resigned in August of 1978,[122] there were no funds to replace him. Hooson had to send a letter requesting help from David Steel, stating that the MCLA was in 'considerable financial difficulties', and that they were no longer able to appoint an organiser and only had a part-time secretary.[123] Following Steel's intervention, the MCLA was sent £450 from the Joseph Rowntree Social Service Trust.[124] What this demonstrates is that the local association of the Welsh Liberal leader, in what was a significant historical seat for Welsh Liberalism,[125] was facing a financial crisis. As pointed out above, Hooson's seat was not unique in being in this situation, but it should have attracted a greater amount of financial assistance from the WLP and the federal party.

John Davies made a flippant remark as to why Hooson lost his seat and Howells's share of the vote fell. He suggested that the farmers of Wales were 'becoming increasingly Conservative and it is likely that some Welsh Liberals, on discovering that their party supported dangerously radical ideas such as devolution, changed from being conservative to Conservative'.[126] This may seem like a throwaway, jokey remark, but the historic conservative nature of the constituency, more than the in-migration from England, is a better explanation as to why Hooson lost his seat. Montgomery was a rural constituency, and during Clement Davies's period as MP, he benefited from a lack of Conservative opposition. Due to his position as a Liberal National in 1931 and 1935, Davies faced no opposition at either general election. It is only when Davies realigned himself with the LPW, a process that happened during the Second World War, that the Conservatives placed a candidate in the seat and we see Davies's majority suffer. He often faced a Labour candidate (a party that was never really in contention for the seat), but it was the presence of the Conservatives that affected Davies's position. Table 29 ably demonstrates this, showing that the Labour candidate's share of the vote never really changed, and it was support for the Conservative candidate that ate into Davies's vote.

Table 29: Montgomeryshire general election results, 1945–59[127]

Party	1945 Votes – %	1950 Votes – %	1951 Votes – %	1955 Votes – %	1959 Votes – %
LPW	14,018 – 56.3%	14,401 – 51.3%	17,075 – 69.2%	16,021 – 68.1%	10,970 – 42.1%
Conservative	10,895 – 43.7%	7,621 – 27.1%	N/A	N/A	8,176 – 31.3%
Labour	N/A	6,070 – 21.6%	7,584 – 30.8%	7,521 – 31.9%	6,950 – 26.6%

Likewise, under Hooson, it was the Conservatives that posed the biggest threat, whilst the presence of a Plaid Cymru candidate did not trouble Hooson, as Plaid usually took votes from Labour. The 1962 by-election was an anomaly, in that Hooson benefited from the goodwill of the constituency following Davies's death, and from a national revival in Liberal fortunes (see tables 30 and 31).

Table 30: Montgomeryshire general election results, 1962–6[128]

Party	1962 by-election Votes – %	1964 Votes – %	1966 Votes – %
LPW	3,181 – 51.3%	10,738 – 42.3%	10,278 – 41.4%
Conservative	5,632 – 21.9%	6,768 – 26.7%	6,784 – 27.4%
Labour	5,299 – 20.6%	5,696 – 22.5%	5,891 – 23.8%
Plaid Cymru	1,594 – 6.2%	2,167 – 8.5%	1,841 – 7.4%

Table 31: Montgomeryshire general election results, 1970–9[129]

Party	1970 Votes – %	February 1974 Votes – %	October 1974 Votes – %	1979 Votes – %
WLP	10,202 – 38.4%	12,495 – 45.4%	11,280 – 43.1%	10,158 – 34.9%
Conservative	7,891 – 29.7%	7,844 – 28.5%	7,421 – 28.4%	11,751 – 40.3%
Labour	5,335 – 20.1%	4,888 – 17.8%	5,031 – 19.2%	4,751 – 16.3%
Plaid Cymru	3,145 – 11.8%	2,274 – 8.3%	2,440 – 9.3%	2,474 – 8.5%

Jones sees the loss of Montgomery as an 'unlikely' win for the Conservatives in 1979. Yet, it was the conservative nature of the seat, which had been in evidence throughout Davies's and Hooson's tenure, which worried the Liberals. Whenever the Conservatives were in the ascendancy nationally or had been in power (as in 1945, 1959 and 1970), we see Davies's and Hooson's vote share begin to suffer. This was even more in evidence with the Conservative onslaught on Wales in 1979. If we can say anything about Morgan's thesis, it is that the in-migration helped the Conservatives, but the seat was already conservative in nature.

Finally, the issue that affected Hooson more than any other, and handed the seat to the Conservatives, was the enthusiastic support that he had shown for devolution and the Lib-Lab Pact. This is something that has been recognised by most historians, including Morgan, Deacon and Jones. Powys, the county which contained Montgomery following the boundary changes, registered one of the largest majorities, 63%, against devolution in the March 1979 referendum.[130] There is no doubt about it that keeping an unpopular Labour government in power, along with the support for its flagship policy, whilst occupying a conservative seat, was just more ammunition for the Conservative candidate. It might well have been a more manageable situation had the Prime Minister, James Callaghan, called a general election in the autumn of 1978, when the polls suggested it would be more favourable for his government. However, the 'Winter of Discontent' showed the folly of not calling a general election then, and Hooson was tarnished by association.

However, it was an odd situation for Hooson to find himself in, as he had been against a pact with Labour throughout his tenure as WLP leader. As previously stated, he blamed Jo Grimond's 'Realignment of the Left' policy for the failure of the BLP to make gains at the 1970 general election. Yet, what Hooson said in public could be quite different from what he said and pursued in private. For example, he was publicly against any deal with Plaid, chastising Laura Grimond when she suggested a pact, stating: 'I am sure that any kind of deal with the Nats. would be a great mistake. We would be accused of having sought an agreement with Labour, then having failed to obtain it, then sought an agreement with the Nationalists.'[131] However, we know that he seriously considered and sounded out Gwynfor Evans in a bid to form a new party, which would be known as the 'Welsh Democratic Party'. Failing that, he suggested that each party could split the constituencies, each putting up eighteen candidates. However, Evans ignored his approaches.[132] It would not have been out of character for Hooson to have said one thing and then done another, especially if there was something to gain, and devolution was a worthy prize.

Although historians have pointed out that devolution was also a factor in losing the constituency, Deacon argues that 'Hooson had become out of touch with the grass roots in his seat, which was quite "conservative" in nature, regarding both the Assembly and other Liberal policy ideas'.[133] However, it must be pointed out that Hooson was not blind to the damage that he was doing to his electoral chances. In a letter to the treasurer of the MCLA, regarding the devolution campaign, he points out that though he will speak at rallies in Montgomeryshire,

> I think there is a great psychological disadvantage for us in appearing with Plaid and Labour on a platform against the Tories. What do you think? The reason for my feeling on this matter is that I surmise that, probably, the majority of people in Mont. are against the Assembly. However, how we get over this, I do not know.[134]

These are not the words of a man who is out of touch with the grass roots of his constituency; on the contrary, he understands them all too well. These are the words of a man that is following his Liberal principles. The whole of the WLP's programme rested on gaining a Welsh parliament, and the proposed Assembly would be a step towards that. Hooson had a strong inkling that he was putting his political future at risk, but it was a risk worth taking if they could secure more devolution for Wales.

Further, Jones states that Hooson's 'long and distinguished career in the House of Commons had come to an unlikely inglorious end'.[135] This does Hooson a disservice, as it would have been 'inglorious' if he had not forfeited his seat standing up for his *Welsh* Liberal principles. As Hooson put it when he introduced his Government of Wales Bill to Parliament on St David's Day 1967,

> I am happy to say that, in many facets of our national life, we are still conscious of that harmony of spirit which unites us as a nation. We inherit a small but distinct culture whose origins are lost in antiquity. Our language is an expressive language of lyrical and emotive beauty. But we are bound by something beyond language, beyond culture only, by that curious blend of romanticism and radicalism which in one way or another finds expression in every son of Wales. This is the peculiar fervour which for well over 1,000 years has enabled us to preserve our individuality and enabled us to make a contribution to life outside Wales as well as within Wales in a distinctive way.[136]

Hooson was a leader who held Wales and Welsh Liberalism at the heart of everything he did. By campaigning for devolution, he understood that he had to do it. He did not forfeit anything 'inglorious[ly]' or needlessly; it was for Wales and Liberalism.

CONCLUSION

This chapter has been framed to show that the WLP was electorally stronger than Plaid, its main competitor in every seat it contested throughout the 1970s. By framing the argument this way, we can show that the WLP has been ignored and written off as an 'also-ran' party by Welsh historians. This chapter challenges the traditional historiography. For too long, the historical narrative has been written by historians interested in the fortunes of the Labour Party or Plaid Cymru, or of both parties. There is a consensus at play here but, for a subject written about by Labour and nationalist historians, this historiographical consensus needs to be challenged. For example, when discussing the February 1974 general elections, Deacon concedes that the immediate (and, by extension, the subsequent) narrative was the surge in north-west Wales, and not the 'Liberal revival in mid-Wales'.[137] This chapter has argued against that narrative and shown that the WLP were in a much better electoral position in 1974 and 1979 than has previously been conceded. Even in 1970, there was cause for some minor optimism. This chapter has shown that the WLP deserves more than a passing mention in the post-war political historiography and electoral map of Wales.

As for Hooson, the loss of his Montgomery seat has been framed in a slightly new way. The chapter argued that many varied factors secured the loss of Hooson's seat, namely the organisational and financial weakness of his local party, the conservative nature of the constituency and his support for the Lib-Lab Pact and devolution. It was seen as an 'inglorious' loss and it was felt that Hooson had lost touch with his party's grass roots. However, Hooson knew the risk he was taking and pushed ahead with his Welsh Liberal principles anyway. Hooson may have faced a perfect storm of events nationally and locally, but he did not lose the seat ingloriously. His elevation to the House of Lords followed the defeat and he remained an active Liberal and, later, Liberal Democrat.

Notes

1   Andrew Edwards, *Labour's Crisis: Plaid Cymru, The Conservatives and the Decline of the Labour Party in North-West Wales, 1960–74* (Cardiff, 2011), p. 9.
2   For example Roy Douglas, *Liberals: The History of the Liberal and Liberal Democrat Parties* (London, 2005), p. 267, or Kenneth O. Morgan, *Rebirth of a Nation: Wales 1880–1980* (Oxford, 1990), p. 342.

3   For example Martin Johnes, *Wales Since 1939* (Manchester, 2012), p. 269, or John Davies, *A History of Wales* (London,1993), p. 673.
4   For example Kenneth O. Morgan, 'Montgomeryshire's Liberal Century', *Welsh History Review*, 16/1 (June 1992), pp. 107–8.
5   NLW, Lord Hooson Papers, Box 42, Letter from Hooson to Mr Watson of Basingstoke, 22 February 1967.
6   Beti Jones, *Welsh Elections 1885–1997* (Talybont, 1999), p. 114.
7   NLW, Lord Hooson Papers, Box 42, Letter from Hooson to Mr Watson of Basingstoke, 22 February 1967.
8   Russell Deacon, *The Welsh Liberals: The History of the Liberal and Liberal Democratic Parties in Wales* (Cardiff, 2014), p. 176.
9   *Western Mail*, 17 July 1968.
10 John Graham Jones, *David Lloyd George and Welsh Liberalism* (Llandysul, 2010), p. 504.
11 NLW, Merfyn Jones Papers 34, 'Our Task in Wales – We Start at Caerphilly', Memo from Hooson, undated but July 1968. My italics.
12 NLW, Lord Hooson Papers, Box 42, Letter from Mr Watson of Basingstoke, 22 February 1967. For example, 'If this is the first outcome of separation of the Welsh Liberals from the rest of us, it was not perhaps a wise move'.
13 NLW, Lord Hooson Box 42, Letter from Hooson to Pratap Chitnis, 24 October 1967.
14 Jones, *Welsh Elections*, pp. 113 and 118. In 1966, Davies took 74.5% of the vote, and in 1970, 51.9%. His Labour opponent in 1970 took 28.7%.
15 Adjusted to 2023 levels, £294.71 at 4.7% inflation p/a.
16 NLW, Lord Hooson Papers, Correspondence between Winifred Whitaker (Freddie) and Angus Donaldson, 14 November 1972.
17 NLW, Lord Hooson Papers, Correspondence between Angus Donaldson and Rhys Gerran Lloyd, 20 November 1972.
18 Adjusted to 2023 levels, £623.42 at 4.9% inflation p/a.
19 NLW, Lord Hooson Papers, Correspondence between Hooson and G. H. Black, 26 July 1972.
20 Adjusted to 2023 levels, £11,334.91 at 4.9% inflation p/a.
21 NLW, Lord Hooson Papers, Box 45, Memorandum from Hooson to Members of the Executive, 12 April 1972. This was written on the eve of the poll.
22 This was the Gower, 16 September 1982, the first by-election contested by an Alliance candidate in Wales, namely Gwynoro Jones.
23 NLW, Lord Hooson Papers, Box 45, Memorandum from Hooson to Members of the Executive, 12 April 1972.
24 Ivor Thomas Rees, *Welsh Hustings 1885–2004* (Llandybie, 2005), multiple pages. This is a 'who's who' of general election, European and Assembly candidates, so all nineteen candidates were spread out alphabetically.
25 NLW, Cardiganshire Liberal Association, File 120, *Welsh Liberal Party Manifesto: The Liberal Case for Wales*.
26 NLW, Lord Ogmore Papers, File 4, Letter from Mary Murphy to Ogmore, 12 October 1967. Annotated at the bottom to say that Ellis had been written to.

27 NLW, Lord Hooson Papers, Box 42, Letter to Tom Crowther from Hooson, 25 October 1967.
28 NLW, Merfyn Jones Papers, File 35, Minutes of the WLP Executive Committee, 20 July 1974.
29 NLW, Merfyn Jones Papers, File 35, Minutes of the WLP Executive Committee, 17 August 1974.
30 NLW, Merfyn Jones Papers, File 35, Minutes of the WLP Executive Committee, 2 November 1974.
31 NLW, Welsh Liberal Papers, File A5, Minutes of the WLP Executive Committee, 2 September 1978.
32 NLW, Merfyn Jones Papers, File 35, Draft Revised Constitution, 1975.
33 Alex Carlile, elected for Montgomeryshire in 1983, was the first Liberal MP since 1945 not to speak Welsh.
34 Rees, *Welsh Hustings*, multiple pages. If a candidate declared that they were Welsh speaking, either on their election leaflet or via the questionnaire he sent out, then Rees has recorded this under their entry. It is likely that more candidates spoke Welsh but did not mention it.
35 David Thomas, a Welsh speaker, had contested Cardiff North in February 1974. The future leader of the Welsh Liberal Democrats, Mike German, contested Cardiff North in October 1974 but was not a Welsh speaker at this stage.
36 *Digest of Welsh Historical Statistics 1700–1974*, ch. 1. These include bilingual speakers, not just monoglot Welsh speakers. Available at: *https://webarchive. nationalarchives.gov.uk/ukgwa/20150402173126/http:/gov.wales/statistics-and-research/digest-welsh-historical-statistics/?lang=en#/statistics-and-research/digest-welsh-historical-statistics/?tab=previous&lang=en* (accessed 1 August 2024).
37 Carmarthen 1970–9 and Merioneth 1974–9.
38 Montgomery 1970–9, Cardigan 1970–9, Denbigh 1974–9.
39 Jones, *Welsh Elections*, pp. 115–18. These contests were in Anglesey, Brecon and Radnor, Cardigan, Carmarthen, Conwy, Denbigh, Llanelli, Merioneth, Montgomery and Wrexham. A note about Brecon and Radnor: together, the total percentage of Welsh speakers was 18%, but individually, Brecon had 22.9% and Radnor had 3.8%. I have included the constituency based on Brecon. The WLP lost their deposits in Anglesey (6.2%), Conwy (6.6%), Llanelli (7.7%) and Wrexham (9.3%). Plaid lost deposits in Brecon and Radnor (5.4%), Conwy (10.8%), Denbigh (11%), Montgomery (6.7%) and Wrexham (9.3%).
40 The threshold for losing a deposit was set at 12.5% of the vote. This changed to 5% of the vote in 1985.
41 Jones, *Welsh Elections*, pp. 119–22. These contests were in Anglesey, Cardigan, Carmarthen, Conwy, Denbigh, Merioneth and Montgomery. The WLP lost its deposit in Anglesey (11.1%). Plaid lost it deposit in Conwy (10.1%), Denbigh (8.1%) and Montgomery (8.3%).
42 Jones, *Welsh Elections*, pp. 123–6. Contests were in Caernarvon, Cardigan, Carmarthen, Conwy, Denbigh, Merioneth and Pembroke. The WLP lost

its deposits in Caernarvon (10.7%) and Carmarthen (10.4%). Plaid lost its deposits in Conwy (11.8%), Denbigh (11.9%) and Montgomery (9.3%).

43 Jones, *Welsh Elections*, pp. 127–30. Contests were in Caernarvon, Cardigan, Carmarthen, Conwy, Denbigh, Llanelli, Merioneth, Montgomery and Pembroke. The WLP lost its deposits in Caernarfon (5.7%), Carmarthen (8%), Llanelli (11.4%), Merioneth (12.1%) and Pembroke (10.1%). Plaid lost its deposits in Conwy (8.6%), Denbigh (9.3%), Llanelli (7.4%), Montgomery (8.5%) and Pembroke (2.5%).
44 Jones, *Welsh Elections*, pp. 115–30.
45 Edwards, *Labour's Crisis*, p. 215.
46 Jones, *Welsh Elections*, pp. 109 and 118.
47 Jones, *Welsh Elections*, p. 109.
48 Jones, *Welsh Elections*, p. 117.
49 Peter Clarke, *Hope and Glory: Britain 1900–2000* (London, 2004), p. 318. Clarke also pointed to a break in the weather and the England football team being knocked out of the World Cup in Mexico.
50 William Wallace, 'Survival and Revival', in Vernon Bogdanor (ed.), *Liberal Party Politics* (Oxford, 1983), p. 65.
51 Tudor Jones, *The Uneven Path of British Liberalism, From Jo Grimond to Brexit* (Manchester, 2019), p. 81.
52 Jones, *Welsh Elections*, pp. 111–14.
53 NLW, Lord Hooson Archive, Box 42, Letter from Hooson to Mr Watson of Basingstoke, 27 February 1967.
54 NLW, Lord Hooson Archive, Box 45, Letter from Hooson to Mr Millington of Stourport-on-Severn, 14 July 1969. Mr Millington was asking to become a PPC.
55 NLW, Lord Hooson Archive, Box 44 – Peter Jacobs Envelope, Letter from Peter Jacobs to Hooson, 17 November 1969.
56 *The Times*, 22 September 1967, 3.
57 NLW, Lord Hooson Archive, Box 44 – Peter Jacobs Envelope, Letter from Hooson to Jacobs, 24 November 1969.
58 *The Times*, 28 July 1969. The others were Peter Bessell, MP for Bodmin, and Alasdair McKenzie, MP for Ross and Cromarty.
59 NLW, Lord Hooson Files, Box 44, Letter from Eluned French to Winston Roddick, 19 March 1970.
60 NLW, Lord Hooson Files, Box 44, Letter from Roddick to Hooson, dated 'Saturday' but likely to be 21 March 1970.
61 NLW, Lord Hooson Files, Box 44, Letter from Hooson to Mrs Edwards, Treasurer of the Anglesey LA, 21 April 1970.
62 NLW, Lord Hooson Files, Box 44, Letter from Mrs Edwards to Hooson, 27 April 1970.
63 NLW, Lord Hooson Files, Box 44, Letter from Mrs Edwards to Hooson, 27 April 1970.

64 NLW, Lord Hooson Files, Box 44, Copy of a Letter from Angus Donaldson to Hooson, forwarded to Hooson by W. A. Powell, Treasurer of Tredegar, 20 January 1970. This letter was forwarded to the Press Association.
65 Robert Ingham, 'Liberal Revival (1956–1974)', in Robert Ingham and Duncan Brack (eds), *Peace, Reform and Liberation: A History of Liberal Politics in Britain, 1679–2011* (London, 2011), pp. 259–60.
66 Roy Douglas, *The History of the Liberal Party 1895–1970* (London, 1971), pp. 285–6.
67 Jones, *The Uneven Path*, pp. 82–3. Jones was quoting from Hooson's 'What's Left for the Liberals?' article in the September/October 1970 issue of the *New Outlook* magazine.
68 Jones, *Welsh Elections*, pp. 116–18.
69 Jones, *Welsh Elections*, pp. 116–18.
70 Morgan, *Rebirth*, p. 396.
71 Morgan, *Rebirth*, p. 397.
72 John Davies, *A History of Wales* (London, 1994), p. 673.
73 Edwards, *Labour's Crisis*, p. 192.
74 Johnes, *Wales*, p. 269.
75 J. Graham Jones, 'Emlyn Hooson and Montgomeryshire Politics 1962–79', *The Montgomeryshire Collections*, 97 (2009), 197–9.
76 Deacon, *Welsh Liberals*, pp. 185–7.
77 Deacon, *Welsh Liberals*, p. 189.
78 Jones, *Welsh Elections*, p. 119.
79 Jones, *Welsh Elections*, p. 83.
80 Jones, *Welsh Elections*, p. 95.
81 Jones, 'Emlyn Hooson and Montgomeryshire Politics', 198.
82 Jones, *Welsh Elections*, p. 123.
83 Jones, *Welsh Elections*, p. 123.
84 Johnes, *Wales*, p. 269. Also, see Edwards, *Labour's Crisis*, for a fuller account that focuses on north-west Wales.
85 Jones, *Welsh Elections*, p. 149. This is from 1997.
86 Jones, *Welsh Elections*, p. 126. This is the 1979 figure.
87 Jones, *Welsh Elections*, p. 131.
88 Jones, *Welsh Elections*, pp. 143 and 149.
89 Edwards, *Labour's Crisis*, p. 215.
90 Jones, *Welsh Elections*, p. 117.
91 Jones, *Welsh Elections*, p. 121.
92 Jones, *Welsh Elections*, p. 125.
93 Jones, *Welsh Elections*, p. 113.
94 Jones, *Welsh Elections*, p. 117.
95 Jones, *Welsh Elections*, p. 121.
96 Jones, *Welsh Elections*, p. 125. The vote share of 7% was the same but the majority decreased slightly, to 2,410 votes.
97 Jones, *Welsh Elections*, pp. 119–22.
98 Jones, *Welsh Elections*, pp. 113–26.

99 Gwynoro Jones and Alun Gibbard, *Whose Wales? The Battle for Welsh Devolution and Nationhood 1880–2020* (Milton Keynes, 2021), p. 332.
100 David Steel, *A House Divided* (London, 1980), p. 93.
101 Mari James and Peter D. Lindley, 'The Parliamentary Passage of the Wales Act 1978', in David Foulkes, J. Barry Jones and R. A. Wilford (eds), *The Welsh Veto: The Wales Act 1978 & The Referendum* (Cardiff, 1983), p. 44.
102 Colin Rallings and Michael Thrasher (eds), *British Electoral Facts 1832–1999* (Aldershot, 2000), p. 11.
103 Jones, *Welsh Elections*, pp. 111–27.
104 Jones, *Welsh Elections*, pp. 127–30.
105 *Belfast Telegraph*, 24 April 1979, 8.
106 NLW, Merfyn Jones Papers, File 37, Minutes of the WLP Executive Committee, 16 August 1977.
107 NLW, Merfyn Jones Papers, File 32, A Report on the 1979 general election.
108 Morgan, 'Montgomeryshire's Liberal Century', 107.
109 Morgan, 'Montgomeryshire's Liberal Century', 108.
110 Jones, 'Emlyn Hooson and Montgomeryshire Politics', 204.
111 *Digest of Welsh Historical Statistics, 1974–96*, ch. 1, p. 7. Available at: https://gov.wales/digest-welsh-historical-statistics-0 (accessed 1 August 2024).
112 [ARCHIVED CONTENT] Welsh Government | Digest of Welsh historical statistics (*nationalarchives.gov.uk*), ch. 1, table 1.9 (accessed 1 August 2024).
113 Jones, *Welsh Elections*, pp. 126 and 130.
114 From 26,172 votes in October 1974 to 29,134 in May 1979, a rise of 2,962 voters.
115 Deacon, *Welsh Liberals*, p. 206. Deacon listed eight reasons as to why Hooson lost Montgomery. There is a reference to in-migration in Russell Deacon, 'The Steady Tapping Breaks the Rock', *Journal of Liberal History*, 22 (Spring 1999), 15. However, as it is left out of his later work, one must surmise that he has revised his opinion that this was a chief cause.
116 Deacon, *Welsh Liberals*, p. 206.
117 Adjusted to 2023 levels, £25,142.49 at 4.6% inflation p/a and £26,796.82 at 4.3% inflation p/a.
118 NLW, Montgomeryshire Liberal Association, File 9, Accounts from 1966 to 1975. Adjusted to 2023 levels, £29,797.14 and £27,034.69, 4.6% inflation p/a and 4.3% inflation p/a, respectively.
119 NLW, Lord Hooson Papers, Box 46, Montgomeryshire County Liberal Association, Memorandum of Election Expenses, 7 July 1978. This is a rundown of the election expenses incurred by each party in October 1974: WLP – £11,423.45, Con – £11,586.77, PC – £11,187.54 and Lab – £7,712.41 at 4.6% inflation p/a.
120 NLW, Lord Hooson Papers, Box 46, Letter from Colin A. Smith to Norman Lewis, 8 March 1978.
121 NLW, Lord Hooson Papers, Box 46, Minutes of the MCLA Executive Committee, 7 July 1978.

122 NLW, Lord Hooson Papers, Box 46, Agenda for a Special Meeting of the Executive Committee on 16/08/1978; item 3 is the resignation of Mr R. E. Griffiths.
123 NLW, Lord Hooson Papers, Box 46, Letter from Hooson to David Steel, 9 January 1979.
124 NLW, Lord Hooson Papers, Box 46, Letter from Major H.P.M. Lewis, Treasurer, to Hooson acknowledging receipt of the amount, 12 February 1979. Adjusted to 2023 levels, £2,120.49, 3.6% inflation p/a.
125 The party had held the seat continuously for ninety-nine years when it fell to the Conservatives.
126 Davies, *A History*, p. 679.
127 Jones, *Welsh Elections*, pp. 90–106. I have not included the pre-war figures, as Davies stood as a Liberal National and did not face an opponent in 1931 and 1935.
128 Jones, *Welsh Elections*, pp. 106–14.
129 Jones, *Welsh Elections*, pp. 118–30.
130 Jones, *Welsh Elections*, p. 160. Only Gwent and Glamorgan South registered larger majorities, 76% and 73.8%, respectively.
131 NLW, Lord Hooson Papers, Box 42, Letter to Laura Grimond, 27 September 1967.
132 NLW, Lord Hooson Papers, Box 42, Letter to Geraint Jenkins from Hooson, 22 November 1967. For a more detailed analysis, see Nicholas Alderton, 'Welsh Liberal Party 1966–70: New Beginnings and the Challenge of Plaid Cymru', *Journal of Liberal History*, 103 (Summer 2019), 20.
133 Deacon, *Welsh Liberals*, p. 206.
134 NLW, Lord Hooson Papers, Box 46, Letter to Colin A. Smith from Hooson, 10 November 1978.
135 Jones, 'Emlyn Hooson and Montgomeryshire Politics', 204.
136 Government of Wales', HC Debate, 1 March 1967, vol. 742, col. 418. Available at: *https://hansard.parliament.uk/Commons/1967-03-01/debates/73586515-ebae-47fe-8160-d1de6a0837a0/GovernmentOfWales*
137 Deacon, *Welsh Liberals*, p. 186.

CONCLUSION

The formation of the WLP was the lifeline needed for Liberalism to survive in Wales. By 1959, the LPW was a party that had been rotting from the inside and was in a terminal decline. The party had been left with just two MPs and by 1966, there would be just one Liberal MP left in Wales. There were several causes of the rot, going back to the nineteenth century. First, was the demise of Cymru Fydd, with Lloyd George focusing his attention elsewhere, which left the organisation of the LPW woefully unprepared to unify the party. Second, the party was split into two federations, the South Wales Liberal Federation and the North Wales Liberal Federation and, as Hooson commented, 'they [the federations], were allegedly co-ordinated by the vaguest possible organisation called the Liberal Party of Wales'.[1] With no strong leader to guide them, the factionalism and mutual suspicion within the party increased. Not only that, but by the middle of the twentieth century, both federations were issuing policies that were diametrically opposite to each other, creating confusion within the party and for voters. The 'traditional' Welsh Liberal policies, which included land reform, support for the Welsh language and devolution, had also been neglected by the leadership. The post-war leadership was more focused on keeping the BLP from collapsing nationally. Emlyn Hooson recognised that Liberalism in Wales was facing an existential crisis of its own making, and in 1948 called for reform of its organisation and policies. Having failed to get elected in either 1950 or 1951, Hooson focused on his legal career and did not stand in either the 1955 or 1959 general elections. Yet, Hooson was still heavily involved in the BLP and LPW, co-authoring the LPW's 1959 general election manifesto. The policies in this manifesto became the basis of Hooson's reform agenda for the LPW, which would come to fruition with the founding of the WLP in 1966. The policies were Welsh and Liberal, and, in the truest sense of both labels, there was a focus on Welshness and they could be described as Welsh nationalist in nature.[2]

This is the crux of this book: Hooson was determined and convinced that reforming the structure of the party, along with its policies, would ensure the survival of Liberalism within Wales and would fend off any challenge by Plaid. Knowing that during the nineteenth and early twentieth centuries the Welsh Liberals had been the engine through which a nascent Welsh consciousness and sense of nationhood had begun to express itself, Hooson believed they could recapture that position. Both terms could be used interchangeably with the concept of Welshness and Welsh nationalism, which was at the heart of the WLP programme. Although he would never have used the latter term to describe the party or himself, it is quite clear that the WLP presented itself as an alternative nationalist party. Yet, with Plaid garnering all the headlines, the disbanding of the LPW was just as much a reaction against the rise of Plaid as it was about making sure Liberalism survived within Wales. As such, the policies that the new party pursued became a valuable tool in defining the Welsh nationalist credentials of the WLP. Federalism, including a law-making Welsh parliament/senedd, was a unique position for the WLP to take: different from the unionist stance of the Conservative and Labour parties, and not as insular as Plaid Cymru's desire for separatism. It was also in keeping with what had come before, notably the Cymru Fydd movement from Lloyd George's early career. Hooson's first statement about the type of nationalism that the WLP would project came on St David's Day in 1967, with the publication of the Government of Wales Bill. Although unsuccessful, the contents of this Bill were to define every WLP policy that followed under Hooson.

The policies of the WLP were predicated on gaining a Welsh parliament within a future federal UK.

'Nationalist' and 'nationalism' were self-confining terms for a man and party with an internationalist outlook. Yet members of the party were not hesitant in admitting there were a lot of similarities between Plaid and the WLP, from Martin Thomas stating that the WLP would focus on economic nationalism, to Geraint Jenkins's belief that the WLP 'go three quarters of the way along the same path and I am certain that the future lies in the formation of a truly radical Welsh Party'.[3] As demonstrated, Hooson was very open to this form of persuasion, and the idea of a 'truly radical Welsh Party' appealed to him enough to reach out to Gwynfor Evans with a suggestion of working together and potentially creating a new party. It was Hooson's good fortune that his request was ignored by Evans, as it could have meant the end of the Welsh Liberal brand. However, amalgamation could have attracted a broader audience for the nationalist cause, and support for a Welsh parliament could have gained traction following the recommendations in the 1973 Royal Commission Report on the Constitution. Yet, it would not be easy for such a party to find common ground on the federalism or independence question. Hooson's other suggestion, for Plaid and WLP to contest eighteen seats each, would have been a better proposition.

Although we know that none of this happened, the fact that the WLP had been formed to revive Liberalism was not a wasted endeavour and was met with a good measure of success.

ADDING TO THE HISTORIOGRAPHY

The archives are often a treasure chest for the historian, but one must realise that you cannot find the treasure without a map. To conduct a thorough investigation without first building a base amount of knowledge about your subject would be like staring at a blank page, thinking it is a map and hoping it will lead you in the right direction. You will soon find yourself lost, looking at information and not knowing where it fits or what it truly means. For this book, my map had to consist of many secondary sources, building a knowledge of how and why things happened. For example, I could not begin to understand what motivated Emlyn Hooson to tackle the depopulation crisis within Wales unless I had an understanding of the root causes of the crisis or how others saw the solution. Likewise, I had to know what Wales meant to Hooson and how his sense of Welshness informed his vision for the WLP. The historian must also know where they stand in relation to the political and personal positions that their subject takes. In essence, you must know your own biases. Finally, you need to know where your work will fit with regards to the research that came before it.

The post-1945 historiography of the Liberal Party of Wales and the Welsh Liberal Party is in its infancy. Kenneth O. Morgan, David Roberts, J. Graham Jones and Russell Deacon have all built upon the other, each producing a body of work that has etched out a valid claim for the Welsh Liberals to be taken seriously by other Welsh historians. This book could not have been written, or researched, in the same way had it been the first to appear. All of the above historians were able to conduct interviews with the leading players, ask the questions and use the archives to support their arguments. Without them building that knowledge base, and if this book had been the first attempt at writing the history of the post-war Welsh Liberals, then it would have been written fifteen years too late. It needed those interviews to have taken place and it needed the archives to be consulted, even if they were only partially available until the 2010s. So much would have been lost if this book was the first to appear in 2025.

So, for the historian who comes after those first vital steps have been taken, it provides their investigation with an established narrative, a map to follow. Along the way, their work and those established narratives can be challenged, expanded upon and revised. In the case of this book, much of the documents and archival material were only able to help produce a more rounded understanding of Hooson's period as leader of the Welsh Liberals because the present study had the map to work with.

Any new work cannot be a rehash of what has come before it; it has to move the historiography forward and be open to challenge, whether that is by the public, the Welsh Liberal community or other historians. This book had to be confident in its approach, research methods arguments and conclusions, so that it created debate; without this approach, the historiography on this period would have stood still. Where the other historians created the foundations and, with Deacon's book, the first brick, this book aims to be the second brick in the study of the Welsh Liberals in the post-1945 period.

So, this study and its conclusions stand to be challenged. The importance of the post-1945 Welsh Liberals on the political history of Wales is too great to be ignored or discounted. The party and its politics have earned the right to be heard.

ELECTORAL 'WHAT IFS'

The main body of this book was not interested in historical 'what ifs', but we can give something of an addendum to the final chapter to further show how the WLP was unfairly disadvantaged by the 'first past the post' (FPTP) electoral system (table 32). Using the D'Hondt electoral method, it can be demonstrated that under a simple proportional system, the WLP would have gained more seats at the 1974 general elections than Plaid. Seats based on their actual vote share would have allowed a different story to emerge, including a less dramatic fall at the 1979 general election (table 33). A proportional result would have produced a different conversation that could have focused on a more robust rise in Welsh nationalism, with both Plaid and the WLP sharing the headlines.

Table 32: WLP and Plaid Cymru seats gained under FPTP, 1970–9 general elections[4]

Party	1970 general election	February 1974 general election	October 1974 general election	1979 general election
WLP	1	2	2	1
Plaid Cymru	0	2	3	2

Table 33: WLP and Plaid Cymru seats allocated under the D'Hondt method, 1970–9 general elections[5]

Party	1970 general election	February 1974 general election	October 1974 general election	1979 general election
WLP	2	6	5	3
Plaid Cymru	4	4	4	3

Whichever way one looks at this period, Hooson was the person Welsh Liberalism needed and he arrived at the right time. Deacon points to Clement Davies's sacrificing the chance of a ministerial career under Churchill as saving the BLP, noting that this was 'the most important act by any Welsh Liberal . . . it was also perhaps the greatest act undertaken by any Liberal'.[6] It would not be out of place to update this and state that the greatest act of any Welsh Liberal was Hooson's root-and-branch reorganisation of the LPW. It ensured the survival of the Liberal name within Wales and breathed new life into Welsh Liberalism. Without this fundamental change, it is doubtful that the LPW would have been able to weather the nationalist tide, as it would have remained a party at war with itself. And survive it did, staying more popular, in terms of the votes received, than Plaid during the rest of the twentieth century. As the Welsh Liberal Democrats, between 2001 and 2003, the party became a coalition partner with Labour in the National Assembly. This would probably not have occurred without the changes undertaken by Hooson.

Additionally, if the WLP had been fighting under a proportional electoral system, it is possible that Hooson's proposal for a Welsh Democratic Party could have received a more favourable reply from Gwynfor Evans. Whether that would have resulted in the new party being formed is another matter, but it could have led to closer cooperation between the two parties of Wales.

This book has also argued that historians, particularly those interested in the Labour Party and Plaid Cymru, have consciously or otherwise ignored the Liberals in the second half of the twentieth century. This has begun to change in the last decade, and this book proudly sits alongside a small historiography of Welsh Liberalism in the second half of the twentieth century. The arguments put forward show that the Welsh Liberals and the party's later incarnations deserve a more prominent place within the Welsh historiography. The WLP should no longer be seen as having little relevance to the Welsh nationalist movement of the late 1960s and 1970s, but should be shown as an integral part of that story. The inclusion of the Welsh Liberals as something more than a footnote can only enrich the sense that the politics of Wales were and are very different from the politics of England. With all of this in mind, it is worth reiterating and pointing out that this book sits within several other historical disciplines: these include the histories of British and Welsh politics, of the Liberal and Welsh Liberal parties, of Welsh nationalism and those of other organisations and political parties in general.

EMLYN HOOSON

The title of this book is 'Emlyn Hooson and the Welsh Liberal Party, 1962–1979' and it has placed Hooson at the centre of the project. As historians, we must approach our subject objectively, eradicating our bias whenever we unintentionally stray. However, the reader should never mistake the historian's genuine appreciation of someone for bias, unless it is blatantly so. For example, it is no secret that Lloyd George is something of a political hero to Kenneth O. Morgan; after all, he has written extensively on the subject and has often praised Lloyd George's 'vision and his greatness'.[7] Yet, no one would accuse Morgan of showing undue bias towards Lloyd George, as his works have always been critical when required. Equally, historians can show admiration or appreciation for controversial leaders such as Margaret Thatcher and Tony Blair, and even grow to like them through their research, without allowing them to escape a critical analysis of their time in office. This is offered as something of a caveat to the last section of this conclusion, as this book has been generous to Hooson when required and critical when deserving of criticism.

Since 2018, Hooson has gained a negative reputation for his role in the Jeremy Thorpe affair and for defending one of the most reviled serial killers in British history, Ian Brady. Much of this can be attributed to the 2018 mini-series *A Very English Scandal* and Jason Watkins's portrayal of Hooson as a sly weasel of a character seeking to dethrone Thorpe and become the leader of the Liberal Party. Whilst it cannot be denied that Hooson played a significant role in the downfall of Thorpe and was Brady's barrister, the artistic licence of the portrayal has given a false impression of Hooson, one that his close friends and colleagues did not recognise.[8] Little titbits of information about Hooson have begun to appear, including a charge by the writer Jonathan Calder that whilst defending Arnold Murray, who was tried alongside Alan Turing for 'acts of gross indecency', Hooson was instrumental in directing the blame towards Turing.[9] However, he does not provide any concrete evidence for this, only conjecture.

Hooson never got round to writing his autobiography, but a volume of essays and reminiscences was published after his death in 2012.[10] If this volume was better known, it might go some way to dispelling the myths that have grown up around Hooson since 2018. It was written by colleagues, friends and historians, and includes many of Hooson's own words. It suggests that Hooson's prominence within legal, political and business circles requires significant re-evaluation. Hooson has often been described as a driven man of intellect who revelled in a challenge. The intellectual challenges he took on, of reorganising the LPW and formulating policies, being the vice-chairman of NATO's political committee or, later in life, the chairman of the Second Severn Crossing group, highlight a man who was not afraid to take that extra step. As Eifion Roberts, a former colleague of Hooson, put it, 'Emlyn had a broad compass',[11] and a biography would make for fascinating reading.

Hooson's place within Welsh politics needs to be better known than it is, and it is hoped that this book has shed some much-needed light on the actual man, rather than the near-fictional portrayal of him in 'A Very English Scandal'. He deserves to be remembered as the intellectual reformer that he was, and not as a sinister caricature.

Notes

1   Lord Emlyn Hooson, *Rebirth or Death?* (Aberystwyth, 1994), p. 5.
2   Russell Deacon, *The Welsh Liberals: The History of the Liberal and Liberal Democratic Parties in Wales* (Cardiff, 2014), p. 148.
3   NLW, Lord Hooson Papers, Box 42, Letter from Geraint Jenkins to Hooson, 16 November 1967.
4   Beti Jones, *Welsh Elections 1885–1997* (Talybont, 1999), pp. 114–27.
5   Election calculator, available at: *https://user.eng.umd.edu/~yavuz/electioncalcEE. html* (accessed 1 August 2024). In most general elections using this method, the threshold is usually set somewhere around 5%. As this is just for illustrative purposes, it is not necessary to set this threshold. Additionally, none of the smaller parties gained more than 1.1% of the vote during these elections. The total number of seats is based on the total number of votes of each party.
6   Russell Deacon, *The Welsh Liberals: The History of the Liberal and Liberal Democratic Parties in Wales* (Cardiff, 2014), p. 138.
7   For example, Kenneth O. Morgan, *The Age of Lloyd George: The Liberal Party and British Politics, 1890–1929* (London, 1978), p. 110.
8   For example, BBC News, 'A Very English Scandal: Former MP Hooson portrayal "unfair"'. Available at: *https://www.bbc.com/news/uk-wales-politics-44302393.*

amp (accessed 1 August 2024). See also Michael Meadowcroft, 'Review of *A Very English Scandal*', *Journal of Liberal History*. Available at: *https://liberalhistory.org.uk/wp-content/uploads/2018/09/100-Review-Meadowcroft-A-Very-English-Scandal.pdf* (accessed 1 August 2024).

9   Liberal England blog, 'Alan Turing and Emlyn Hooson', 26 September 2016. Although, elsewhere in the blog, Calder is more even-handed on Hooson. Available at: *https://liberalengland.blogspot.com/2016/09/alan-turing-and-emlyn-hooson.html* (accessed 1 August 2024).

10 Derec Llwyd Morgan (ed.), *Emlyn Hooson: Essays and Reminiscences* (Llandysul, 2014).

11 Eifion Roberts, 'Emlyn in the Law', in Morgan (ed.), *Emlyn Hooson*, pp. 33, 64.

BIBLIOGRAPHY

PRIMARY SOURCES

ARCHIVES

National Library of Wales
Cardiganshire Liberal Association
Clement Davies Papers
Lord Hooson Papers
Merfyn Jones Papers
Lord Ogmore Papers
Welsh Liberal Party Papers

ONLINE ARCHIVES

Hansard
Hansard: *Hansard's Parliamentary Debates*, vol. 721, cols 1236–352. HC Deb 30 November 1965, col. 1248. Available at: *https://api.parliament.uk/historic-hansard/commons/1965/nov/30/agriculture-bill#column_1267* (accessed 1 August 2024).
HC Debate, 1 March 1967, vol. 742, col. 418. Available at: *https://hansard.parliament.uk/Commons/1967-03-01/debates/73586515-ebae-47fe-8160-d1de6a0837a0/GovernmentOfWales* (accessed 1 August 2024).
HL Debate, 30 January 1968, Fifth Series, vol. 288, col. 737. Available at: *https://hansard.parliament.uk/Lords/1968-01-30/debates/f6458a99-f92c-4cce-97e4-2ed65bd47394/GovernmentOfWalesBillHl* (accessed 1 August 2024).

Internet archive
Royal Commission on the Constitution, Minutes of Evidence I, 19 November 1969, p. 17. Available at: https://archive.org/details/op1267081-1001/page/n15/mode/2up?q=The+Structure+of+the+Welsh+Economy (accessed 1 August 2024).

Legislation
Agricultural Act 1967 – Available at: https://www.legislation.gov.uk/ukpga/1967/22/part/III/crossheading/special-measures-for-certain-areas/enacted (accessed 1 August 2024).

British Online Archives
'Grimond and Thorpe's Liberal revival, 1954–1976'
https://microform.digital/boa/collections/81/volumes/585/grimond-and-thorpes-liberal-revival-1954-1976 (accessed 1 May 2024).
'National executive committee 1954–1976'
https://microform.digital/boa/documents/10863/national-executive-committee-1954-1976 (accessed 1 May 2024).

The National Archives
Digest of Welsh Historical Statistics 1700–1974: https://webarchive.nationalarchives.gov.uk/ukgwa/20150402173126/http:/gov.wales/statistics-and-research/digest-welsh-historical-statistics/?lang=en#/statistics-and-research/digest-welsh-historical-statistics/?tab=previous&lang=en (accessed 1 August 2024).
Digest of Welsh Historical Statistics, 1974–96: https://webarchive.nationalarchives.gov.uk/ukgwa/20150402173126/http:/gov.wales/statistics-and-research/digest-welsh-historical-statistics/?lang=en#/statistics-and-research/digest-welsh-historical-statistics/?lang=en (accessed 1 August 2024).

National Library of Wales Viewer
Reports of the Commissioners of Inquiry into the State of Education in Wales Part II & III
Available at: https://viewer.library.wales/4753689#?c=&m=&s=&cv=&manifest=https%3A%2F%2Fdamsssl.llgc.org.uk%2Fiiif%2F2.0%2F4753689%2Fmanifest.json&xywh=-1412%2C-1%2C5839%2C4742 (accessed 1 August 2024).

Parliamentary papers

Report of the Committee on Financial Aid to Political Parties, British Parliamentary Papers (1976). Available at: *https://parlipapers.proquest.com/parlipapers/docview/t70.d75.1975-066534* (accessed 1 May 2024).

Government of Wales Bill 1967 Available at: *https://parlipapers-proquest-com.abc.cardiff.ac.uk/parlipapers/result/pqpdocumentview?accountid=9883&groupid=107330&pgId=8a093b74-2547-43c6-8d56-3d58304175d7&rsId=17FDA5675AC* (accessed 1 May 2024).

Cymdeithas Hanes Plaid Cymru History Society

'water water everywhere: alwen efyrnwy tryweryn elan claerwen clywedog – dulas?' Available at: *www.hanesplaidcymru.org/taflenni-cyn-1970/nggallery/thumbnails?lang=en* (accessed 1 August 2024).

Evans, Gwynfor, *Argyfwng Amaethyddiaeth Cymru / The Crisis of Welsh Agriculture* (Cardiff, 1975). Available at: *http://www.hanesplaidcymru.org/filebase/llyfrynnau/1975%20Argyfwng%20Amaethyddiaeth.pdf* (accessed 1 August 2024).

PERSONAL CORRESPONDENCE

John Summers, former *Daily Telegraph* columnist, March 2006.

GOVERNMENT PUBLICATIONS

HMSO, *Royal Commission on the Constitution, 1969–1973* (London, 1973), volume 1.

HMSO, *Royal Commission on the Constitution, 1969–1973* (London, 1973), volume 2: *Memorandum of Dissent*.

HMSO, *A New Town in Mid-Wales: Consultants' Proposals* (London, 1966).

NEWSPAPERS

https://www.britishnewspaperarchive.co.uk/ (accessed 1 August 2024). Unless otherwise stated, copies of newspapers were obtained from this site.

Belfast Telegraph
Birmingham Daily Post

Coventry Evening Telegraph
Daily Mirror
Daily Post Available at: *https://www.dailypost.co.uk* (accessed 1 August 2024).
The Daily Telegraph
London Daily News
The North Wales Weekly News
Sunday Telegraph
The Times Available at: *www.thetimes.co.uk/archive* (accessed 1 August 2024).
The Western Mail and South Wales News
Western Mail

ONLINE MANIFESTOS

1959 Conservative Party Manifesto
Available at: *http://www.conservativemanifesto.com/1959/1959-conservative-manifesto.shtml* (accessed 1 August 2024).
1964 Conservative Party Manifesto
Available at: *http://www.conservativemanifesto.com/1964/1964-conservative-manifesto.shtml* (accessed 1 August 2024).
1966 Conservative Party Manifesto
Available at: *http://www.conservativemanifesto.com/1966/1966-conservative-manifesto.shtml* (accessed 1 August 2024).
1970 Conservative Party Manifesto
Available at: *http://www.conservativemanifesto.com/1970/1970-conservative-manifesto.shtml* (accessed 1 August 2024).

Plaid Cymru publications
Plaid Cymru Research Group, *An Economic Plan for Wales* (Cardiff, 1970).

TELEVISION ARCHIVES

'Farmers Against the EEC' (BBC, 15 October 1971). Available at: *https://bbcrewind.co.uk/asset/61f971e00fde0c002214dc23?q=Farmers%20against%20the%20EEC* (accessed 1 August 2024).

WLP PUBLICATIONS

Hooson, Emlyn and Jenkins, Geraint, *The Heartland: A Plan for Mid-Wales* (London, 1965).
Life to a Nation: An Economic Policy for Wales (1969).
Welsh Liberal Party Manifesto: The Liberal Case for Wales (1970).

SECONDARY SOURCES

BOOKS

Balsom, Denis and Burch, Martin (eds), *A Political and Electoral Handbook for Wales* (Hants, 1980).
Blaxland, Sam, *The Conservative Party in Wales, 1945–1997* (Cardiff, 2024).
Butt Philip, Alan, *The Welsh Question: Nationalism in Welsh Politics 1945–1970* (Cardiff, 1975).
Burnham, Peter, Gilland Lutz, Karin, Grant, Wyn and Layton-Henry, Zig (eds), *Research Methods in Politics* (Basingstoke, 2008).
Clarke, P. F., *Lancashire and the New Liberalism* (Cambridge, 1971).
Clarke, Peter, *Hope and Glory: Britain 1900–2000* (London, 2004).
Dale, Iain (ed.), *Liberal Party General Election Manifestos, 1900–1997* (London, 2000).
Dangerfield, George, *The Strange Death of Liberal England* (London, 1997).
Davies, Charlotte Aull, *Welsh Nationalism in the Twentieth Century: The Ethnic Option and the Modern State* (New York, 1989).
Davies, John, *A History of Wales* (London, 1994).
Deacon, Russell, *The Welsh Liberals: The History of the Liberal and Liberal Democratic Parties in Wales* (Cardiff, 2014).
Douglas, Roy, *The History of the Liberal Party 1895–1970* (London, 1971).
Douglas, Roy, *Liberals: The History of the Liberal and Liberal Democrat Parties* (London, 2005).
Dutton, David, *A History of the Liberal Party* (Basingstoke, 2004).
Edwards, Andrew, *Labour's Crisis: Plaid Cymru, The Conservatives and the Decline of the Labour Party in North-West Wales, 1960–74* (Cardiff, 2011).
Foulkes, David, Jones, J. Barry and Wilford, R. A. (eds), *The Welsh Veto: The Wales Act 1978 & The Referendum* (Cardiff, 1983).

Green, Anna and Troup, Kathleen, *The Houses of History* (Manchester, 2012).
Hattersley, Roy, *David Lloyd George* (London, 2010).
Hooson, Lord Emlyn, *Rebirth or Death?* (Aberystwyth, 1994).
Ingham, Robert and Brack, Duncan (eds), *Peace, Reform and Liberation: A History of Liberal Politics in Britain, 1679–2011* (London, 2011).
Johnes, Martin, *Wales Since 1939* (Manchester, 2012).
Jones, Beti, *Welsh Elections 1885–1997* (Talybont, 1999).
Jones, Gwynoro and Gibbard, Alun, *Whose Wales? The Battle for Welsh Devolution and Nationhood 1880–2020* (Milton Keynes, 2021).
Jones, John Graham, *David Lloyd George and Welsh Liberalism* (Llandysul, 2010).
Jones, Tudor, *The Uneven Path of British Liberalism, From Jo Grimond to Brexit* (Manchester, 2019).
Joyce, Peter, *Realignment of the Left?* (Basingstoke, 1999).
McAllister, Laura, *Plaid Cymru: The Emergence of a Political Party* (Bridgend, 2001).
Morgan, Derec Llwyd (ed.), *Emlyn Hooson: Essays and Reminiscences* (Llandysul, 2014).
Morgan, Kenneth O., *The Age of Lloyd George: The Liberal Party and British Politics, 1890–1929* (London, 1983).
Morgan, Kenneth O., *Wales in British Politics, 1868–1922* (Cardiff, 1980).
Morgan, Kenneth O., *Rebirth of a Nation: Wales 1880–1980* (Oxford, 1990).
Morgan, Kenneth O., *Modern Wales: Politics, Places and People* (Cardiff, 1995).
Osmond, John (ed.), *The National Question Again: Welsh Political Identity in the 1980s* (Llandysul, 1985).
Parry, Cyril, *The Radical Tradition in Welsh Politics: A Study of Liberal and Labour politics in Gwynedd 1900–1920* (Hull, 1970).
Pierce, Roger, *Research Methods in Politics: A Practical Guide* (London, 2008).
Pinto-Duschinsky, Michael, *British Political Finance 1830–1980* (London, 1981).
Rallings, Colin and Thrasher, Michael (eds), *British Electoral Facts 1832–1999* (Aldershot, 2000).
Rasmussen, Jorgen Scott, *The Liberal Party* (London, 1965).

Rees, Ivor Thomas, *Welsh Hustings 1885–2004* (Llandybie, 2005).
Shipton, Martin, *Political Chameleon: In Search of George Thomas* (Cardiff, 2017).
Steel, David, *A House Divided* (London, 1980).
Tanner, Duncan, *Political Change and the Labour Party 1900–1918* (Cambridge, 1990).
Tanner, Duncan, Williams, Chris and Hopkin, Deian (eds), *The Labour Party in Wales 1900–2000 (*Cardiff, 2000).
Tanner, Duncan, Williams, Chris, Griffith, W. P and Edwards, Andrew (eds), *Debating Nationhood and Governance in Britain, 1885–1939* (Manchester, 2006).
Thomas, Wyn, *Hands Off Wales: Nationhood and Militancy* (Llandysul, 2013).
Williams, John, *Digest of Welsh Historical Statistics, Vol. 1* (Pontypool, 1985).
Wilson, Trevor, *The Downfall of the Liberal Party, 1914–1935* (London, 2011).
Wyburn-Powell, Alun, *Clement Davies: Liberal Leader* (London, 2003).

JOURNALS

Belzak, Steve, 'Swinging in the '60s to the Liberals: Mary Murphy and Pontypridd Urban District Council', *Journal of Liberal History*, 68 (Autumn 2010).
Cook, C. P., 'Wales and the General Election of 1923', *Welsh History Review*, 4/2 (1968).
Deacon, Russell, 'The Steady Tapping Breaks the Rock', *Journal of Liberal History*, 22 (Spring 1999).
Deacon, Russell, 'Interview with Lord Geraint of Ponterwyd', *Journal of Liberal History*, 44 (Autumn 2004).
Deacon, Russell, 'The Slow Death of Liberal Wales 1906–1979', *Journal of Liberal History*, 49 (Winter 2005–6).
Douglas, Enid H., 'Oral History and Public History', *The Oral History Review*, 8 (1980).
Hooson, Emlyn, 'Clement Davies: An Underestimated Welshman and Politician', *Journal of Liberal Democrat History*, 24 (Autumn 1999).
Jones, J. Graham, 'The Parliament for Wales Campaign, 1950–1956', *Welsh History Review*, 16/2 (1992).

Jones, J. Graham, 'The Liberal Party and Wales, 1945–79', *Welsh History Review*, 16/3 (June 1993).
Jones, J. Graham, 'Emlyn Hooson's Parliamentary Debut: The Montgomeryshire By-Election of 1962', *The Montgomeryshire Collections*, 81 (1993).
Jones, J. Graham, 'Emlyn Hooson and Montgomeryshire Politics 1962–79', *The Montgomeryshire Collections*, 97 (2009).
Jones, J. Graham, 'Emlyn Hooson (1925–2012)', *Journal of Liberal History*, 86 (Spring 2015).
Jones, J. Graham, 'The Union Jack, the Red Flag and the Welsh Dragon: The Dilemmas of Goronwy Roberts and James Griffiths', *Llafur: Journal of Welsh People's History*, 12/1 (2016).
Jones, J. Graham, 'Emlyn Hooson, The Devolution Debate and the General Election of May 1979', *The Montgomeryshire Collections*, 106 (2018).
Jones, J. Graham, 'The Cardiganshire Election of 1966', *Llafur: Journal of Welsh People's History*, 9/1 (2004).
Jones, R. Merfyn, 'Beyond Identity? The Reconstruction of the Welsh', *Journal of British Studies*, 31/4 (October 1992).
Morgan, Kenneth O., 'The new Liberalism and the challenge of Labour, 1885–1929', *Welsh History Review*, 6/3 (June 1973).
Morgan, Kenneth O., 'Montgomeryshire's Liberal Century', *Welsh History Review*, 16/1 (June 1992).
Thomas, Ian C., 'The Beginnings of an Economic Development Policy in Mid-Wales: The Mid-Wales Industrial Development Association, 1957–1974', *Welsh History Review*, 17/3 (1995).

ONLINE JOURNALS

Journal of Liberal History

Robinson, Emily, 'Whatever happened to Orpington Man? Report of a Liberal Democrat History Group meeting at the National Liberal Club, 23 January 2012, with Dr Mark Egan and Professor Dennis Kavanagh. Chair, Duncan Brack', *Journal of Liberal History*, 74 (Spring 2012). Available at: *https://liberalhistory.org.uk/events/whatever-happened-to-orpington-man/* (accessed 1 August 2024).
Meadowcroft, Michael, 'Review of *A Very English Scandal*', *Journal of Liberal History* (September 2018). Available at: *https://liberalhistory.*

org.uk/wp-content/uploads/2018/09/100-Review-Meadowcroft-A-Very-English-Scandal.pdf (accessed 1 August 2024).

Wales Magazine

'Charter for Wales', *Wales Magazine*, 41 (1959), 12–13. No author given. Available at: *https://journals.library.wales/view/1214989/1218069/#?xywh=-2068%2C-201%2C6483%2C4005* (accessed 1 August 2024).

WEBSITES AND BLOGS

Aberystwyth population statistics, 2001 – Available at: *https://www.citypopulation.de/en/uk/wales/admin/ceredigion/W04000359__aberystwyth/* (accessed 5 March 2025).

Appalachian Regional Commission – Available at: *https://web.archive.org/web/20160407014958/http://www.arc.gov/about/archistory.asp* (accessed 1 August 2024).

Bank of England inflation calculator – Available at: *https://www.bankofengland.co.uk/monetary-policy/inflation/inflation-calculator* (accessed 1 August 2024).

BBC News, 'A Very English Scandal: Former MP Hooson portrayal "unfair"', 30 May 2018. Available at: *https://www.bbc.com/news/uk-wales-politics-44302393.amp* (accessed 1 August 2024).

Cambridge English Dictionary, 'Devolution' – Available at: *https://dictionary.cambridge.org/dictionary/english/devolution* (accessed 1 August 2024).

Cardiff University blog, Davies, Nye, 'The difference between sheep: Bevan and the "Welsh Day" debate', 26 April 2017. Available at: *https://blogs.cardiff.ac.uk/thinking-wales/the-difference-between-sheep-bevan-and-the-welsh-day-debate/* (accessed 1 August 2024).

Election calculator – Available at: *https://user.eng.umd.edu/~yavuz/electioncalcEE.html* (accessed 1 August 2024).

Independent, Stephens, Meic, 'Glyn Tegai Hughes, obituary: esteemed literary critic who championed Welsh writing', 12 September 2017. Available at: *https://www.independent.co.uk/news/obituaries/glyn-tegai-hughes-obituary-literary-critic-who-championed-welsh-writing-a7748841.html* (accessed 1 August 2024).

Independent, Clayton, George, 'Obituary, Professor E. T. Nevin CORRECTED', 20 and 23 September 1992. Available at:

https://www.independent.co.uk/news/people/obituary-professor-e-t-nevin-corrected-1552650.html (accessed 1 August 2024).

Liberal England blog, 'Alan Turing and Emlyn Hooson', 26 September 2016. Available at: *https://liberalengland.blogspot.com/2016/09/alan-turing-and-emlyn-hooson.html* (accessed 1 August 2024).

The London Gazette, 'Llanelli Borough Council: Change of Name of Borough', 4 March 1966. Available at: *https://www.thegazette.co.uk/London/issue/43915/page/2444* (accessed 1 August 2024).

Merriam-Webster dictionary, 'Welshness' – Available at: *https://www.merriam-webster.com/dictionary/Welshness* (accessed 1 August 2024).

INDEX

A Very English Scandal (2018 TV Mini-Series)
    Portrayal of Hooson 4, 254, 255
Abse, Leo 140
Anderson, Donald
    Critical of Justice of Peace 181
Anglesey 215
Ashford, Gwyneth 105
    Reduction in hours 121
    Resignation 122
    Role and oversight by WLP 105
    Treatment by the WLP 118
Asquith, H. H. 37
    Liberal schism 33
    Resignation as Prime Minister 28
Attlee, Clement 140

Bailey, Christopher
Stands down in favour of Conservatives 230
Beacham Committee 150
Bevan, Aneurin 140
Blair, Tony 254
Blaxland, Sam 136, 138
Bonham-Carter, Lady Violet 40
Bonham-Carter, Mark 51
    Bowen, Roderic 43, 68, 76, 153, 226
    Deputy Speaker 58
    Indifference to devolution 145
    Loses to Labour 59
    Loss of Cardigan Seat 24
Brady, Ian 254
Brecon and Radnor General Election Committee (BRGEC)
    Recognised by WLP 211
Brecon and Radnor Liberal Association (BRLA)
    Not contesting 1979 General Election 211
British Liberal Party (BLP) 1, 2, 4, 11, 23, 78
    1923 Liberal reunification 34
    1931 Three-way Liberal split 29
    1959 'A New Deal for Wales' 57
    Decentralisation of party 63
    Devolution 228
    Funding WLP 112
    Liberal Revival 1974 3
    Policy overhaul under Grimond 51
British Newspaper Archive (BNA) 14
Butt-Philip, Alan 44, 160–1
    The Welsh Question 18
By-elections
    1921 Cardiganshire 34
    1922 Newport
    1945–59 49
    1957 Carmarthen 49
    1958 Torrington 51
    1960 Ebbw Vale 51
    1962 Blackpool North 52
    1962 Derbyshire West 53

1962 Middlesborough West 53
1962 Montgomery 51–3
1962 Orpington 3, 51, 52, 53
1963 Swansea 51
1966 Carmarthen 60, 206
1967 Rhondda West 205
1968 Caerphilly 136, 205
1972 Merthyr Tydfil 205, 207

Caernarvonshire 226
Caersws 151
Calder, Jonathan 254
Callaghan, James 3, 236
Cardiff
  1955 becomes capital city of Wales 54
Cardiff South East Liberal Association Disaffiliation 231
Cardigan 224
Carmarthen 214, 226
  Changing hands 214
Churchill, Winston 252
  Desire for closer working with BLP 43
  Offers Clement Davies role in Government 40
  Promise of Cabinet Minister for Wales 137
Committee on Financial Aid to Political Parties 115
Conservative Party 1, 3, 11, 19, 28, 29, 51, 54, 135, 203, 229, 235, 236
  1962 Montgomery by-election 53
  Cardiff as capital of Wales 55
  Coalition with Liberal Democrats 3
  Mention of Wales in 1960s Manifestos 138
  Overtakes the Liberals 36
  Payments to areas providing water to England 180
  The Charter for Wales policy document 137
  Wales into the 70s policy document 139
  Welsh policies 137
  Welsh Policy Group 138
  Work for Wales/Gwaith i Gymru policy proposals 138
Council for Wales and Monmouthshire
  1949 establishment of 55
Crowther, Tom 210
Cymdeithas yr Iaith Gymraeg/Welsh Language Society (WLS) 56, 142, 181
Cymru Fydd (Young Wales) 247

Dangerfield, George
  The Strange Death of Liberal Britain 30
Davies, Chris
  Honorary Treasurer 115
Davies, Clement 41, 43, 48, 54, 76, 234, 236, 252
  As Montgomery MP (1929–62) 4
  Courts Hooson as Montgomery successor 45
  Death of 24, 45, 52
  Electoral Record 52
  Indifference to devolution 145
  Leadership of the BLP 40
  Neglect of the LPW 43
  Resigns as leader of BLP 45
  Shifts BLP to the right 43
Davies, Edward
  Funding the Policy Directorate 167
Davies, John 234
Davies, S. O. 140, 207

Deacon, Russell 11–12, 15, 26, 49, 65, 72, 94, 205, 224, 232, 236, 237, 249, 252
    Four reasons for Welsh Liberal decline after 1945 32
    Liberal Schisms of 1916 and 1931 18, 33
    'The Slow Death of Liberal Wales' 18
    'The Steady Tapping Breaks the Rock' 17
    The Welsh Liberals 9, 17–18, 32
Defence of the Realm Act (1914) 28
Denbigh 209, 213
Devolution 39, 228
    1979 Referendum 3, 229
    Royal Commission on the Constitution 93
    Scotland-Wales Bill 228
Disestablishment of the Church in Wales 26
Donaldson, Angus 207, 222
Douglas, Roy 222

Education Acts
    1870 27
    1902 27
Education in Wales 26
    1847 'Reports of the Commissioners of Enquiry into the State of Education in Wales' 27
Edwards, Andrew 15, 56, 136, 138, 161, 203, 224
    Labour's Crisis 18, 89
Electoral Systems
    D'Hondt 251
    First Past the Post (FPTP) 251
Ellis, Tom 27
Ellis, W. Armon 209

European Economic Community (EEC) 78
    1975 Referendum 14, 116, 171
    Hooson's Opposition to 4
Evans, Gwynfor 142, 177, 214, 237, 249, 253
    1966 Carmarthen by-election 61
    Ignores Hooson's offer of a pact 237

Famers Union of Wales (FUW)
    Recognised by Labour Government 4
Federalism 39
First World War 28, 32
Free Wales Army 142

General Elections 216
    1906 28
    1918 28–9
    1922 18, 29, 35
    1923 29, 35
    1924 29, 37
    1929 29, 30, 225
    1931 28, 29, 36, 52
    1935 30, 33, 36, 52, 225
    1945 47
    1950 247
    1951 42, 43, 44, 223, 225, 247
    1955 43, 48, 52, 247
    1959 30, 42, 48, 50, 52, 61, 217, 247
    1964 60, 140, 223
    1966 60, 217, 229
    1970 13, 93, 167, 169, 183, 205, 216, 222, 223, 225, 226, 236
    1974 106, 115, 171, 183, 184, 223, 252
    1974 Feb 223, 225, 226, 239
    1974 Oct 210, 223, 226, 227, 229, 230, 233

1979 173, 229, 233, 252
1992 226
1997 226
2010 3
2015 31
Gibbard, Alun 228
Gibbs, Jennie 64, 155
   Challenges council election result 72
Gibbs, John 155
   Campaign against new Welsh Liberal Party 70, 71
   Secretary of the SWLF 64
   Halts campaign against WLP 72
Griffiths, Gwyn 173
   Reforming the Policy Directorate 1979 174
   Transport Policy 185
   Welsh language policy 185
Griffiths, James 140
   Reads *The Heartland* 157
Grimond, Jo 3, 4, 77
   Becomes leader of BLP 45
   'Realignment of the Left' policy 24, 57, 59, 222, 236
   Suez Crisis 51
   Threat to Welsh Liberals 57
Grimond, Laura 236

Hando, David 171, 210
Hansard 15
Hobsbawm, Eric 12
Holyhead 229
Hooson, Emlyn 253–5
   1962 Montgomery by-election 52, 53
   1967 BLP leadership manifesto 58
   Government of Wales Bill (1967) 15, 93, 175, 207, 248
   1967 Rhondda West by-election 205
   Admiration for Appalachian Regional Development Act (1965) 148
   Admiration of Britain's Industrial Future 148
   Affects BLP Policy 4
   Animosity towards Jo Grimond 58
   Anonymous donations 112
   Background 45
   Belief in a Liberal revival 146
   Death of 9
   Devolution 93, 204, 228
   Differs from Plaid Cymru 48
   Directs blame towards Alan Turing 255
   Dulas Valley 56
   Electoral record 204
   Elevation to the House of Lords 239
   Events leading to loss of Montgomery 232
   Five-point policy plan 47
   Formation of the Welsh Liberal Party (WLP) 68
   Hooson's role in WLP 90
   Influence of Lloyd George 45, 46
   Leader role 92
   Legal career 93
   Lib-Lab Pact 93, 204, 232
   Loses Montgomery seat 230, 238–9
   Marked as Clement Davies's successor 45
   On LPW leadership after 1945 41
   Opposition to joining EEC 93, 220
   President role 92
   Prosecutes members of Welsh Language Society 181
   Reorganisation of the LPW 67

INDEX 271

Role in Jeremy Thorpe resignation 93
Role in revived Policy Directorate 172
Second Severn Crossing Group 255
Seeks pact with Plaid Cymru 237
Self-government for Wales 48
Spokesman portfolio for BLP 93
Survival of Liberalism in Wales 248
Welsh Democratic Party 237
Welsh Liberal principles 238
Welsh policies 189
'Welsh Yellow Book' 47
WLP reorganisation 1972 93
WLP to emphasises its Welshness 143
Hopkin Morris, Rhys 40, 43
Death of 34, 49
Wins Cardiganshire Seat in 1923 34
Wins Carmarthenshire seat 1945 34
House of Commons
1944 'Welsh Day' inaugurated 54
Howells, Geraint 12, 186, 226, 230, 251
1970 General Election finances 118
Affects Labour Government Agricultural Policy 4
Devolution spokesperson for BLP 228
Farmers Union of Wales (FUW) 188
Funding for Organiser role 120
Opposes Hooson as President 92
Takes Ceredigion 1974 213
Hughes, Cledwyn 140
Hughes, Glyn Tegai 51, 145
Co-Authors 'A New Deal for Wales' 49
The Weekend Schools 165
Hughes-Evans, Idris 210
Hylton-Foster, Harry
Death of 59

Independent Labour Party 31
Ingham, Robert 222
Internet Archive 15
Iwan, Dafydd
Imprisonment for defacing road signs 181

Jacobs, Peter 219
Jenkins, Geraint
The Heartland 156
Johnes, Martin 2, 15, 56, 224
Wales Since 1939 19
Johnson, Lyndon
Appalachian Regional Development Act (1965) 148
Jones, Gwynoro 140, 228
Jones, J. Graham 12–13, 15–16, 31, 72, 94, 205, 224, 236, 250
'The Liberal Party and Wales, 1945–79' 15
Jones, Kenner 207
Jones, Leslie 169
Jones, Merfyn 10, 13
Jones, R. Merfyn (academic) 25
Jones, Tudor 222
Joseph Rowntree Social Service Trust
Finances Montgomeryshire County Liberal Association 234
Journals
Journal of Liberal History 17
Montgomeryshire Collections 17

Keith-Lucas, Bryan
  The Heartland 157

Labour Party 1, 11, 18–19, 28, 31, 36, 54, 135, 139, 203, 224, 229, 239, 253
  1968 Caerphilly by-election 206
  1979 Devolution Referendum 141
  Council for Wales and Monmouthshire 139
  Establishes Secretary of State for Wales 140
  Hostility to Welsh devolution 140
  Overtakes the Liberals 29
  Royal Commission on the Constitution 140
  Support for a Welsh Water Board 180
  Welsh Language Act 1967 140
  'Winter of Discontent' 229, 236
Lewis, Norman 121
  Honorary Treasurer 122
Lewis, Robyn 226
Liberal Democrats 2, 3
  Coalition with the Conservative Party (2010–15) 3
Liberal Nationals/National Liberals 36
Liberal Party of Wales (LPW) 1, 16, 19, 30, 247
  Denbigh Association 60
  1966 General Election 217
  LPW Manifesto 'A New Deal for Wales' 48, 49
  'A New Deal for Wales' 48–9, 76
  Charter for Wales 148
  Complaints about 'Council for Wales' commitment 60
  Lack of policies 46, 47
  Largest section of Parliamentary Liberal Party in 1951 42
  LPW Federations (NWLF and SWLF) 41
  Maesteg/Ogmore Constituency Association 64
  North Wales Liberal Federation (NWLF) 24, 65
  Organisation 39, 63
  Organisational and financial issues 65, 66
  Polarisation after 1945 40
  South Wales Liberal Federation (SWLF) 24
  The Heartland 76, 147, 167, 178–9, 187, 189, 217
Lib-Lab Pact 3, 228
Llanelli 215
Lloyd George, David 2, 15, 27, 28, 37, 76, 78, 145, 187, 225, 254
  1909 'People's Budget' 3
  1918 'Coupon Election' 28
  Britain's Industrial Future 143, 148
  Cymru Fydd 27, 38, 247
  Disestablishment of the Church in Wales 3
  Failure to reform the LPW 39
  Family group 30
  Home Rule for Wales Campaign 24
  Influence on Emlyn Hooson 45, 46
  Liberal schisms 33
  Neglect of the LPW 37
  Ousted as Prime Minister 29
  Policy documents of the 1920s 31
  Political Fund 37
  Prime Minister 28
  The Land and the Nation 144
Lloyd George, Gwilym 30
Lloyd George, Megan 30, 40, 94, 214
  1957 Carmarthen by-election 50

Death of 60
Defection to Labour 34
Loses seat 44
Parliament for Wales campaign 145
Lloyd, Jennifer
Revives Policy Directorate 171
Lord Lloyd, Rhys, 1st Baron of Kilgerran 7, 12, 98, 123, 171, 250
Honorary Treasurer 91, 108
Loan scheme 111
Resignation 104
Running of Cardiff HQ 100
Unofficial payments to WLP 114
Worries about Emlyn Thomas 98
Lord Ogmore, David, 1st Baron Ogmore 10, 13, 17, 92, 95, 111, 167, 178, 210
House of Lords, 1968 Government of Wales Bill 178
Lowe, R 10–11
Lubbock, Eric
Orpington by-election 51

MacDonald, Ramsay
Labour Prime Minister 29
National government Prime Minister 29
Masterman, Charles 76
McAllister, Laura 15, 142
Plaid Cymru: The Emergence of a Political Party 89
Merioneth 214, 226
Mid-Wales Industrial Development Association (MWIDA) 149, 151, 154
Military Service Act (1916)
Conscription 28

Minister of Welsh Affairs 55
Montgomery 214, 224
Montgomeryshire County Liberal Association (MCLA) 232
Financial situation 233
Morgan, Gareth
Revives Policy Directorate 171
Morgan, John
Chairman of the Executive 104
WLP finances 114
Morgan, Kenneth O. 3, 15, 17, 25, 31, 36, 223, 231, 236, 254
Modern Wales 23
'Montgomeryshire's Liberal Century' 18
Murphy, Mary 171, 209
General Secretary 90, 94, 95
Pontypridd Councillor 65
Resignation as General Secretary 95
Murray, Arnold
Tried alongside Alan Turing 254

National Farmers Union (NFU) 188
National League of Young Liberals (NLYL) 219
'Stop the Tour' protests 216, 221
National Library of Wales 13, 17, 26
Newtown
Inward migration 232
Nevin, Edward
Criticism of The Heartland 154
Influence on Plaid Cymru's *Economic Plan* 160
Scepticism of *The Heartland* 150
New Liberalism 143
Newport 229
Newspapers
Birmingham Daily Post 156
Coventry Evening Telegraph

1962 Montgomery by-election 53
Daily Mirror 15
Sunday Telegraph
   1962 Montgomery by-election 52
Times 151
Western Mail 14
Non-Conformism 26
North Atlantic Treaty Organization (NATO) 255
North Wales Liberal Federation (NWLF) 247

Oral history 12–13
Oral History Association 13
Owen, Cecil
   Alderman and Mayor of Aberystwyth 156

Parliament for Wales Campaign 44, 48, 49
   Plaid Cymru 141
Parry, Cyril 26
   The Radical Tradition in Welsh Politics 31
Pinto-Duschinsky, Michael 112
Plaid Cymru 1, 2, 4, 11, 16, 19, 20, 24, 31, 34, 48, 49, 54, 55, 56, 57, 77, 141, 151, 203, 207, 224, 227, 235, 239, 248, 252
   1962 Montgomery by-election 52
   1968 Caerphilly by-election 206
   1970 *An Economic Plan for Wales* 142, 159–60, 179
   Appeals to same base as LPW 50
   Devolution 228
   Electoral Performance 1
   Electoral record 225
   Finances 166

National Water Board policy 180
   Organisational and policy resurgence 142
   Policy formation 142
   Reorganisation of party 61
   Tryweryn 50
Powell, Enoch
   The Charter for Wales 137
Prince Charles
   Investiture bombing 55

Report of the Committee on Financial Aid to Political Parties 165
Roberts, David 16–17, 250
   The National Question Again 15
Roberts, Eifion 255
Roberts, Emrys 40
   Loses seat 44
Roberts, Helen 9
Roberts, John 106
Roddick, Winston 221
   PPC for Anglesey 220
Royal Commission on the Constitution 140, 184, 228, 249
Royal Commission on the NHS
   WLP evidence to commission 184
Rural depopulation in Wales 147

Sadler, Peter
   1968 Caerphilly by-election 206
Samuel, Herbert
   Leader of the BLP 30
Scott, Norman 229
Scottish Liberal Party (SLP) 68, 77, 228
Scottish National Party (SNP) 138
   Devolution 228
Second World War 32
Secretary of State for Wales

1959 Labour pledges Secretary of State for Wales 55
Silkin, John
   Farmers Union of Wales 188
Simon, Sir John
   Leader of Liberal Nationals 30
Smith, Colin A.
   Montgomery Association finances 117
Social Democratic Party (SDP) 3, 226
   The Alliance 18
South Wales Liberal Federation (SWLF) 247
Spiller, John 119, 172
   Resignation 121
Steel, David 233

Tanner, Duncan 35
Thatcher, Margaret 229, 254
The Government of Wales Bill (1967) 15, 176, 177
The Heartland
   Aberystwyth 154
   Criticism 154
   Differences with Plaid Cymru's *Economic Plan* 161
   Enthusiastic response 156
   Recommendations 151
   Similarities in Plaid Cymru's *Economic Plan* 160
   Similarities to 1965 White Paper 157
   Welsh outlook 153
Thomas, Dafydd Elis 214
Thomas, Emlyn 13, 122, 172, 209, 250
   Causing financial issues of WLP 6, 111
   General Secretary 90, 96
   Resignation as General Secretary 98

Thomas, George 140
Thomas, Iorwerth
   Death of 205
Thomas, Mair
   The Weekend Schools 165
Thomas, Maldwyn
   The Weekend Schools 165
Thomas, Martin 12, 178, 249
   Vision for the WLP 175
Thorpe, Jeremy 3, 4, 93, 222, 254
   Resignation 106
   Trial 229
Tryweryn 20
   Capel Celyn 50, 55
   Plaid Cymru 141
Turing, Alan
   Gross indecency trial 255

Watkins, Jason
   Portrayal of Emlyn Hooson 254
Welsh Church Act (1914)
   Disestablishment of the Church in Wales 144
Welsh Democratic Party 253
Welsh Home Rule 27
Welsh Liberal Democrats 19, 252
Welsh Liberal Party (WLP) 1–2
   1968 Caerphilly by-election 206
   1970 General Election Manifesto 157
   1974 General Election Manifestos 184
   Aberystwyth Headquarters 91
   Affiliation fee rise 117
   Agricultural policy 186–8
   Anglesey Liberal Association 220
   Brecon and Radnor Association finances 118
   Brecon and Radnor Liberal Association 211
   Candidate selection 209, 211

Candidates Committee 106, 210
Cardiff Headquarters 91, 99
Cardiff South East Liberal Association 230
Celtic Sea oil levy policy 184
Collapse of constituency organisations 107
Critical of Welsh Language Society 181
Devolution 228
Election funding 112
Electoral record 203, 205, 218 226, 227
Electoral record against Plaid Cymru 212, 213
Executive officers 105
Finances 98, 108, 113, 115, 118
Finances of Policy Directorate 163, 164, 167, 172–3
Formation of 68, 69
The Heartland 168
Lack of oversight of Emlyn Thomas 100
Life to a Nation – An Economic Policy for Wales 92, 167, 168, 178, 179, 187, 189, 217
Local Associations 231
Membership subscriptions 109
Merthyr Tydfil Liberal Association 208
New constitution 106
New executive after 1974 104
Opposition to formation of WLP 72
Organisation 73, 75, 90
Organisation of Local Associations 102
Policies 169
Policy Directorate (PD) 161–2, 189

Policy Directorate constitution 172
Recognises Brecon and Radnor General Election Committee (BRGEC) 211
Spokespersons 168–70
Steering Committee 91, 205
Tenby Association 109
The Weekend Schools 165
Transport policy 185
Treatment of female staff 103
Tryweryn 179
Welsh cultural policies 181
Welsh Development Fund policy 180
Welsh Language Act (1967) 140
Welsh language policy 182, 183, 185
Welsh nationalist credentials 249
Welsh policies 248
Welsh speaking PPCs 212
Welsh Water Board policy 179
Water Act (1973)
  Welsh National Water Development Authority 181
Welsh Courts Act (1941) 54
Welsh Radical Group (WRG) 146, 150
  The Heartland 150
'Welshness' 2, 248
  Conservative Party 138
  Cultural policies of WLP 181
  Cultural reassessment 55
  Definition of 5, 146
  Depoliticisation of the Welsh language 142
  Hooson reasserts Welshness 62
  Sense of Identity 27
  Welsh Liberal Party (WLP) 2
  Welsh Liberals as defenders of Wales and Welshness 26

INDEX

Welsh national consciousness 1
WLP emphasises its Welshness 143, 146
Whitaker, Winifred 'Freddie' 6, 91, 122
Liaising with local associations 101
Organisational success 104
Role at Cardiff HQ 101
Wigley, Dafydd 226
Williams, O. Glyn
Letter to Hooson 68
Williams, Phil, 142
1968 Carmarthen by-election 206
Wilson, Harold
Establishes Secretary of State for Wales 140
Offer's deputy speaker role to Bowen 59

277